S0-AGJ-589

SCOTT
1994 U.S. POCKET STAMP CATALOGUE

VICE PRESIDENT/PUBLISHER	Stuart J. Morrissey
EDITOR	William W. Cummings
ASSISTANT EDITOR	William H. Hatton
VALUING EDITOR	Martin J. Frankevicz
NEW ISSUES EDITOR	David C. Akin
COMPUTER CONTROL COORDINATOR	Denise Oder
VALUING ANALYST	Jose R. Capote
EDITORIAL ASSISTANTS	Judith E. Bertrand, Beth Brown
CONTRIBUTING EDITOR	Joyce Nelson
ART/PRODUCTION DIRECTOR	Janine C. S. Apple
PRODUCTION COORDINATOR	Philip A. Miller
SALES MANAGER	Bill Fay
ADVERTISING	David Lodge
CIRCULATION/PRODUCT PROMOTION MANAGER	Tim Wagner

CONTENTS

4A

6A

7A

9A

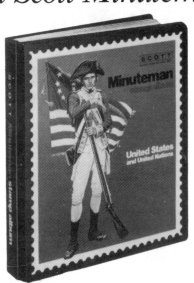

14A

16A

20A

AN OVERVIEW OF THE WORLD'S MOST POPULAR HOBBY

A fascinating hobby, an engrossing avocation and a universal pastime, stamp collecting is pursued by millions. Young and old, and from all walks of life, stamp collectors are involved in the indoor sport known as "the paper chase."

It was more than 150 years ago that Rowland Hill's far-reaching postal reforms became a reality and the world's first adhesive postage stamp, the Penny Black, was placed on sale at post offices in Great Britain. Not long after, a hobby was born that has continued to grow since.

Although there were only four stamp issues in England from 1840-47, the Penny Black, two types of the 2-penny blue and the 1-penny red, there were people who saved them. One story relates that a woman covered a wall in a room of her home with copies of the Penny Black.

As country after country began to issue postage stamps, the fraternity of stamp collectors flourished. Today, collectors number in the millions, while the number of stamp-issuing entities has exceeded 650.

The hobby of stamp collecting may take many forms. There are those people who collect the stamps of a single country. Others collect a single issue, such as the current U.S. Transportation coils. Others specialize in but a single stamp, with all its nuances and variations. Some collectors save one type of postage stamp, such as airmails, commemoratives or other types. Another type of collection would consist only of covers (envelopes) bearing a stamp with a postmark from the first day of that stamp's issue.

Most popular, however, is collecting by country, especially one's own country. This catalogue is designed to aid in forming just such a collection. It lists the postage stamps of the United States and is a simplified edition of information found in Volume I of the *Scott Standard Postage Stamp Catalogue*.

Catalogue Information

The number (1581) in the first column of the example below is the stamp's identifying Scott number. Each stamp issued by the United States has a unique number. The letter-number combination in the second column (A984) indicates the design type and refers to the illustration with the same designation. Following in the same line are the denomination of the stamp, its color or other description along with the color of the paper (in italic type) if other than white, and the catalogue value both unused and used.

Scott Number	Illustration Design No.	Denomination	Color or Description	Color of the Stamp Paper	Unused Value	Used Value
1581	A984	1c	dark blue	*greenish*	15	15

About this edition

The Scott Catalogue values stamps on the basis of the cost of purchasing them individually. You will find packets, mixtures and collections where the unit cost of the material will be substantially less than the total catalogue value of the component stamps.

Catalogue value

Scott Catalogue value is a retail price; what you could expect to pay for a sound stamp in a grade of Fine to Very Fine. The value listed is a reference that reflects recent actual dealer selling prices.

Dealer retail price lists, public auction results, published prices in advertising and individual solicitation of retail prices from dealers, collectors and specialty organizations have been used in establishing the values found in this catalogue.

Use this catalogue as a guide in your own buying and selling. The actual price you pay for a stamp may be higher or lower than the catalogue value because of one or more of the following factors: the grade and condition of the actual stamp; the amount of personal service a dealer offers; increased interest in the country or topic represented by the stamp or set; whether an item is a "loss leader," part of a special sale, or is otherwise being sold for a short period of time at a lower price; or if at a public auction you are able to obtain an item inexpensively because of little interest in the item at that time.

Unused stamps are valued never-hinged beginning with Nos. 772, C18, E17, FA1, J88, O127, RW1 and all of Marshall Islands, Micronesia and Palau.

23A

Grade

A stamp's grade and condition are crucial to its value. Values quoted in this catalogue are for stamps graded at Fine to Very Fine, and with no faults. Exceptions are noted in the text. The accompanying illustrations show an example of a Fine to Very Fine grade between the grades immediately below and above it: Fine and Very Fine.

FINE stamps have the design noticeably off-center on two sides. Imperforate stamps may have small margins and earlier issues may show the design touching one edge of the stamp. Used stamps may have heavier than usual cancellations.

FINE to VERY FINE stamps may be somewhat off-center on one side, or only slightly off-center on two sides. Imperforate stamps will have two margins at least normal size and the design will not touch the edge. *Early issues of a country may be printed in such a way that the design is naturally very close to the edges.* Used stamps will not have a cancellation that detracts from the design. This is the grade used to establish Scott Catalogue values.

VERY FINE stamps may be slightly off-center on one side, with the design well clear of the edge. Imperforate stamps will have three margins at least normal size. Used stamps will have light or otherwise neat cancellations.

It should be noted that many imperforate stamps are priced as pairs only, since it is an easy matter to trim perforations from a normal stamp.

FINE

Scott Catalogues value stamps in **FINE-VERY FINE** condition.

VERY FINE

Condition

The definitions given with the illustrations describe *grade,* which is centering and, for used stamps, cancellation. *Condition* refers to the soundness of the stamp; that is, faults, repairs and other factors influencing price.

Copies of a stamp that are of a lesser grade or condition trade at lower prices. Those of exceptional quality often command higher than catalogue prices.

Factors that can increase the value of a stamp include exceptionally wide margins, particularly fresh color and, in the case of older stamps, the presence of selvage (sheet margin).

Factors other than faults that decrease the value of a stamp include loss of gum or regumming, hinge remnants, foreign objects adhering to gum, natural inclusions, or straight edges.

Faults include a missing piece, tear, clipped perforation, pin or other hole, surface scuff, thin spot, crease, toning, oxidation or other form of color changeling, short or pulled perforation, stains or such man-made changes as reperforation or the chemical removal or lightening of a cancellation.

Scott Publishing Co. recognizes that there is no formal, enforced grading scheme for postage stamps, and that the final price you pay for a stamp or obtain for a stamp you are selling will be determined by individual agreement at the time of the transaction.

Forming a collection

Methods of collecting stamps are many and varied. A person may begin by attempting to gather a single specimen of every face-different stamp issued by a country. An extension of that approach is to include the different types of each stamp, such as perforation varieties, watermark varieties, different printings and color changes. The stamps may be collected on cover (envelope) complete with postal markings, thus showing postal rates, types of cancellations and other postal information.

Collections also may be limited to types of stamps. The stamps issued by most countries are divided into such categories as regular postage (made up of definitives and commemoratives), airmail stamps, special delivery stamps, postage due stamps and others. Any of those groups may provide the basis for a good collection.

Definitive stamps are those regular issues used on most mail sent out on a daily basis. They are normally issued in extended sets, sometimes over a period of years. The sets feature a rising series of face values that allows a mailer to meet any current postal rate. Definitive stamps may be printed in huge quantities and are often kept in service by the Postal Service for long periods of time.

Commemorative stamps meet another need. They are primarily issued to celebrate an important event, honor a famous person or promote a special project or cause. Such stamps are issued on a limited basis for a limited time. They are usually more colorful and are often of a larger size than definitives, making them of special interest to collectors.

Although few airmail stamps are currently issued by the United States, they continue to remain very popular among collectors. Just as with regular issues, airmail stamps are subject to several types of collecting. In addition to amassing the actual stamps, airmail enthusiasts pursue first-flight covers, airport dedication covers and even crash covers.

Not as popular, but still collected as a unit, are special delivery and postage due stamps. Special delivery stamps ensured speedier delivery of a letter once it reached its destination post office through normal postal means. Postage due stamps were used when a letter or parcel did not carry enough postage to pay for its delivery, subjecting the recipient to a fee to make up the difference. The United States no longer issues postage due stamps.

The resurgence in 1983 of Official Mail stamps—those used only by departments and offices of the federal government—has also brought about a resurgence of interest in them by stamp collectors. Originally issued between 1873 and 1911, Official Mail stamps were obsolete until recently. To be legally used, they must be on cards, envelopes or parcels that bear the return address of a federal office or facility.

"Topical" collecting is becoming more and more popular. Here the paramount attraction to the collector is the subject depicted on the stamp. The topics or themes from which to choose are virtually unlimited, other than by your own imagination. Animals, flowers, music, ships, birds and famous people on stamps make interesting collections. The degree of specialization is limitless, leading to such topics as graduates of a specific college or university, types of aircraft or the work of a specific artist.

There are several ways to obtain topical information, one of which is through the "By Topic" section of the *Scott Stamp Monthly*. "By Topic" is a regular feature of the magazine that divides the stamps of the world into more than 130 topical areas. Scott also presents, in each edition of the *Scott Standard Postage Stamp Catalogue*, selected topical listings based on individual handbooks published by the American Topical Association.

The album

To be displayed at their best, stamps should be properly housed. A quality album not only achieves this, but gives protection from dirt, loss and damage. When choosing an album, consider these three points: Is it within your means, does it meet your special interests and is it the best you can afford?

The Scott *Pony Express* and *Minuteman* albums are ideal companions to this Catalogue. Scott also publishes the National Album series for United States stamps, with much more specialization.

Looseleaf albums are recommended for all collectors beyond the novice level. Not only do looseleaf albums allow for expansion of a collection, but the pages may be removed for mounting stamps as well as for display. A special advantage of a loose-leaf album is that in many cases it may be kept current with supplements published annually on matching pages. All Scott albums noted are looseleaf and are supplemented annually.

Mounts and hinges

Mounts and hinges specially manufactured for collectors are used to affix stamps to album pages. Most stamp mounts are pre-gummed, clear plastic containers that hold a stamp safely and may be affixed to an album page with minimum effort. They are available in sizes to fit any stamp, block or even complete envelopes. Mounts are particularly important with unused stamps when there is a desire to not disturb the gum.

Although the mount is important, so is the venerable hinge. Innumerable stamps have been ruined beyond redemption by being glued to an album page. Hinges are inexpensive and effective. Use only peelable hinges. These may be removed from a stamp or album page without leaving an unsightly mark or causing damage to either.

Hinges are perfect for less-expensive stamps, used stamps and stamps that previously have been hinged. The use of stamp hinges is simple: Merely fold back, adhesive side out, about a quarter of the hinge (if it is not pre-folded). Lightly moisten the shorter side and affix it near the top of the back of the stamp. Then, holding the stamp with a pair of tongs, moisten the longer side of the hinge and place it (with stamp attached) in its proper place on the album page.

Stamp tongs

As previously noted, stamp tongs are a simple but important accessory and should always be used when handling a stamp. Fingers can easily damage or soil a stamp. Tongs cost little and will quickly pay for themselves. They come in a variety of styles. Beginners should start with tongs having a blunt or rounded tip. Those with sharp ends may inadvertently cause damage to a stamp. With just a little practice you will find tongs easier to work with than using your fingers . . . and your stamps will be better for it.

Magnifying glass

A good magnifying glass for scrutinizing stamps in detail is another useful philatelic tool. It allows you to see variations in stamps that may otherwise be invisible to the naked eye. Also, a magnifying glass makes minute parts of a stamp design large enough to see well. Your first glass should be at least 5- to 10-power magnification, with edge-to-edge clarity. Stronger magnifications are available and may also be useful.

Perforation gauge and watermark detector

Although many stamps appear to be alike, they are not. Even though the design may be the same and the color identical, there are at least two other areas where differences occur, and where specialized devices are needed for such identification. These are perforation measurement and watermark detection. A ruler that measures in millimeters is also useful.

The perforation gauge, printed on plastic, cardboard or metal, contains a graded scale that enables you to measure the number of perforation "teeth" in two centimeters. To determine the perforation measurement, place the stamp on the gauge and move the former along the scale until the points on one entry of the scale align perfectly with the teeth of the stamp's perforations. A stamp may have different perforations horizontally and vertically.

Watermarks are a bit more difficult to detect. They are letters or designs impressed into the paper at the time of manufacture. A watermark may occasionally be seen by holding a stamp up to the light, but a watermark detector is often necessary. The simplest of the many types of detectors available consists of a small black tray (glass or hard plastic). The stamp is placed face down in the tray and watermark detection fluid is poured over it. If there is a watermark, or a part of one, it should become visible when the stamp becomes soaked with the fluid.

There are a number of other liquids that over the years have been recommended for use to detect watermarks. The currently available fluids made specifically for that purpose are the safest—to the stamp and the collector. We do not recommend anything other than such watermark detection fluids for that use.

Benjamin
Franklin
A1

George
Washington
A2

A3

A4

Reproductions (found in Special Printings section). The letters R. W. H. & E. at the bottom of each stamp are less distinct on the reproductions than on the originals.

5c. On the originals the left side of the white shift frill touches the oval on a level with the top of the "F" of "Five." On the reproductions it touches the oval about on a level with the top of the figure "5."

10c. On the reproductions, line of coat at left points to right tip of "X" and line of coat at right points to center of "S" of CENTS. On the originals, line of coat points to "T" of TEN and between "T" and "S" of CENTS. On the reproductions the eyes have a sleepy look, the line of the mouth is straighter, and in the curl of hair near the left cheek is a strong black dot, while the originals have only a faint one.

Franklin
A5

A5

ONE CENT.

Type I. Has complete curved lines outside the labels with "U.S. Postage" and "One Cent." The scrolls below the lower label are turned under, forming little balls. The ornaments at top are substantially complete.

Type Ib. Same as I but balls below the bottom label are not so clear. The plume-like scrolls at bottom are not complete.

A6

Type Ia. Same as I at bottom but top ornaments and outer line at top are partly cut away.

A7

Type II. The little balls of the bottom scrolls and the bottoms of the lower plume ornaments are missing. The side ornaments are complete.

A8

Type III. The top and bottom curved lines outside the labels are broken in the middle. The side ornaments are complete.

Type IIIa. Similar to type III with the outer line broken at top or bottom but not both.

A9

Type IV. Similar to type II, but with the curved lines outside the labels recut at top or bottom or both.

Prices for types I and III are for stamps showing the marked characteristics plainly. Copies of type I showing the balls indistinctly and of type III with the lines only slightly broken, sell for much lower prices.

2

UNITED STATES

Scott No.	Illus No.	Description	Unused Value	Used Value	//////
1847, Imperf.					
1	A1	5c red brown, *bluish*	4,500.	425.00	☐☐☐☐☐
a.		5c dark brown, *bluish*	4,500.	425.00	☐☐☐☐☐
b.		5c orange brown, *bluish*	5,000.	525.00	☐☐☐☐☐
c.		5c red orange, *bluish*	*10,000.*	*3,500.*	☐☐☐☐☐
d.		Double impression		—	☐☐☐☐☐
2	A2	10c black, *bluish*	*20,000.*	900.00	☐☐☐☐☐
a.		Diagonal half used as 5c on cover		*10,000.*	☐☐☐☐☐
b.		Vert. half used as 5c on cover		*20,000.*	☐☐☐☐☐
c.		Horiz. half used as 5c on cover		—	☐☐☐☐☐

1875, Reproductions, Bluish Paper Without Gum, Imperf.

Scott No.	Illus No.	Description	Unused Value	Used Value	//////
3	A3	5c red brown	700.00		☐☐☐☐☐
4	A4	10c black	900.00		☐☐☐☐☐

1851-57, Imperf.

Scott No.	Illus No.	Description	Unused Value	Used Value	//////
5	A5	1c blue, type I	*200,000.*	*17,500.*	☐☐☐☐☐
5A	A5	1c blue, type Ib	*8,500.*	*2,500.*	☐☐☐☐☐
6	A6	1c blue, type Ia	*22,500.*	*6,500.*	☐☐☐☐☐
b.		Type Ic	*5,000.*	*1,200.*	☐☐☐☐☐
7	A7	1c blue, type II	575.00	110.00	☐☐☐☐☐
8	A8	1c blue, type III	*6,500.*	*1,500.*	☐☐☐☐☐
8A	A8	1c blue, type IIIa	*2,500.*	*600.00*	☐☐☐☐☐
9	A9	1c blue, IV	425.00	90.00	☐☐☐☐☐
a.		Printed on both sides, reverse inverted		—	☐☐☐☐☐
10	A10	3c orange brown, type I	1,250.	40.00	☐☐☐☐☐
a.		Printed on both sides		—	☐☐☐☐☐

Washington
A10

Thomas Jefferson
A11

A13

Type II. The design is complete at the top. The outer line at the bottom is broken in the middle. The shells are partly cut away.

A10

THREE CENTS.

Type I. There is an outer frame line at top and bottom.

A11

FIVE CENTS.

Type I. There are projections on all four sides.

A12

A14

Type III. The outer lines are broken above the top label and the "X" numerals. The outer line at the bottom and the shells are partly cut away, as in Type II.

A15

Type IV. The outer lines have been recut at top or bottom or both.

Types I, II, III and IV have complete ornaments at the sides of the stamps and three pearls at each outer edge of the bottom panel.

A12

TEN CENTS.

Type I. The "shells" at the lower corners are practically complete. The outer line below the label is very nearly complete. The outer lines are broken above the middle of the top label and the "X" in each upper corner.

A16

Same Designs as 1851-56 Issues.

Franklin
A20

ONE CENT.

Type V. Similar to type III of 1851-56 but with side ornaments partly cut away.

A21

THREE CENTS.

Type II. The outer frame line has been removed at top and bottom. The side frame lines were recut so as to be continuous from the top to the bottom of the plate.

Type IIa. The side frame lines extend only to the top and bottom of the stamp design.

A22

A22

FIVE CENTS.

Type II. The projections at top and bottom are partly cut away.

A23
(Two typical examples).

TEN CENTS.

Type V. The side ornaments are slightly cut away. Usually only one pearl remains at each end of the lower label but some copies show two or three pearls at the right side. At the bottom the outer line is complete and the shells nearly so. The outer lines at top are complete except over the right " X ".

A17   **A18**

A19

TWELVE CENTS.

Plate I. Outer frame lines complete.

Plate III. Outer frame lines noticeably uneven or broken, sometimes partly missing.

5

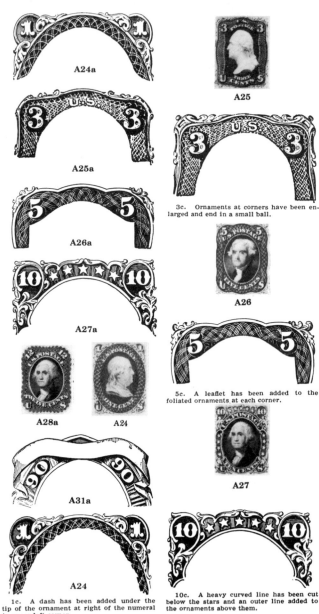

A24a

A25

A25a

3c. Ornaments at corners have been enlarged and end in a small ball.

A26a

A26

A27a

5c. A leaflet has been added to the foliated ornaments at each corner.

A28a   A24

A27

A31a

A24

1c. A dash has been added under the tip of the ornament at right of the numeral in upper left corner.

10c. A heavy curved line has been cut below the stars and an outer line added to the ornaments above them.

Scott No.	Illus No.		Description	Unused Value	Used Value	/ / / / / /
11	A10	3c	dull red, type I	130.00	7.00	☐☐☐☐☐
c.			Vert. half used as 1c on cover		7,500.	☐☐☐☐☐
d.			Diagonal half used as 1c on cover		7,000.	☐☐☐☐☐
e.			Double impression	—		☐☐☐☐☐
12	A11	5c	red brown, type I	8,500.	875.00	☐☐☐☐☐
13	A12	10c	green, type I	9,000.	575.00	☐☐☐☐☐
14	A13	10c	green, type II	2,000.	190.00	☐☐☐☐☐
15	A14	10c	green, type III	2,000.	190.00	☐☐☐☐☐
16	A15	10c	green, type IV	12,500.	1,100.	☐☐☐☐☐
17	A16	12c	black	2,500.	225.00	☐☐☐☐☐
a.			Diagonal half used as 6c on cover		2,000.	☐☐☐☐☐
b.			Vert. half used as 6c on cover		8,500.	☐☐☐☐☐
c.			Printed on both sides		5,500.	☐☐☐☐☐

1857-61, Perf. 15½

Scott No.	Illus No.		Description	Unused Value	Used Value	/ / / / / /
18	A5	1c	blue, type I	800.00	325.00	☐☐☐☐☐
19	A6	1c	blue, type Ia	11,500.	2,750.	☐☐☐☐☐
b.			Type Ic	1,500.	500.00	☐☐☐☐☐
20	A7	1c	blue, type II	450.00	150.00	☐☐☐☐☐
21	A8	1c	blue, type III	5,000.	1,250.	☐☐☐☐☐
22	A8	1c	blue, type IIIa	800.00	275.00	☐☐☐☐☐
b.			Horiz. pair, imperf. btwn.		5,000.	☐☐☐☐☐
23	A9	1c	blue, type IV	2,750.	325.00	☐☐☐☐☐
24	A20	1c	blue, type V	120.00	25.00	☐☐☐☐☐
b.			Laid paper		—	☐☐☐☐☐
25	A10	3c	rose, type I	900.00	30.00	☐☐☐☐☐
b.			Vert. pair, imperf. horiz. ..		10,000.	☐☐☐☐☐
26	A21	3c	dull red, type II	45.00	3.00	☐☐☐☐☐
a.		3c	dull red, type IIa	110.00	20.00	☐☐☐☐☐
b.			Horiz. pair, imperf. vert., type II	—	—	☐☐☐☐☐
c.			Vert. pair, imperf. horiz., type II		—	☐☐☐☐☐
d.			Horiz. pair, imperf. between, type II		—	☐☐☐☐☐
e.			Double impression, type II		—	☐☐☐☐☐
27	A11	5c	brick red, type I	9,000.	675.00	☐☐☐☐☐
28	A11	5c	red brown, type I	1,350.	250.00	☐☐☐☐☐
b.		5c	bright red brown	1,850.	400.00	☐☐☐☐☐
28A	A11	5c	Indian red, type I	12,000.	1,750.	☐☐☐☐☐
29	A11	5c	brown, type I	850.00	200.00	☐☐☐☐☐
30	A22	5c	orange brown, type II	750.00	1,000.	☐☐☐☐☐

Scott No.	Illus No.		Description	Unused Value	Used Value	/ / / / / /
30A	A22	5c	brown, type II	475.00	185.00	☐☐☐☐☐
b.			Printed on both sides	3,750.	3,000.	☐☐☐☐☐
31	A12	10c	green, type I	6,750.	500.00	☐☐☐☐☐
32	A13	10c	green, type II	2,500.	165.00	☐☐☐☐☐
33	A14	10c	green, type III	2,500.	165.00	☐☐☐☐☐
34	A15	10c	green, type IV	17,500.	1,400.	☐☐☐☐☐
35	A23	10c	green, type V	200.00	50.00	☐☐☐☐☐
36	A16	12c	black, plate 1	375.00	85.00	☐☐☐☐☐
a.			Diagonal half used as 6c on cover (1)		17,500.	☐☐☐☐☐
b.		12c	black, plate 3	350.00	110.00	☐☐☐☐☐
c.			Horiz. pair, imperf. between (1)	—		☐☐☐☐☐
37	A17	24c	gray lilac	675.00	200.00	☐☐☐☐☐
a.		24c	gray	675.00	200.00	☐☐☐☐☐
38	A18	30c	orange	750.00	300.00	☐☐☐☐☐
39	A19	90c	blue	1,150.	5,000.	☐☐☐☐☐

1875, Reprints, Without Gum, Perf. 12

40	A5	1c	bright blue	425.00		☐☐☐☐☐
41	A10	3c	scarlet	2,000.		☐☐☐☐☐
42	A22	5c	orange brown	900.00		☐☐☐☐☐
43	A12	10c	blue green	1,750.		☐☐☐☐☐
44	A16	12c	greenish black	2,000.		☐☐☐☐☐
45	A17	24c	black violet	2,000.		☐☐☐☐☐
46	A18	30c	yellow orange	2,000.		☐☐☐☐☐
47	A19	90c	deep blue	3,250.		☐☐☐☐☐

1861

62B	A27a	10c	dark green	5,000.	450.00	☐☐☐☐☐

1861-62

63	A24	1c	blue	140.00	15.00	☐☐☐☐☐
a.		1c	ultramarine	250.00	40.00	☐☐☐☐☐
b.		1c	dark blue	350.00	25.00	☐☐☐☐☐
c.			Laid paper	—	—	☐☐☐☐☐
d.			Vert. pair, imperf. horiz. ..	—	—	☐☐☐☐☐
e.			Printed on both sides	—	2,500.	☐☐☐☐☐
64	A25	3c	pink	4,500.	350.00	☐☐☐☐☐
a.		3c	pigeon blood pink	—	1,750.	☐☐☐☐☐
b.		3c	rose pink	300.00	45.00	☐☐☐☐☐
65	A25	3c	rose	70.00	1.00	☐☐☐☐☐
b.			Laid paper	—	—	☐☐☐☐☐
d.			Vert. pair, imperf. horiz. ..	1,200.	750.00	☐☐☐☐☐
e.			Printed on both sides	1,650.	1,000.	☐☐☐☐☐
f.			Double impression		1,200.	☐☐☐☐☐

8

Scott No.	Illus No.		Description	Unused Value	Used Value	||||||
67	A26	5c	buff	*6,000.*	425.00	☐☐☐☐☐
a.		5c	brown yellow	*6,000.*	425.00	☐☐☐☐☐
b.		5c	olive yellow	*6,000.*	425.00	☐☐☐☐☐
68	A27	10c	yellow green	275.00	30.00	☐☐☐☐☐
a.		10c	dark green	290.00	31.00	☐☐☐☐☐
b.			Vert. pair, imperf. horiz. ..		*3,500.*	☐☐☐☐☐
69	A28	12c	black	550.00	55.00	☐☐☐☐☐
70	A29	24c	red lilac	700.00	80.00	☐☐☐☐☐
a.		24c	brown lilac	600.00	67.50	☐☐☐☐☐
b.		24c	steel blue	4,000.	300.00	☐☐☐☐☐
c.		24c	violet, thin paper	6,500.	550.00	☐☐☐☐☐
d.		24c	grayish lilac, thin paper ...	1,400.	350.00	☐☐☐☐☐
71	A30	30c	orange	625.00	70.00	☐☐☐☐☐
a.			Printed on both sides	—		☐☐☐☐☐
72	A31	90c	blue	1,450.	250.00	☐☐☐☐☐
a.		90c	pale blue	1,450.	250.00	☐☐☐☐☐
b.		90c	dark blue	1,600.	275.00	☐☐☐☐☐

1861-66

Scott No.	Illus No.		Description	Unused Value	Used Value	||||||
73	A32	2c	black	175.00	22.50	☐☐☐☐☐
a.			Half used as 1c on cover, diagonal, vert. or horiz.		*1,250.*	☐☐☐☐☐
d.			Laid paper	—	—	☐☐☐☐☐
e.			Printed on both sides		*5,000.*	☐☐☐☐☐
75	A26	5c	red brown	1,450.	225.00	☐☐☐☐☐
76	A26	5c	brown	375.00	60.00	☐☐☐☐☐
a.		5c	dark brown	425.00	72.50	☐☐☐☐☐
b.			Laid paper	—		☐☐☐☐☐
77	A33	15c	black	575.00	70.00	☐☐☐☐☐
78	A29	24c	lilac	300.00	50.00	☐☐☐☐☐
a.		24c	grayish lilac	300.00	50.00	☐☐☐☐☐
b.		24c	gray	300.00	50.00	☐☐☐☐☐
c.		24c	black violet	*17,500.*	*1,100.*	☐☐☐☐☐
d.			Printed on both sides		*3,500.*	☐☐☐☐☐

1867, Perf. 12, Grill with points up
A. Grill covering the entire stamp

Scott No.	Illus No.		Description	Unused Value	Used Value	||||||
79	A25	3c	rose	2,000.	475.00	☐☐☐☐☐
b.			Printed on both sides	—		☐☐☐☐☐
80	A26	5c	brown	—	—	☐☐☐☐☐
a.		5c	dark brown		—	☐☐☐☐☐
81	A30	30c	orange		—	☐☐☐☐☐

B. Grill about 18x15mm (22 by 18 points)

Scott No.	Illus No.		Description	Unused Value	Used Value	||||||
82	A25	3c	rose		45,000.	☐☐☐☐☐

A28

12c. Ovals and scrolls have been added to the corners.

A29   **A30**

    Grill

A31

A31

90c. Parallel lines form an angle above the ribbon with "U. S. Postage"; between these lines a row of dashes has been added and a point of color to the apex of the lower pair.

A32   **A33**

A34   **A35**

A36   **A37**

A38   **A39**

A40   **A41**

A42   **A43**

A40

FIFTEEN CENTS. Type I. Picture unframed.

A40a

Type II. Picture framed.

Type III. Same as type I but without fringe of brown shading lines around central vignette.

Scott No.	Illus No.	Description	Unused Value	Used Value	//////

Grill with points down

C. Grill about 13x16mm (16 to 17 by 18 to 21 points)

Scott No.	Illus No.	Description	Unused Value	Used Value	
83	A25	3c rose	2,250.	425.00	☐☐☐☐☐

D. Grill about 12x14mm (15 by 17 to 18 points)

Scott No.	Illus No.	Description	Unused Value	Used Value	
84	A32	2c black	4,500.	1,100.	☐☐☐☐☐
85	A25	3c rose	1,900.	450.00	☐☐☐☐☐

Z. Grill about 11x14mm (13 to 14 by 17 to 18 points)

Scott No.	Illus No.	Description	Unused Value	Used Value	
85A	A24	1c blue		—	☐☐☐☐☐
85B	A32	2c black	1,750.	400.00	☐☐☐☐☐
85C	A25	3c rose	5,000.	950.00	☐☐☐☐☐
85D	A27	10c green		25,000.	☐☐☐☐☐
85E	A28	12c black	2,500.	575.00	☐☐☐☐☐
85F	A33	15c black		100,000.	☐☐☐☐☐

E. Grill about 11x13mm (14 by 15 to 17 points)

Scott No.	Illus No.	Description	Unused Value	Used Value	
86	A24	1c blue	1,000.	250.00	☐☐☐☐☐
a.		1c dull blue	1,000.	250.00	☐☐☐☐☐
87	A32	2c black	450.00	70.00	☐☐☐☐☐
a.		Half used as 1c on cover, diagonal or vert.		2,000.	☐☐☐☐☐
88	A25	3c rose	350.00	10.00	☐☐☐☐☐
a.		3c lake red	400.00	12.50	☐☐☐☐☐
89	A27	10c green	1,750.	175.00	☐☐☐☐☐
90	A28	12c black	2,000.	200.00	☐☐☐☐☐
91	A33	15c black	5,000.	450.00	☐☐☐☐☐

F. Grill about 9x13mm (11 to 12 by 15 to 17 points)

Scott No.	Illus No.	Description	Unused Value	Used Value	
92	A24	1c blue	450.00	100.00	☐☐☐☐☐
a.		1c pale blue	450.00	100.00	☐☐☐☐☐
93	A32	2c black	175.00	25.00	☐☐☐☐☐
a.		Half used as 1c on cover, diagonal or vert.		1,250.	☐☐☐☐☐
c.		Horiz. half used as 1c on cover		1,750.	☐☐☐☐☐
94	A25	3c red	125.00	2.50	☐☐☐☐☐
a.		3c rose	125.00	2.50	☐☐☐☐☐
c.		Vert. pair, imperf. horiz.	1,000.		☐☐☐☐☐
d.		Printed on both sides	1,100.		☐☐☐☐☐
95	A26	5c brown	1,500.	225.00	☐☐☐☐☐
a.		5c dark brown	1,600.	250.00	☐☐☐☐☐
96	A27	10c yellow green	900.00	110.00	☐☐☐☐☐
a.		10c dark green	900.00	110.00	☐☐☐☐☐
97	A28	12c black	900.00	125.00	☐☐☐☐☐
98	A33	15c black	900.00	135.00	☐☐☐☐☐
99	A29	24c gray lilac	1,700.	425.00	☐☐☐☐☐
100	A30	30c orange	2,500.	375.00	☐☐☐☐☐
101	A31	90c blue	5,000.	750.00	☐☐☐☐☐

A44 A45 A48 A49

A44

A48

A45

A49

A46

A50

A46

A51

A47

A50

A47

A51

12

Scott No.	Illus No.		Description	Unused Value	Used Value	//////

1875, Reprints, Without Gum, Perf. 12

Scott No.	Illus No.		Description	Unused Value	Used Value	
102	A24	1c	blue	500.00	800.00	☐☐☐☐☐
103	A32	2c	black	2,250.	4,000.	☐☐☐☐☐
104	A25	3c	brown red	2,500.	4,250.	☐☐☐☐☐
105	A26	5c	brown	1,850.	2,250.	☐☐☐☐☐
106	A27	10c	green	2,000.	3,750.	☐☐☐☐☐
107	A28	12c	black	2,750.	4,500.	☐☐☐☐☐
108	A33	15c	black	2,750.	4,750.	☐☐☐☐☐
109	A29	24c	deep violet	3,750.	6,000.	☐☐☐☐☐
110	A30	30c	brownish orange	4,250.	6,000.	☐☐☐☐☐
111	A31	90c	blue	5,250.	20,000.	☐☐☐☐☐

1869, Perf. 12
G. Grill measuring 9½x9mm

Scott No.	Illus No.		Description	Unused Value	Used Value	
112	A34	1c	buff	275.00	65.00	☐☐☐☐☐
b.			Without grill	750.00		☐☐☐☐☐
113	A35	2c	brown	200.00	25.00	☐☐☐☐☐
b.			Without grill	600.00		☐☐☐☐☐
c.			Half used as 1c on cover, diagonal, vert. or horiz.		—	☐☐☐☐☐
d.			Printed on both sides		—	☐☐☐☐☐
114	A36	3c	ultramarine	175.00	7.00	☐☐☐☐☐
a.			Without grill	600.00	—	☐☐☐☐☐
b.			Vert. one third used as 1c on cover		—	☐☐☐☐☐
c.			Vert. two thirds used as 2c on cover		—	☐☐☐☐☐
d.			Double impression		—	☐☐☐☐☐
115	A37	6c	ultramarine	825.00	95.00	☐☐☐☐☐
b.			Vert. half used as 3c on cover		—	☐☐☐☐☐
116	A38	10c	yellow	900.00	85.00	☐☐☐☐☐
117	A39	12c	green	850.00	95.00	☐☐☐☐☐
118	A40	15c	brown & blue, Type I	2,250.	325.00	☐☐☐☐☐
a.			Without grill	3,500.		☐☐☐☐☐
119	A40a	15c	brown & blue, type II	1,000.	150.00	☐☐☐☐☐
b.			Center inverted	175,000.	14,000.	☐☐☐☐☐
c.			Center double, one inverted	—	—	☐☐☐☐☐
120	A41	24c	green & violet	2,400.	500.00	☐☐☐☐☐
a.			Without grill	5,000.		☐☐☐☐☐
b.			Center inverted	150,000.	15,000.	☐☐☐☐☐
121	A42	30c	blue & carmine	2,400.	250.00	☐☐☐☐☐
a.			Without grill	3,750.		☐☐☐☐☐
b.			Flags inverted	165,000.	55,000.	☐☐☐☐☐
122	A43	90c	carmine & black	5,000.	1,150.	☐☐☐☐☐
a.			Without grill	10,000.		☐☐☐☐☐

A52

A53

A54

A44a

1c.   In pearl at left of numeral "1" is a small crescent.

A45a

2c.   Under the scroll at the left of "U. S." there is a small diagonal line. This mark seldom shows clearly. The stamp, No. 157, can be distinguished by its color.

A46a

3c.   The under part of the upper tail of the left ribbon is heavily shaded.

A47a

6c.   The first four vertical lines of the shading in the lower part of the left ribbon have been strengthened.

A48a

7c.   Two small semi-circles are drawn around the ends of the lines which outline the ball in the lower right hand corner.

A49a

10c.   There is a small semi-circle in the scroll at the right end of the upper label.

Scott No.	Illus No.		Description	Unused Value	Used Value	//////

1875, Re-issues, Without Gum, Hard White Paper

Scott No.	Illus No.		Description	Unused Value	Used Value	//////
123	A34	1c	buff	325.00	225.00	☐☐☐☐☐
124	A35	2c	brown	375.00	325.00	☐☐☐☐☐
125	A36	3c	blue	3,000.	10,000.	☐☐☐☐☐
126	A37	6c	blue	850.00	550.00	☐☐☐☐☐
127	A38	10c	yellow	1,400.	1,200.	☐☐☐☐☐
128	A39	12c	green	1,500.	1,200.	☐☐☐☐☐
129	A40	15c	brown & blue, type III	1,300.	550.00	☐☐☐☐☐
a.			Imperf. horiz., single	1,600.	—	☐☐☐☐☐
130	A41	24c	green & violet	1,250.	550.00	☐☐☐☐☐
131	A42	30c	blue & carmine	1,750.	1,000.	☐☐☐☐☐
132	A43	90c	carmine & black	4,000.	4,250.	☐☐☐☐☐

1880, Soft Porous Paper

Scott No.	Illus No.		Description	Unused Value	Used Value	//////
133	A34	1c	buff	200.00	175.00	☐☐☐☐☐
a.		1c	brown orange	175.00	150.00	☐☐☐☐☐

1870-71, Perf. 12, With Grill

Scott No.	Illus No.		Description	Unused Value	Used Value	//////
134	A44	1c	ultramarine	800.00	60.00	☐☐☐☐☐
135	A45	2c	red brown	475.00	37.50	☐☐☐☐☐
a.			Diagonal half used as 1c on cover	—		☐☐☐☐☐
136	A46	3c	green	365.00	10.00	☐☐☐☐☐
137	A47	6c	carmine	1,850.	300.00	☐☐☐☐☐
138	A48	7c	vermilion	1,350.	275.00	☐☐☐☐☐
139	A49	10c	brown	1,600.	450.00	☐☐☐☐☐
140	A50	12c	dull violet	13,000.	1,750.	☐☐☐☐☐
141	A51	15c	orange	2,750.	750.00	☐☐☐☐☐
142	A52	24c	purple	—	11,500.	☐☐☐☐☐
143	A53	30c	black	5,250.	950.00	☐☐☐☐☐
144	A54	90c	carmine	6,750.	800.00	☐☐☐☐☐

1870-71, Perf. 12, Without grill

Scott No.	Illus No.		Description	Unused Value	Used Value	//////
145	A44	1c	ultramarine	200.00	7.50	☐☐☐☐☐
146	A45	2c	red brown	125.00	5.00	☐☐☐☐☐
a.			Half used as 1c on cover, diagonal or vert.	—		☐☐☐☐☐
c.			Double impression	—		☐☐☐☐☐
147	A46	3c	green	150.00	50	☐☐☐☐☐
a.			Printed on both sides		1,500.	☐☐☐☐☐
b.			Double impression		1,000.	☐☐☐☐☐
148	A47	6c	carmine	290.00	12.00	☐☐☐☐☐
a.			Vert. half used as 3c on cover	—		☐☐☐☐☐
b.			Double impression		1,250.	☐☐☐☐☐
149	A48	7c	vermilion	375.00	55.00	☐☐☐☐☐
150	A49	10c	brown	290.00	12.00	☐☐☐☐☐
151	A50	12c	dull violet	625.00	65.00	☐☐☐☐☐

A50a

12c. The balls of the figure "2" are crescent shaped.

A51a

15c. In the lower part of the triangle in the upper left corner two lines have been made heavier forming a "V". This mark can be found on some of the Continental and American (1879) printings, but not all stamps show it.

Secret marks were added to the dies of the 24c, 30c and 90c but new plates were not made from them. The various printings of these stamps can be distinguished only by the shades and paper.

A55   **A56**

A44b

1c. The vertical lines in the upper part of the stamp have been so deepened that the background often appears to be solid. Lines of shading have been added to the upper arabesques.

A46b

3c. The shading at the sides of the central oval appears only about one-half the previous width. A short horizontal dash has been cut about 1mm. below the "TS" of "CENTS."

A47b

6c. On the original stamps four vertical lines can be counted from the edge of the panel to the outside of the stamp. On the re-engraved stamps there are but three lines in the same place.

A49b

10c. On the original stamps there are five vertical lines between the left side of the oval and the edge of the shield. There are only four lines on the re-engraved stamps. In the lower part of the latter, also, the horizontal lines of the background have been strengthened.

Scott No.	Illus No.		Description	Unused Value	Used Value	//////
152	A51	15c	bright orange	600.00	62.50	
a.			Double impression		—	
153	A52	24c	purple	700.00	85.00	
154	A53	30c	black	1,200.	100.00	
155	A54	90c	carmine	1,600.	185.00	

1873, Perf. 12

Scott No.	Illus No.		Description	Unused Value	Used Value	//////
156	A44a	1c	ultramarine	75.00	1.75	
e.			With grill	1,400.		
f.			Imperf., pair	—	500.00	
157	A45a	2c	brown	210.00	10.00	
c.			With grill	1,100.	600.00	
d.			Double impression	—	—	
e.			Vert. half used as 1c on cover		—	
158	A46a	3c	green	65.00	15	
e.			With grill	175.00		
h.			Horiz. pair, imperf. vert.		—	
i.			Horiz. pair, imperf. btwn.		1,300.	
j.			Double impression		600.00	
k.			Printed on both sides		—	
159	A47a	6c	dull pink	235.00	10.00	
b.			With grill	1,000.		
160	A48a	7c	orange vermilion	465.00	57.50	
a.			With grill	1,500.		
161	A49a	10c	brown	285.00	11.50	
c.			With grill	2,000.		
d.			Horiz. pair, imperf. btwn.		2,500.	
162	A50a	12c	black violet	775.00	67.50	
a.			With grill	3,000.		
163	A51a	15c	yellow orange	700.00	62.50	
a.			With grill	3,000.		
164	A52	24c	purple		—	
165	A53	30c	gray black	800.00	65.00	
c.			With grill	3,000.		
166	A54	90c	rose carmine	1,600.	185.00	

1875, Re-issues, Without Gum, Hard White Paper, Perf. 12

Scott No.	Illus No.		Description	Unused Value	Used Value	//////
167	A44a	1c	ultra	7,500.		
168	A45a	2c	dark brown	3,500.		
169	A46a	3c	blue green	9,500.	—	
170	A47a	6c	dull rose	8,500.		
171	A48a	7c	reddish vermilion	2,250.		
172	A49a	10c	pale brown	8,250.		
173	A50a	12c	dark violet	3,000.		
174	A51a	15c	bright orange	8,250.		
175	A52	24c	dull purple	1,850.		

17

A57   A58   A59

A60   A61   A62

A63   A64   A65

A66   A67   A68   A69   A70

HOW TO USE THIS BOOK

The number in the first column is its Scott number or identifying number. The letter and number that come next (A41) indicate the design and refer to the illustration so designated. Following that is the denomination of the stamp and its color. Finally, the value, unused and used is shown.

Scott No.	Illus No.		Description	Unused Value	Used Value	/ / / / / /
176	A53	30c	greenish black	7,500.		▢▢▢▢▢
177	A54	90c	violet carmine	7,500.		▢▢▢▢▢

Yellowish Wove Paper, Perf. 12

178	A45a	2c	vermilion	190.00	5.00	▢▢▢▢▢
b.			Half used as 1c on cover..		—	▢▢▢▢▢
c.			With grill	300.00		▢▢▢▢▢
179	A55	5c	blue	235.00	9.00	▢▢▢▢▢
c.			With grill	400.00		▢▢▢▢▢

Re-issues, Without Gum, Hard White Paper, Perf. 12

180	A45a	2c	carmine vermilion	17,500.		▢▢▢▢▢
181	A55	2c	bright blue	27,500.		▢▢▢▢▢

1879, Perf. 12, Soft Paper

182	A44a	1c	dark ultra	160.00	1.25	▢▢▢▢▢
183	A45a	2c	vermilion	70.00	1.25	▢▢▢▢▢
a.			Double impression	—	500.00	▢▢▢▢▢
184	A46a	3c	green	55.00	15	▢▢▢▢▢
b.			Double impression		—	▢▢▢▢▢
185	A55	5c	blue	300.00	8.00	▢▢▢▢▢
186	A47a	6c	pink	550.00	13.00	▢▢▢▢▢
187	A49	10c	brown (without secret mark)	875.00	15.00	▢▢▢▢▢
188	A49a	10c	brown (with secret mark)	600.00	16.00	▢▢▢▢▢
189	A51a	15c	red orange	200.00	15.00	▢▢▢▢▢
190	A53	30c	full black	575.00	35.00	▢▢▢▢▢
191	A54	90c	carmine	1,200.	155.00	▢▢▢▢▢

1880

Special Printing, Without Gum, Soft Porous Paper, Perf. 12

192	A44a	1c	dark ultra	10,000.		▢▢▢▢▢
193	A45a	2c	black brown	6,000.		▢▢▢▢▢
194	A46a	3c	blue green	15,000.		▢▢▢▢▢
195	A47a	6c	dull rose	11,000.		▢▢▢▢▢
196	A48a	7c	scarlet vermilion	2,250.		▢▢▢▢▢
197	A49a	10c	deep brown	10,000.		▢▢▢▢▢
198	A50a	12c	black purple	3,500.		▢▢▢▢▢
199	A51a	15c	orange	11,000.		▢▢▢▢▢
200	A52	24c	dark violet	3,500.		▢▢▢▢▢
201	A53	30c	greenish black	8,500.		▢▢▢▢▢
202	A54	90c	dull carmine	9,000.		▢▢▢▢▢
203	A45a	30c	scarlet vermilion	18,000.		▢▢▢▢▢
204	A55	90c	deep blue	30,000.		▢▢▢▢▢

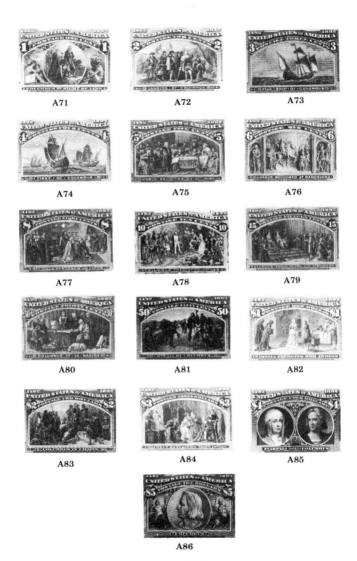

A71   A72   A73

A74   A75   A76

A77   A78   A79

A80   A81   A82

A83   A84   A85

A86

TWO CENTS.

Type I. The horizontal lines of the ground work run across the triangle and are of the same thickness within it as without.

Type II. The horizontal lines cross the triangle but are thinner within it than without.

Type III. The horizontal lines do not cross the double frame lines of the triangle. The lines within the triangle are thin, as in type II.

Scott No.	Illus No.		Description	Unused Value	Used Value	/ / / / / /
1882, Perf. 12						
205	A56	5c	yellow brown	135.00	4.50	☐☐☐☐☐

Special Printing, Soft Porous Paper, Without Gum

205C	A56	5c	gray brown	*20,000.*		☐☐☐☐☐

1881-82, Perf. 12						
206	A44b	1c	gray blue	40.00	40	☐☐☐☐☐
207	A46b	3c	blue green	45.00	15	☐☐☐☐☐
c.			Double impression		—	☐☐☐☐☐
208	A47b	6c	rose	250.00	45.00	☐☐☐☐☐
a.		6c	brown red	225.00	55.00	☐☐☐☐☐
209	A49b	10c	brown	90.00	2.50	☐☐☐☐☐
b.		10c	black brown	140.00	10.00	☐☐☐☐☐
c.			Double impression		—	☐☐☐☐☐

1883, Perf. 12						
210	A57	2c	red brown	37.50	15	☐☐☐☐☐
211	A58	4c	blue green	160.00	8.00	☐☐☐☐☐

Special Printing, Soft Porous Paper, Without Gum

211B	A57	2c	pale red brown	*600.00*	—	☐☐☐☐☐
c.			Horiz. pair, imperf. btwn.	*2,000.*	—	☐☐☐☐☐
211D	A58	4c	deep blue green	*15,000.*		☐☐☐☐☐

1887, Perf. 12						
212	A59	1c	ultramarine	65.00	65	☐☐☐☐☐
213	A57	2c	green	25.00	15	☐☐☐☐☐
b.			Printed on both sides		—	☐☐☐☐☐
214	A46b	3c	vermilion	50.00	37.50	☐☐☐☐☐

1888, Perf. 12						
215	A58	4c	carmine	160.00	11.00	☐☐☐☐☐
216	A56	5c	indigo	160.00	6.50	☐☐☐☐☐
217	A53	30c	orange brown	360.00	75.00	☐☐☐☐☐
218	A54	90c	purple	750.00	130.00	☐☐☐☐☐

1890-93, Perf. 12						
219	A60	1c	dull blue	18.50	15	☐☐☐☐☐
219D	A61	2c	lake	150.00	45	☐☐☐☐☐
220	A61	2c	carmine	15.00	15	☐☐☐☐☐
a.			Cap on left "2"	35.00	1.00	☐☐☐☐☐
c.			Cap on both "2s"	125.00	8.00	☐☐☐☐☐
221	A62	3c	purple	50.00	4.50	☐☐☐☐☐
222	A63	4c	dark brown	50.00	1.50	☐☐☐☐☐
223	A64	5c	chocolate	50.00	1.50	☐☐☐☐☐
224	A65	6c	brown red	55.00	15.00	☐☐☐☐☐
225	A66	8c	lilac	40.00	8.50	☐☐☐☐☐

A87   A88   A89   A90

A91   A92   A93   A94

A95   A96   A97   A98

A99

ONE DOLLAR.

Type I. The circles enclosing "$1" are broken where they meet the curved line below "One Dollar." The fifteen left vertical rows of impressions from plate 76 are Type I, the balance being Type II.

Type II. The circles are complete.

TEN CENTS

Type I. Tips of foliate ornaments do not impinge on white curved line below "TEN CENTS".

Type II. Tips of ornaments break curved line below "E" of "TEN" and "T" of "CENTS".

A100   A101   A102

A103   A104   A105

A106   A107   A108

22

Scott No.	Illus No.		Description	Unused Value	Used Value	//////
226	A67	10c	green	95.00	1.75	☐☐☐☐☐
227	A68	15c	indigo	150.00	15.00	☐☐☐☐☐
228	A69	30c	black	225.00	20.00	☐☐☐☐☐
229	A70	90c	orange	350.00	95.00	☐☐☐☐☐

1893, Perf. 12

Scott No.	Illus No.		Description	Unused Value	Used Value	//////
230	A71	1c	deep blue	21.00	25	☐☐☐☐☐
231	A72	2c	brown violet	19.00	15	☐☐☐☐☐
232	A73	3c	green	50.00	12.50	☐☐☐☐☐
233	A74	4c	ultra	70.00	5.50	☐☐☐☐☐
a.		4c	blue (error)	_10,000._	_4,000._	☐☐☐☐☐
234	A75	5c	chocolate	75.00	6.50	☐☐☐☐☐
235	A76	6c	purple	70.00	18.00	☐☐☐☐☐
a.		6c	red violet	70.00	18.00	☐☐☐☐☐
236	A77	8c	magenta	60.00	8.00	☐☐☐☐☐
237	A78	10c	black brown	115.00	5.50	☐☐☐☐☐
238	A79	15c	dark green	190.00	50.00	☐☐☐☐☐
239	A80	30c	orange brown	260.00	70.00	☐☐☐☐☐
240	A81	50c	slate blue	450.00	120.00	☐☐☐☐☐
241	A82	$1	salmon	1,350.	525.00	☐☐☐☐☐
242	A83	$2	brown red	1,400.	450.00	☐☐☐☐☐
243	A84	$3	yellow green	2,400.	800.00	☐☐☐☐☐
a.		$3	olive green	2,400.	800.00	☐☐☐☐☐
244	A85	$4	crimson lake	2,900.	1,000.	☐☐☐☐☐
a.		$4	rose carmine	2,900.	1,000.	☐☐☐☐☐
245	A86	$5	black	3,250.	1,200.	☐☐☐☐☐

1894, Perf. 12, Unwatermarked

Scott No.	Illus No.		Description	Unused Value	Used Value	//////
246	A87	1c	ultramarine	16.00	2.00	☐☐☐☐☐
247	A87	1c	blue	40.00	85	☐☐☐☐☐
248	A88	2c	pink, type I	12.50	1.50	☐☐☐☐☐
249	A88	2c	carmine lake, type I	77.50	1.00	☐☐☐☐☐
250	A88	2c	carmine, type I	15.00	25	☐☐☐☐☐
a.			Vert. pair, imperf. horiz.	_1,500._		☐☐☐☐☐
b.			Horiz, pair, imperf. btwn.	_1,500._		☐☐☐☐☐
251	A88	2c	carmine, type II	125.00	1.50	☐☐☐☐☐
252	A88	2c	carmine, type III	70.00	2.00	☐☐☐☐☐
a.			Horiz. pair, imperf. vert.	_1,350._		☐☐☐☐☐
b.			Horiz. pair, imperf. btwn.	_1,500._		☐☐☐☐☐
253	A89	3c	purple	52.50	4.25	☐☐☐☐☐
254	A90	4c	dark brown	60.00	2.00	☐☐☐☐☐
255	A91	5c	chocolate	50.00	2.50	☐☐☐☐☐
c.			Vert. pair, imperf. horiz.	_1,000._		☐☐☐☐☐
256	A92	6c	dull brown	90.00	12.00	☐☐☐☐☐
a.			Vert. pair, imperf. horiz.	_850.00_		☐☐☐☐☐
257	A93	8c	violet brown	80.00	8.00	☐☐☐☐☐
258	A94	10c	dark green	115.00	5.00	☐☐☐☐☐
259	A95	15c	dark blue	185.00	30.00	☐☐☐☐☐

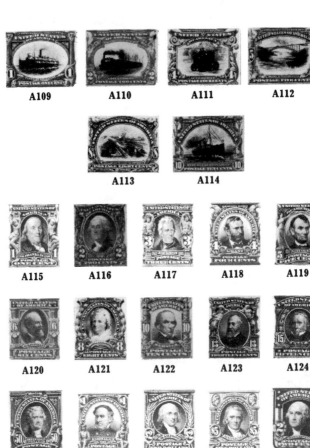

A109 A110 A111 A112

A113 A114

A115 A116 A117 A118 A119

A120 A121 A122 A123 A124

A125 A126 A127 A128 A129

A130 A131 A132

A133 A134

Scott No.	Illus No.		Description	Unused Value	Used Value	//////
260	A96	50c	orange	250.00	60.00	☐☐☐☐☐
261	A97	$1	black, type I	500.00	160.00	☐☐☐☐☐
261A	A97	$1	black, type II	1,300.	350.00	☐☐☐☐☐
262	A98	$2	bright blue	1,700.	400.00	☐☐☐☐☐
263	A99	$5	dark green	2,250.	750.00	☐☐☐☐☐

1895, Watermark 191, Perf. 12

Scott No.	Illus No.		Description	Unused Value	Used Value	//////
264	A87	1c	blue	3.50	15	☐☐☐☐☐
265	A88	2c	carmine, type I	18.00	40	☐☐☐☐☐
266	A88	2c	carmine, type II	15.00	1.75	☐☐☐☐☐
267	A88	2c	carmine, type III	3.00	15	☐☐☐☐☐
268	A89	3c	purple	22.50	65	☐☐☐☐☐
269	A90	4c	dark brown	24.00	75	☐☐☐☐☐
270	A91	5c	chocolate	22.50	1.20	☐☐☐☐☐
271	A92	6c	dull brown	42.50	2.50	☐☐☐☐☐
a.			Wmkd. USIR	2,250.	350.00	☐☐☐☐☐
272	A93	8c	violet brown	35.00	65	☐☐☐☐☐
a.			Wmkd. USIR	1,750.	110.00	☐☐☐☐☐
273	A94	10c	dark green	45.00	80	☐☐☐☐☐
274	A95	15c	dark blue	125.00	5.50	☐☐☐☐☐
275	A96	50c	orange	175.00	14.00	☐☐☐☐☐
a.		50c	red orange	195.00	16.00	☐☐☐☐☐
276	A97	$1	black, type I	425.00	45.00	☐☐☐☐☐
276A	A97	$1	black, type II	875.00	95.00	☐☐☐☐☐
277	A98	$2	bright blue	675.00	225.00	☐☐☐☐☐
a.		$2	dark blue	650.00	235.00	☐☐☐☐☐
278	A99	$5	dark green	1,350.	300.00	☐☐☐☐☐

1898, Watermark 191, Perf. 12

Scott No.	Illus No.		Description	Unused Value	Used Value	//////
279	A87	1c	deep green	6.00	15	☐☐☐☐☐
279B	A88	2c	red, type III	5.50	15	☐☐☐☐☐
c.		2c	rose carmine, type III	185.00	25.00	☐☐☐☐☐
d.		2c	orange red, type III	6.50	15	☐☐☐☐☐
e.			Booklet pane of 6	350.00	200.00	☐☐☐☐☐
f.		2c	deep red, type III	12.50	75	☐☐☐☐☐
280	A90	4c	rose brown	20.00	45	☐☐☐☐☐
a.		4c	lilac brown	20.00	45	☐☐☐☐☐
b.		4c	orange brown	20.00	45	☐☐☐☐☐
281	A91	5c	dark blue	22.50	40	☐☐☐☐☐
282	A92	6c	lake	32.50	1.40	☐☐☐☐☐
a.		6c	purple lake	35.00	1.65	☐☐☐☐☐
282C	A94	10c	brown, type I	125.00	1.20	☐☐☐☐☐
283	A94	10c	org brown, type II	75.00	1.00	☐☐☐☐☐
284	A95	15c	olive green	100.00	4.50	☐☐☐☐☐
285	A100	1c	dark yellow green	21.00	4.00	☐☐☐☐☐
286	A101	2c	copper red	19.00	1.00	☐☐☐☐☐

Scott No.	Illus No.		Description	Unused Value	Used Value	//////
287	A102	4c	orange	110.00	16.00	☐☐☐☐☐
288	A103	5c	dull blue	95.00	14.00	☐☐☐☐☐
289	A104	8c	violet brown	140.00	30.00	☐☐☐☐☐
a.			Vert. pair, imperf. horiz.	13,500.		☐☐☐☐☐
290	A105	10c	gray violet	135.00	18.00	☐☐☐☐☐
291	A106	50c	sage green	400.00	150.00	☐☐☐☐☐
292	A107	$1	black	1,050.	400.00	☐☐☐☐☐
293	A108	$2	orange brown	1,700.	700.00	☐☐☐☐☐

1901, Watermark 191, Perf. 12

Scott No.	Illus No.		Description	Unused Value	Used Value	//////
294	A109	1c	green & black	16.00	2.50	☐☐☐☐☐
a.			Center inverted	9,000.	5,500.	☐☐☐☐☐
295	A110	2c	carmine & black	15.00	75	☐☐☐☐☐
a.			Center inverted	30,000.	13,500.	☐☐☐☐☐
296	A111	4c	deep red brown & black	75.00	12.50	☐☐☐☐☐
a.			Center inverted	12,500.		☐☐☐☐☐
297	A112	5c	ultra & black	90.00	11.00	☐☐☐☐☐
298	A113	8c	brown violet & black	100.00	45.00	☐☐☐☐☐
299	A114	10c	yellow brown & black	160.00	20.00	☐☐☐☐☐

1902-03, Watermark 191, Perf. 12

Scott No.	Illus No.		Description	Unused Value	Used Value	//////
300	A115	1c	blue green	6.00	15	☐☐☐☐☐
b.			Booklet pane of 6	450.00	250.00	☐☐☐☐☐
301	A116	2c	carmine	8.00	15	☐☐☐☐☐
c.			Booklet pane of 6	400.00	250.00	☐☐☐☐☐
302	A117	3c	bright violet	30.00	2.00	☐☐☐☐☐
303	A118	4c	brown	30.00	90	☐☐☐☐☐
304	A119	5c	blue	35.00	1.10	☐☐☐☐☐
305	A120	6c	claret	40.00	2.00	☐☐☐☐☐
306	A121	8c	violet black	27.50	1.50	☐☐☐☐☐
307	A122	10c	pale red brown	30.00	70	☐☐☐☐☐
308	A123	13c	purple black	27.50	5.00	☐☐☐☐☐
309	A124	15c	olive green	90.00	3.75	☐☐☐☐☐
310	A125	50c	orange	285.00	17.50	☐☐☐☐☐
311	A126	$1	black	450.00	45.00	☐☐☐☐☐
312	A127	$2	dark blue	675.00	140.00	☐☐☐☐☐
313	A128	$5	dark green	2,000.	450.00	☐☐☐☐☐

1906-08, Imperf.

Scott No.	Illus No.		Description	Unused Value	Used Value	//////
314	A115	1c	blue green	20.00	15.00	☐☐☐☐☐
314A	A118	4c	brown	18,500.	11,000.	☐☐☐☐☐
315	A119	5c	blue	300.00	350.00	☐☐☐☐☐

1908, Coil Stamps, Perf. 12 Horizontally

Scott No.	Illus No.		Description	Unused Value	Used Value	//////
316	A115	1c	blue green, pair	50,000.	—	☐☐☐☐☐
317	A119	5c	blue, pair	6,000.	—	☐☐☐☐☐

| A135 | A136 | A137 |

| Franklin A138 | Washington A139 | Washington A140 | Franklin A148 | A141 |

| A142 | A143 |

| A144 | A145 | A146 | A147 |

TYPE I

THREE CENTS.

Type I. The top line of the toga rope is weak and the rope shading lines are thin. The fifth line from the left is missing.
The line between the lips is thin.
Used on both flat plate and rotary press printings.

28

Scott No.	Illus No.		Description	Unused Value	Used Value	/ / / / / /
Perf. 12 Vertically						
318	A115	1c	blue green, pair	*5,000.*	—	☐☐☐☐☐
1903, Watermark 191, Perf. 12						
319	A129	2c	carmine (I)	4.00	15	☐☐☐☐☐
a.		2c	lake (I)	—	—	☐☐☐☐☐
b.		2c	carmine rose (I)	6.00	20	☐☐☐☐☐
c.		2c	scarlet (I)	4.00	15	☐☐☐☐☐
d.			Vert. pair, imperf. horiz. ..	*2,000.*		☐☐☐☐☐
e.			Vert. pair, imperf. btwn. ..	*950.00*		☐☐☐☐☐
f.		2c	lake (II)	5.00	20	☐☐☐☐☐
g.			Booklet pane of 6, car (I) .	90.00	*50.00*	☐☐☐☐☐
h.			As "g" (II)	150.00		☐☐☐☐☐
i.		2c	carmine (II)	17.50	—	☐☐☐☐☐
j.		2c	carmine rose (II)	8.00	50	☐☐☐☐☐
k.		2c	scarlet (II)	5.00	30	☐☐☐☐☐
m.			As "g," lake (I)	—		☐☐☐☐☐
n.			As "g," carmine rose (I) ..	120.00		☐☐☐☐☐
p.			As "g," scarlet (I)	90.00	50.00	☐☐☐☐☐
q.			As "g," lake (II)	125.00		☐☐☐☐☐
1906, Imperf.						
320	A129	2c	carmine	17.50	11.00	☐☐☐☐☐
a.		2c	lake (II)	50.00	35.00	☐☐☐☐☐
b.		2c	scarlet	16.00	12.00	☐☐☐☐☐
c.		2c	carmine rose	60.00	40.00	☐☐☐☐☐
1908, Coil Stamps, Perf. 12 Horizontally						
321	A129	2c	carmine, pair	*55,000.*	—	☐☐☐☐☐
Perf. 12 Vertically						
322	A129	2c	carmine, pair	*6,000.*	—	☐☐☐☐☐
1904, Watermark 191, Perf. 12						
323	A130	1c	green	19.50	3.00	☐☐☐☐☐
324	A131	2c	carmine	17.00	1.00	☐☐☐☐☐
a.			Vert. pair, imperf. horiz. ..	*6,750.*		☐☐☐☐☐
325	A132	3c	violet	65.00	24.00	☐☐☐☐☐
326	A133	5c	dark blue	67.50	15.00	☐☐☐☐☐
327	A134	10c	red brown	130.00	21.00	☐☐☐☐☐
1907, Watermark 191, Perf. 12						
328	A135	1c	green	13.00	2.00	☐☐☐☐☐
329	A136	2c	carmine	17.00	1.75	☐☐☐☐☐
330	A137	5c	blue	72.50	16.00	☐☐☐☐☐

TYPE I

TYPE II

TYPE I

TWO CENTS.
Type I. There is one shading line in the first curve of the ribbon above the left "2" and one in the second curve of the ribbon above the right "2."

The button of the toga has a faint outline.

The top line of the toga rope, from the button to the front of the throat, is also very faint.

The shading lines at the face terminate in front of the ear with little or no joining, to form a lock of hair.

Used on both flat and rotary press printings.

TYPE II

TWO CENTS.
Type II. Shading lines in ribbons as on type I.

The toga button, rope, and shading lines are heavy.

The shading lines of the face at the lock of hair end in a strong vertical curved line.

Used on rotary press printings only.

TYPE III

TWO CENTS.
Type III. Two lines of shading in the curves of the ribbons.

Other characteristics similar to type II.

Used on rotary press printings only.

HOW TO USE THIS BOOK

The number in the first column is its Scott number or identifying number. The letter and number that come next (A41) indicate the design and refer to the illustration so designated. Following that is the denomination of the stamp and its color. Finally, the value, unused and used is shown.

Scott No.	Illus No.		Description	Unused Value	Used Value	//////

1908-09, Watermark 191, Perf. 12

331	A138	1c	green	4.75	15	☐☐☐☐☐
a.			Booklet pane of 6	165.00	*35.00*	☐☐☐☐☐
332	A139	2c	carmine	4.50	15	☐☐☐☐☐
a.			Booklet pane of 6	100.00	*35.00*	☐☐☐☐☐
333	A140	3c	deep violet, type I	21.00	1.75	☐☐☐☐☐
334	A140	4c	orange brown	25.00	55	☐☐☐☐☐
335	A140	5c	blue	32.50	1.50	☐☐☐☐☐
336	A140	6c	red orange	40.00	3.50	☐☐☐☐☐
337	A140	8c	olive green	30.00	1.75	☐☐☐☐☐
338	A140	10c	yellow	47.50	1.00	☐☐☐☐☐
339	A140	13c	blue green	27.50	14.00	☐☐☐☐☐
340	A140	15c	pale ultra	42.50	3.75	☐☐☐☐☐
341	A140	50c	violet	190.00	10.00	☐☐☐☐☐
342	A140	$1	violet brown	350.00	50.00	☐☐☐☐☐

Imperf.

343	A138	1c	green	5.50	3.00	☐☐☐☐☐
344	A139	2c	carmine	7.50	2.00	☐☐☐☐☐
345	A140	3c	deep violet, type I	14.00	15.00	☐☐☐☐☐
346	A140	4c	orange brown	24.00	17.50	☐☐☐☐☐
347	A140	5c	blue	42.50	30.00	☐☐☐☐☐

1908-10, Coil Stamps, Perf. 12 Horizontally

348	A138	1c	green	21.00	10.00	☐☐☐☐☐
349	A139	2c	carmine	37.50	6.00	☐☐☐☐☐
350	A140	4c	orange brown	80.00	60.00	☐☐☐☐☐
351	A140	5c	blue	90.00	90.00	☐☐☐☐☐

Perf. 12 Vertically

352	A138	1c	green	40.00	25.00	☐☐☐☐☐
353	A139	2c	carmine	40.00	6.00	☐☐☐☐☐
354	A140	4c	orange brown	100.00	45.00	☐☐☐☐☐
355	A140	5c	blue	110.00	65.00	☐☐☐☐☐
356	A140	10c	yellow	1,500.	750.00	☐☐☐☐☐

1909, Bluish paper, Perf. 12

357	A138	1c	green	80.00	65.00	☐☐☐☐☐
358	A139	2c	carmine	75.00	55.00	☐☐☐☐☐
359	A140	3c	deep violet, type I	1,500.	*1,300.*	☐☐☐☐☐
360	A140	4c	orange brown	*13,500.*		☐☐☐☐☐
361	A140	5c	blue	3,250.	*3,500.*	☐☐☐☐☐
362	A140	6c	red orange	1,000.	850.00	☐☐☐☐☐
363	A140	8c	olive green	*13,500.*		☐☐☐☐☐
364	A140	10c	yellow	1,100.	1,000.	☐☐☐☐☐
365	A140	13c	blue green	2,250.	*1,250.*	☐☐☐☐☐
366	A140	15c	pale ultra	1,000.	800.00	☐☐☐☐☐

TYPE Ia

TYPE Ia

TWO CENTS.

Type Ia. Design characteristics similar to type I except that all lines of design are stronger.

The toga button, toga rope and rope shading lines are heavy. The latter characteristics are those of type II, which, however, occur only on impressions from rotary plates.

Used only on flat plates 10208 and 10209.

TYPE II

TYPE II

THREE CENTS.

Type II. The top line of the toga rope is strong and the rope shading lines are heavy and complete.

The line between the lips is heavy.

Used on both flat plate and rotary press printings.

TYPE IV

TYPE IV

TWO CENTS.

Type IV. Top line of toga rope is broken. Shading lines in toga button are so arranged that the curving of the first and last form "ƆIƆ".

Line of color in left "2" is very thin and usually broken.

Used on offset printings only.

Scott No.	Illus No.		Description	Unused Value	Used Value	//////

1909, Watermark 191, Perf. 12

| 367 | A141 | 2c carmine | 4.25 | 1.40 | ☐☐☐☐☐ |

Imperf.

| 368 | A141 | 2c carmine | 20.00 | 16.00 | ☐☐☐☐☐ |

Bluish paper

| 369 | A141 | 2c carmine | 170.00 | 175.00 | ☐☐☐☐☐ |

Perf. 12

| 370 | A142 | 2c carmine | 7.50 | 1.25 | ☐☐☐☐☐ |

Imperf.

| 371 | A142 | 2c carmine | 27.50 | 20.00 | ☐☐☐☐☐ |

Perf. 12

| 372 | A143 | 2c carmine | 10.00 | 3.25 | ☐☐☐☐☐ |

Imperf.

| 373 | A143 | 2c carmine | 32.50 | 22.50 | ☐☐☐☐☐ |

1910-11, Watermark 190, Perf. 12

374	A138	1c green	5.00	15	☐☐☐☐☐
a.		Booklet pane of 6	110.00	*30.00*	☐☐☐☐☐
375	A139	2c carmine	5.00	15	☐☐☐☐☐
a.		Booklet pane of 6	95.00	*25.00*	☐☐☐☐☐
376	A140	3c deep violet, type I	11.50	1.00	☐☐☐☐☐
377	A140	4c brown	20.00	30	☐☐☐☐☐
378	A140	5c blue	17.50	30	☐☐☐☐☐
379	A140	6c red orange	25.00	40	☐☐☐☐☐
380	A140	8c olive green	75.00	8.50	☐☐☐☐☐
381	A140	10c yellow	70.00	2.50	☐☐☐☐☐
382	A140	15c pale ultra	190.00	11.50	☐☐☐☐☐

1910, Imperf.

| 383 | A138 | 1c green | 2.25 | 2.00 | ☐☐☐☐☐ |
| 384 | A139 | 2c carmine | 3.50 | 1.75 | ☐☐☐☐☐ |

1910, Coil Stamps, Perf. 12 Horizontally

| 385 | A138 | 1c green | 18.00 | 10.00 | ☐☐☐☐☐ |
| 386 | A139 | 2c carmine | 32.50 | 12.50 | ☐☐☐☐☐ |

1910-11, Perf. 12 Vertically

387	A138	1c green	60.00	30.00	☐☐☐☐☐
388	A139	2c carmine	550.00	200.00	☐☐☐☐☐
389	A140	3c deep violet, type I	*15,000.*	*7,000.*	☐☐☐☐☐

TYPE V

TWO CENTS.

Type V. Top line of toga is complete.
Five vertical shading lines in toga
button.
Line of color in left "2" is very thin
and usually broken.
Shading dots on the nose and lip are as
indicated on the diagram.
Used on offset printings only.

TYPE Va

TWO CENTS.

Type Va. Characteristics same as type
V, except in shading dots of nose. Third
row from bottom has 4 dots instead of 6.
Overall height of type Va is 1/3 mm. less
than type V.

Used on offset printings only.

TYPE VI

TWO CENTS.

Type VI. General characteristics same
as type V, except that line of color in left
"2" is very heavy.

Used on offset printings only.

HOW TO USE THIS BOOK

The number in the first column is its Scott number or identifying number.
The letter and number that come next (A41) indicate the design and refer to
the illustration so designated. Following that is the denomination of the stamp
and its color. Finally, the value, unused and used is shown.

Scott No.	Illus No.		Description	Unused Value	Used Value	//////
1910, Perf. 8½ Horizontally						
390	A138	1c	green	3.00	4.00	☐☐☐☐☐
391	A139	2c	carmine	20.00	6.75	☐☐☐☐☐
1910-13, Perf. 8½ Vertically						
392	A138	1c	green	12.00	14.00	☐☐☐☐☐
393	A139	2c	carmine	24.00	5.50	☐☐☐☐☐
394	A140	3c	deep violet, type I	32.50	40.00	☐☐☐☐☐
395	A140	4c	brown	32.50	30.00	☐☐☐☐☐
396	A140	5c	blue	32.50	30.00	☐☐☐☐☐
1913, Watermark 190, Perf. 12						
397	A144	1c	green	11.00	85	☐☐☐☐☐
398	A145	2c	carmine	12.50	30	☐☐☐☐☐
399	A146	5c	blue	52.50	6.50	☐☐☐☐☐
400	A147	10c	orange yellow	95.00	14.00	☐☐☐☐☐
400A	A147	10c	orange	175.00	10.50	☐☐☐☐☐
1914-15, Perf. 10						
401	A144	1c	green	16.00	4.00	☐☐☐☐☐
402	A145	2c	carmine	55.00	1.00	☐☐☐☐☐
403	A146	5c	blue	120.00	11.00	☐☐☐☐☐
404	A147	10c	orange	825.00	42.50	☐☐☐☐☐
1912-14, Watermark 190, Perf. 12						
405	A140	1c	green	4.00	15	☐☐☐☐☐
a.			Vert. pair, imperf. horiz.	*650.00*	—	☐☐☐☐☐
b.			Booklet pane of 6	50.00	*7.50*	☐☐☐☐☐
406	A140	2c	carmine, type I	3.75	15	☐☐☐☐☐
a.			Booklet pane of 6	60.00	*17.50*	☐☐☐☐☐
b.			Double impression	—		☐☐☐☐☐
407	A140	7c	black	60.00	8.00	☐☐☐☐☐
1912, Imperf.						
408	A140	1c	green	90	50	☐☐☐☐☐
409	A140	2c	carmine, type I	1.00	50	☐☐☐☐☐
Coil Stamps, Perf. 8½ Horizontally						
410	A140	1c	green	4.50	3.00	☐☐☐☐☐
411	A140	2c	carmine, type I	6.00	2.50	☐☐☐☐☐
Coil Stamps, Perf. 8½ Vertically						
412	A140	1c	green	15.00	3.75	☐☐☐☐☐
413	A140	2c	carmine, type I	24.00	75	☐☐☐☐☐
1912-14, Watermark 190, Perf. 12						
414	A148	8c	pale olive green	27.50	85	☐☐☐☐☐
415	A148	9c	salmon red	35.00	9.50	☐☐☐☐☐

TYPE VII

TWO CENTS.

Type VII. Line of color in left "2" is invariably continuous, clearly defined, and heavier than in type V or Va, but not as heavy as in type VI.

Additional vertical row of dots has been added to the upper lip.

Numerous additional dots have been added to hair on top of head.

Used on offset printings only.

TYPE III

THREE CENTS.

Type III. The top line of the toga rope is strong but the fifth shading line is missing as in type I.

Center shading line of the toga button consists of two dashes with a central dot.

The "P" and "O" of "POSTAGE" are separated by a line of color.

The frame line at the bottom of the vignette is complete.

Used on offset printings only.

TYPE IV

THREE CENTS.

Type IV. Shading lines of toga rope are complete.

Second and fourth shading lines in toga button are broken in the middle and the third line is continuous with a dot in the center.

"P" and "O" of "POSTAGE" are joined.

Frame line at bottom of vignette is broken.

Used on offset printings only.

Scott No.	Illus No.		Description	Unused Value	Used Value	//////
416	A148	10c	orange yellow	30.00	25	
417	A148	12c	claret brown	30.00	3.00	
418	A148	15c	gray	55.00	2.00	
419	A148	20c	ultra	125.00	9.00	
420	A148	30c	orange red	90.00	10.00	
421	A148	50c	violet	325.00	10.00	

1912, Watermark 191, Perf. 12

422	A148	50c	violet	175.00	9.50	
423	A148	$1	violet brown	400.00	40.00	

1914-15, Watermark 190, Perf. 10

424	A140	1c	green	1.60	15	
a.			Perf. 12x10	*600.00*	*500.00*	
b.			Perf. 10x12		250.00	
c.			Vert. pair, imperf. horiz.	425.00	250.00	
d.			Booklet pane of 6	3.50	75	
e.			Vert. pair, imperf. btwn. at top	—		
425	A140	2c	rose red, type I	1.50	15	
c.			Perf. 10x12		—	
d.			Perf. 12x10	—	*600.00*	
e.			Booklet pane of 6	12.50	3.00	
426	A140	3c	deep violet, type I	10.00	90	
427	A140	4c	brown	26.00	30	
428	A140	5c	blue	22.50	30	
a.			Perf. 12x10		*1,000.*	
429	A140	6c	red orange	35.00	90	
430	A140	7c	black	65.00	2.50	
431	A148	8c	pale olive green	27.50	1.10	
432	A148	9c	salmon red	37.50	5.00	
433	A148	10c	orange yellow	35.00	20	
434	A148	11c	dark green	16.00	5.50	
435	A148	12c	claret brown	18.00	2.75	
a.			12c copper red	19.00	2.75	
437	A148	15c	gray	87.50	4.50	
438	A148	20c	ultra	165.00	2.50	
439	A148	30c	orange red	190.00	10.00	
440	A148	50c	violet	475.00	10.00	

1914, Coil Stamps, Perf. 10 Horizontally

441	A140	1c	green	55	80	
442	A140	2c	carmine, type I	6.00	4.50	

Perf. 10 Vertically

443	A140	1c	green	15.00	4.00	
444	A140	2c	carmine, type I	21.00	1.00	
445	A140	3c	violet, type I	175.00	100.00	

Scott No.	Illus No.		Description	Unused Value	Used Value	//////
446	A140	4c	brown	90.00	24.00	☐☐☐☐☐
447	A140	5c	blue	30.00	17.50	☐☐☐☐☐

1914-16, Coil Stamps, Perf. 10 Horizontally
Rotary Press Printing
448	A140	1c	green	4.25	2.25	☐☐☐☐☐
449	A140	2c	red, type I	1,750.	250.00	☐☐☐☐☐
450	A140	2c	carmine, type III	7.00	2.25	☐☐☐☐☐

1914-16, Coil Stamps, Perf. 10 Vertically
452	A140	1c	green	7.50	1.40	☐☐☐☐☐
453	A140	2c	carmine rose, type I	90.00	3.25	☐☐☐☐☐
454	A140	2c	red, type II	72.50	7.50	☐☐☐☐☐
455	A140	2c	carmine, type III	7.00	75	☐☐☐☐☐
456	A140	3c	violet, type I	190.00	75.00	☐☐☐☐☐
457	A140	4c	brown	19.00	15.00	☐☐☐☐☐
458	A140	5c	blue	22.50	15.00	☐☐☐☐☐

1914, Imperf.
459	A140	2c	carmine, type I	375.00	*750.00*	☐☐☐☐☐

1915, Watermark 191, Perf. 10
460	A148	$1	violet black	600.00	55.00	☐☐☐☐☐

1915, Watermark 190, Perf. 11
461	A140	2c	pale carmine red, type I	75.00	*150.00*	☐☐☐☐☐

1916-17, Perf. 10, Unwatermarked
462	A140	1c	green	5.00	15	☐☐☐☐☐
a.			Booklet pane of 6	7.50	*1.00*	☐☐☐☐☐
463	A140	2c	carmine, type I	3.25	15	☐☐☐☐☐
a.			Booklet pane of 6	85.00	*20.00*	☐☐☐☐☐
464	A140	3c	violet, type I	57.50	8.00	☐☐☐☐☐
465	A140	4c	orange brown	32.50	1.00	☐☐☐☐☐
466	A140	5c	blue	57.50	1.00	☐☐☐☐☐
467	A140	5c	carmine (error in plate of 2c)	475.00	525.00	☐☐☐☐☐
468	A140	6c	red orange	70.00	5.00	☐☐☐☐☐
469	A140	7c	black	92.50	7.50	☐☐☐☐☐
470	A148	8c	olive green	42.50	3.75	☐☐☐☐☐
471	A148	9c	salmon red	45.00	9.50	☐☐☐☐☐
472	A148	10c	orange yellow	85.00	75	☐☐☐☐☐
473	A148	11c	dark green	25.00	11.00	☐☐☐☐☐
474	A148	12c	claret brown	40.00	3.50	☐☐☐☐☐
475	A148	15c	gray	135.00	7.00	☐☐☐☐☐
476	A148	20c	light ultra	200.00	7.50	☐☐☐☐☐
476A	A148	30c	orange red	*3,500.*	—	☐☐☐☐☐
477	A148	50c	light violet	875.00	40.00	☐☐☐☐☐

Scott No.	Illus No.	Description	Unused Value	Used Value	//////
478	A148	$1 violet black	600.00	11.00	☐☐☐☐☐
479	A127	$2 dark blue	290.00	30.00	☐☐☐☐☐
480	A128	$5 light green	225.00	32.50	☐☐☐☐☐

Imperf.

481	A140	1c green	65	45	☐☐☐☐☐
482	A140	2c carmine, type I	1.25	1.00	☐☐☐☐☐
482A	A140	2c deep rose, type Ia		*7,500.*	☐☐☐☐☐
483	A140	3c violet, type I	9.50	6.50	☐☐☐☐☐
484	A140	3c violet, type II	7.00	3.00	☐☐☐☐☐
485	A140	5c car (error in plate of 2c) ...	*7,500.*		☐☐☐☐☐

1916-22, Coil Stamps, Perf. 10 Horizontally, Rotary Press Printing

486	A140	1c green	65	20	☐☐☐☐☐
487	A140	2c carmine, type II	12.00	2.50	☐☐☐☐☐
488	A140	2c carmine, type III	2.00	1.35	☐☐☐☐☐
489	A140	3c violet, type I	4.00	1.00	☐☐☐☐☐

1916-22, Coil Stamps, Perf. 10 Vertically

490	A140	1c green	40	15	☐☐☐☐☐
491	A140	2c carmine, type II	1,500.	450.00	☐☐☐☐☐
492	A140	2c carmine, type III	6.50	15	☐☐☐☐☐
493	A140	3c violet, type I	13.50	2.00	☐☐☐☐☐
494	A140	3c violet, type II	7.50	1.00	☐☐☐☐☐
495	A140	4c orange brown	8.00	3.00	☐☐☐☐☐
496	A140	5c blue	2.75	90	☐☐☐☐☐
497	A148	10c orange yellow	16.00	9.00	☐☐☐☐☐

Types of 1912-14 Issue
1917-19, Perf. 11

498	A140	1c green	30	15	☐☐☐☐☐
a.		Vert. pair, imperf. horiz. ..	175.00		☐☐☐☐☐
b.		Horiz. pair, imperf. btwn.	75.00		☐☐☐☐☐
c.		Vert. pair, imperf. btwn. ..	*450.00*	—	☐☐☐☐☐
d.		Double impression	150.00		☐☐☐☐☐
e.		Booklet pane of 6	2.00	*35*	☐☐☐☐☐
f.		Booklet pane of 30	*600.00*		☐☐☐☐☐
499	A140	2c rose, type I	35	15	☐☐☐☐☐
a.		Vert. pair, imperf. horiz. ..	150.00		☐☐☐☐☐
b.		Horiz. pair, imperf. vert. ..	200.00	*100.00*	☐☐☐☐☐
c.		Vert. pair, imperf. btwn. ..	*500.00*	*225.00*	☐☐☐☐☐
e.		Booklet pane of 6	3.00	*50*	☐☐☐☐☐
f.		Booklet pane of 30	*11,500.*		☐☐☐☐☐
g.		Double impression	125.00	—	☐☐☐☐☐

Scott No.	Illus No.		Description	Unused Value	Used Value	//////
500	A140	2c	deep rose, type Ia	200.00	110.00	
501	A140	3c	light violet, type I	8.00	15	
b.			Booklet pane of 6	50.00	*15.00*	
c.			Vert. pair, imperf. horiz.	300.00		
d.			Double impression	200.00		
502	A140	3c	dark violet, type II	11.00	15	
b.			Booklet pane of 6	42.50	*10.00*	
c.			Vert. pair, imperf. horiz.	250.00	125.00	
d.			Double impression	200.00		
503	A140	4c	brown	7.50	15	
b.			Double impression	—		
504	A140	5c	blue	6.50	15	
a.			Horiz. pair, imperf. btwn.	*2,500.*	—	
505	A140	5c	rose (error in plate of 2c)	350.00	400.00	
506	A140	6c	red orange	10.00	20	
507	A140	7c	black	20.00	85	
508	A148	8c	olive bister	9.00	40	
b.			Vert. pair, imperf. btwn.	—	—	
509	A148	9c	salmon red	11.00	1.40	
510	A148	10c	orange yellow	13.00	15	
511	A148	11c	light green	7.00	2.00	
512	A148	12c	claret brown	7.00	30	
a.		12c	brown carmine	7.50	35	
513	A148	13c	apple green	8.50	4.75	
514	A148	15c	gray	30.00	80	
515	A148	20c	light ultra	37.50	20	
b.			Vert. pair, imperf. btwn.	*325.00*		
c.			Double impression	*400.00*		
516	A148	30c	orange red	30.00	60	
b.			Double impression	—		
517	A148	50c	red violet	60.00	45	
b.			Vert. pair, imperf. btwn. at bottom	*1,750.*	*1,000.*	
518	A148	$1	violet brown	45.00	1.20	
b.		$1	deep brown	*1,000.*	*450.00*	

1917-19, Watermark 191

519	A139	2c	carmine	225.00	*450.00*	

1918, Perf. 11, Unwatermarked

523	A149	$2	orange red & black	600.00	200.00	
524	A149	$5	deep green & black	200.00	27.50	

1918-20, Perf. 11, Offset Printing

525	A140	1c	gray green	1.50	35	
a.		1c	dark green	1.65	75	
c.			Horiz. pair, imperf. btwn.	100.00		
d.			Double impression	15.00	15.00	

Scott No.	Illus No.		Description	Unused Value	Used Value	//////
526	A140	2c	carmine, type IV	21.00	2.75	□□□□□
527	A140	2c	carmine, type V	11.50	60	□□□□□
a.			Double impression	55.00	10.00	□□□□□
b.			Vert. pair, imperf. horiz. ..	*600.00*		□□□□□
c.			Horiz. pair, imperf. vert. ..	*1,000.*	—	□□□□□
528	A140	2c	carmine, type Va	6.00	15	□□□□□
c.			Double impression	25.00		□□□□□
g.			Vert. pair, imperf. btwn. ..	*1,000.*		□□□□□
528A	A140	2c	carmine, type VI	37.50	1.00	□□□□□
d.			Double impression	150.00	—	□□□□□
f.			Vert. pair, imperf. horiz. ..	—		□□□□□
h.			Vert. pair, imperf. btwn. ..	*1,000.*		□□□□□
528B	A140	2c	carmine, type VII	14.00	30	□□□□□
e.			Double impression	55.00		□□□□□
529	A140	3c	violet, type III	2.25	15	□□□□□
a.			Double impression	30.00	—	□□□□□
b.			Printed on both sides	*350.00*		□□□□□
530	A140	3c	purple, type IV	1.00	15	□□□□□
a.			Double impression	20.00	6.00	□□□□□
b.			Printed on both sides	250.00		□□□□□

Imperf.

Scott No.	Illus No.		Description	Unused Value	Used Value	//////
531	A140	1c	green	7.00	7.00	□□□□□
532	A140	2c	carmine rose, type IV	35.00	25.00	□□□□□
533	A140	2c	carmine, type V	175.00	65.00	□□□□□
534	A140	2c	carmine, type Va	9.00	6.00	□□□□□
534A	A140	2c	carmine, type VI	32.50	20.00	□□□□□
534B	A140	2c	carmine, type VII	1,250.	600.00	□□□□□
535	A140	3c	violet, type IV	7.00	4.50	□□□□□
a.			Double impression	100.00	—	□□□□□

Perf. 12½

Scott No.	Illus No.		Description	Unused Value	Used Value	//////
536	A140	1c	gray green	11.00	14.00	□□□□□
a.			Horiz. pair, imperf. vert. ..	*500.00*		□□□□□

1919, Perf. 11, Flat Plate Printing

Scott No.	Illus No.		Description	Unused Value	Used Value	//////
537	A150	3c	violet	7.50	2.75	□□□□□
a.		3c	deep red violet	*350.00*	*50.00*	□□□□□
b.		3c	light reddish violet	7.50	2.75	□□□□□
c.		3c	red violet	30.00	7.50	□□□□□

1919, Perf. 11x10, Rotary Press Printings,
Size: 19½ to 20mm wide by 22 to 22¼mm high

Scott No.	Illus No.		Description	Unused Value	Used Value	//////
538	A140	1c	green	7.50	6.00	□□□□□
a.			Vert. pair, imperf. horiz. ..	50.00	*100.00*	□□□□□
539	A140	2c	carmine rose, type II	2,750.	*2,000.*	□□□□□

A149

A150

A151

A152

A153

A154

A155

A156

A157

A158

A159

A160

A161

A162

A163

A164

A165

A166

A167

A168

A169

42

Scott No.	Illus No.		Description	Unused Value	Used Value	//////
540	A140	2c	carmine rose, type III	7.50	6.00	☐☐☐☐☐
a.			Vert. pair, imperf. horiz. ..	50.00	*100.00*	☐☐☐☐☐
b.			Horiz. pair, imperf. vert. ..	*550.00*		☐☐☐☐☐
541	A140	3c	violet, type II	22.50	20.00	☐☐☐☐☐

1920, Perf. 10x11, Size: 19mmx22½-22¾mm

542	A140	1c	green	6.50	65	☐☐☐☐☐

1921, Perf. 10, Size: 19x22½mm

543	A140	1c	green	35	15	☐☐☐☐☐
a.			Horiz. pair, imperf. btwn.	*550.00*		☐☐☐☐☐

1922, Perf. 11, Size: 19x22½mm

544	A140	1c	green	*12,500.*	*2,750.*	☐☐☐☐☐

1921, Perf. 11, Size: 19½-20x22mm

545	A140	1c	green	95.00	110.00	☐☐☐☐☐
546	A140	2c	carmine rose, type III	60.00	*110.00*	☐☐☐☐☐

1920, Perf. 11

547	A149	$2	carmine & black	175.00	32.50	☐☐☐☐☐
548	A151	1c	green	3.50	1.65	☐☐☐☐☐
549	A152	2c	carmine rose	5.50	1.25	☐☐☐☐☐
550	A153	5c	deep blue	35.00	10.00	☐☐☐☐☐

1922-25, Perf. 11

551	A154	½c	olive brown	15	15	☐☐☐☐☐
552	A155	1c	deep green	1.25	15	☐☐☐☐☐
a.			Booket pane of 6	4.50	*50*	☐☐☐☐☐
553	A156	1½c	yellow brown	2.25	15	☐☐☐☐☐
554	A157	2c	carmine	1.25	15	☐☐☐☐☐
a.			Horiz. pair, imperf. vert. ..	175.00		☐☐☐☐☐
b.			Vert. pair, imperf. horiz. ..	*500.00*		☐☐☐☐☐
c.			Booklet pane of 6	6.00	*1.00*	☐☐☐☐☐
555	A158	3c	violet	15.00	85	☐☐☐☐☐
556	A159	4c	yellow brown	15.00	20	☐☐☐☐☐
a.			Vert. pair, imperf. horiz. ..	—		☐☐☐☐☐
557	A160	5c	dark blue	15.00	15	☐☐☐☐☐
a.			Imperf., pair	*1,250.*		☐☐☐☐☐
b.			Horiz. pair, imperf. vert. ..	—		☐☐☐☐☐
558	A161	6c	red orange	27.50	75	☐☐☐☐☐
559	A162	7c	black	7.00	45	☐☐☐☐☐
560	A163	8c	olive green	37.50	35	☐☐☐☐☐
561	A164	9c	rose	12.00	90	☐☐☐☐☐
562	A165	10c	orange	16.00	15	☐☐☐☐☐
a.			Vert. pair, imperf. horiz. ..	*1,250.*		☐☐☐☐☐
b.			Imperf., pair	*1,500.*		☐☐☐☐☐

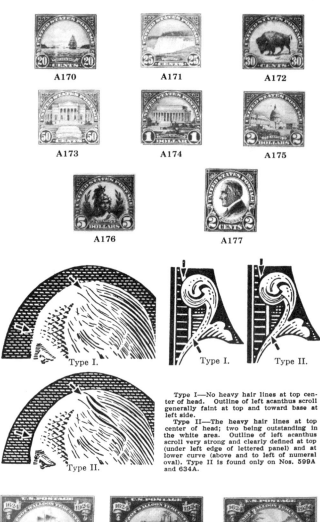

A170   A171   A172

A173   A174   A175

A176   A177

Type I.   Type I.   Type II.

Type II.

Type I—No heavy hair lines at top center of head. Outline of left acanthus scroll generally faint at top and toward base at left side.

Type II—The heavy hair lines at top center of head; two being outstanding in the white area. Outline of left acanthus scroll very strong and clearly defined at top (under left edge of lettered panel) and at lower curve (above and to left of numeral oval). Type II is found only on Nos. 599A and 634A.

A178   A179   A180

Scott No.	Illus No.		Description	Unused Value	Used Value	//////
563	A166	11c	light blue	1.25	25	
d.			Imperf., pair		—	
564	A167	12c	brown violet	5.50	15	
a.			Horiz. pair, imperf. vert.	*1,000.*		
b.			Imperf., pair			
565	A168	14c	blue	3.50	65	
566	A169	15c	gray	19.00	15	
567	A170	20c	carmine rose	19.00	15	
a.			Horiz. pair, imperf. vert.	*1,500.*		
568	A171	25c	yellow green	17.00	38	
b.			Vert. pair, imperf. horiz.	*850.00*		
569	A172	30c	olive brown	30.00	30	
570	A173	50c	lilac	50.00	15	
571	A174	$1	violet black	40.00	35	
572	A175	$2	deep blue	87.50	8.00	
573	A176	$5	carmine & blue	175.00	12.50	

1923-25, Imperf.

Scott No.	Illus No.		Description	Unused Value	Used Value	//////
575	A155	1c	green	7.00	3.50	
576	A156	1½c	yellow brown	1.50	1.00	
577	A157	2c	carmine	1.50	1.25	

Rotary Press Printings, Perf. 11x10, Size: 19¾x22¼mm

Scott No.	Illus No.		Description	Unused Value	Used Value	//////
578	A155	1c	green	70.00	110.00	
579	A157	2c	carmine	60.00	100.00	

Perf. 10

Scott No.	Illus No.		Description	Unused Value	Used Value	//////
581	A155	1c	green	7.00	55	
582	A156	1½c	brown	3.50	45	
583	A157	2c	carmine	1.75	15	
a.			Booklet pane of 6	75.00	*25.00*	
584	A158	3c	violet	19.00	1.75	
585	A159	4c	yellow brown	11.50	30	
586	A160	5c	blue	12.00	18	
a.			Horiz. pair, imperf. btwn.		—	
587	A161	6c	red orange	5.50	25	
588	A162	7c	black	8.00	4.25	
589	A163	8c	olive green	17.50	2.75	
590	A164	9c	rose	3.75	1.90	
591	A165	10c	orange	47.50	15	

Perf. 11

Scott No.	Illus No.		Description	Unused Value	Used Value	//////
594	A155	1c	green	*10,000.*	4,000.	
595	A157	2c	carmine	200.00	225.00	
596	A155	1c	green		*22,500.*	

A181

A182

A183

A184

A185

A186

A187

A188

A190

A189

A191

A192

A193

46

Scott No.	Illus No.	Description	Unused Value	Used Value	//////

1923-29, Coil Stamps, Perf. 10 Vertically, Rotary Press Printing

Scott No.	Illus No.	Description	Unused Value	Used Value
597	A155	1c green	25	15
598	A156	1½c brown	60	15
599	A157	2c carmine, type I	30	15
599A	A157	2c carmine, type II	100.00	9.50
600	A158	3c violet	5.50	15
601	A159	4c yellow brown	2.75	30
602	A160	5c dark blue	1.25	15
603	A165	10c orange	2.75	15

Perf. 10 Horizontally

Scott No.	Illus No.	Description	Unused Value	Used Value
604	A155	1c yellow green	20	15
605	A156	1½c yellow brown	25	15
606	A157	2c carmine	25	15

1923, Perf. 11, Flat Plate Printing, Size: 19¼x22¼mm

Scott No.	Illus No.	Description	Unused Value	Used Value
610	A177	2c black	55	15
a.		Horiz. pair, imperf. vert.	1,100.	

Imperf.

Scott No.	Illus No.	Description	Unused Value	Used Value
611	A177	2c black	6.50	4.25

1923, Sept. 12, Perf. 10, Rotary Press Printing, Size: 19¼x22¾mm

Scott No.	Illus No.	Description	Unused Value	Used Value
612	A177	2c black	12.00	1.50

1923, Perf. 11

Scott No.	Illus No.	Description	Unused Value	Used Value
613	A177	2c black		15,000.

1924-26, Perf. 11

Scott No.	Illus No.	Description	Unused Value	Used Value
614	A178	1c dark green	2.50	3.00
615	A179	2c carmine rose	5.00	2.00
616	A180	5c dark blue	25.00	11.00
617	A181	1c deep green	2.50	2.25
618	A182	2c carmine rose	5.00	3.75
619	A183	5c dark blue	24.00	12.50
620	A184	2c carmine & black	3.50	2.75
621	A185	5c dark blue & black	14.00	10.50
622	A186	13c green	12.00	40
623	A187	17c black	13.00	20

1926, Perf. 11

Scott No.	Illus No.	Description	Unused Value	Used Value
627	A188	2c carmine rose	2.75	40
628	A189	5c gray lilac	5.50	2.75
629	A190	2c carmine rose	1.75	1.50
a.		Vert. pair, imperf. btwn.	—	
630	A190	2c carmine rose, sheet of 25	350.00	375.00

Scott No.	Illus No.		Description	Unused Value	Used Value	//////

1926, Imperf., Rotary Press Printings

631	A156	1½c	yellow brown	1.75	1.60	☐☐☐☐☐

1926-34, Perf. 11x10½

632	A155	1c	green	15	15	☐☐☐☐☐
a.			Booklet pane of 6	4.50	25	☐☐☐☐☐
b.			Vert. pair, imperf. btwn. ..	200.00	125.00	☐☐☐☐☐
633	A156	1½c	yellow brown	1.60	15	☐☐☐☐☐
634	A157	2c	carmine, type I	15	15	☐☐☐☐☐
b.		2c	carmine lake	3.00	1.00	☐☐☐☐☐
c.			Horiz. pair, imperf. btwn.	2,000.		☐☐☐☐☐
d.			Booklet pane of 6	1.75	15	☐☐☐☐☐
634A	A157	2c	carmine, type II	300.00	12.50	☐☐☐☐☐
635	A158	3c	violet	35	15	☐☐☐☐☐
a.		3c	bright violet	25	15	☐☐☐☐☐
636	A159	4c	yellow brown	2.00	15	☐☐☐☐☐
637	A160	5c	dark blue	1.90	15	☐☐☐☐☐
638	A161	6c	red orange	2.00	15	☐☐☐☐☐
639	A162	7c	black	2.00	15	☐☐☐☐☐
a.			Vert. pair, imperf. btwn. ..	150.00	80.00	☐☐☐☐☐
640	A163	8c	olive green	2.00	15	☐☐☐☐☐
641	A164	9c	orange red	2.00	15	☐☐☐☐☐
642	A165	10c	orange	3.25	15	☐☐☐☐☐

1927, Perf. 11

643	A191	2c	carmine rose	1.25	75	☐☐☐☐☐
644	A192	2c	carmine rose	3.00	1.90	☐☐☐☐☐

1928, Perf. 11

645	A193	2c	carmine rose	90	35	☐☐☐☐☐

1928, Perf. 11x10½, Rotary Press Printing

646	A157	2c	carmine	95	95	☐☐☐☐☐
647	A157	2c	carmine	3.75	3.75	☐☐☐☐☐
648	A160	5c	dark blue	11.00	11.00	☐☐☐☐☐

1928, Perf. 11

649	A194	2c	carmine rose	1.00	75	☐☐☐☐☐
650	A195	5c	blue	4.50	3.00	☐☐☐☐☐

1929, Perf. 11

651	A196	2c	carmine & black	55	40	☐☐☐☐☐

Perf. 11x10½, Rotary Press Printing

653	A154	½c	olive brown	15	15	☐☐☐☐☐

1929, Perf. 11

654	A197	2c	carmine rose	60	60	☐☐☐☐☐

Scott No.	Illus No.		Description	Unused Value	Used Value	//////
Perf. 11x10½, Rotary Press Printing						
655	A197	2c	carmine rose	55	15	☐☐☐☐☐
Coil Stamp, Perf. 10 Vertically, Rotary Press Printing						
656	A197	2c	carmine rose	11.50	1.25	☐☐☐☐☐
1929, Perf. 11						
657	A198	2c	carmine rose	60	50	☐☐☐☐☐
1929, Perf. 11x10½, Rotary Press Printing, Overprinted						
658	A155	1c	green	1.50	1.35	☐☐☐☐☐
a.			Vert. pair, one without ovpt.	*300.00*		☐☐☐☐☐
659	A156	1½c	brown	2.25	1.90	☐☐☐☐☐
a.			Vert. pair, one without ovpt.	*325.00*		☐☐☐☐☐
660	A157	2c	carmine	2.75	75	☐☐☐☐☐
661	A158	3c	violet	12.50	10.00	☐☐☐☐☐
a.			Vert. pair, one without ovpt.	*400.00*		☐☐☐☐☐
662	A159	4c	yellow brown	12.50	6.00	☐☐☐☐☐
a.			Vert. pair, one without ovpt.	*400.00*		☐☐☐☐☐
663	A160	5c	deep blue	9.00	6.50	☐☐☐☐☐
664	A161	6c	red orange	19.00	12.00	☐☐☐☐☐
665	A162	7c	black	18.00	18.00	☐☐☐☐☐
a.			Vert. pair, one without ovpt.	*400.00*		☐☐☐☐☐
666	A163	8c	olive green	60.00	50.00	☐☐☐☐☐
667	A164	9c	light rose	9.00	7.50	☐☐☐☐☐
668	A165	10c	orange yellow	15.00	8.00	☐☐☐☐☐
669	A155	1c	green	2.25	1.50	☐☐☐☐☐
a.			Vert. pair, one without ovpt.	*275.00*		☐☐☐☐☐
670	A156	1½c	brown	2.00	1.65	☐☐☐☐☐
671	A157	2c	carmine	2.00	85	☐☐☐☐☐
672	A158	3c	violet	8.50	7.50	☐☐☐☐☐
a.			Vert. pair, one without ovpt.	*400.00*		☐☐☐☐☐
673	A159	4c	yellow brown	13.00	9.50	☐☐☐☐☐
674	A160	5c	deep blue	11.00	9.50	☐☐☐☐☐
675	A161	6c	red orange	27.50	15.00	☐☐☐☐☐
676	A162	7c	black	15.00	11.50	☐☐☐☐☐
677	A163	8c	olive green	20.00	16.00	☐☐☐☐☐
678	A164	9c	light rose	24.00	18.00	☐☐☐☐☐
a.			Vert. pair, one without ovpt.	*600.00*		☐☐☐☐☐
679	A165	10c	orange yellow	70.00	14.00	☐☐☐☐☐

No. 634
Overprinted **MOLLY PITCHER**

SCOTT 646

Nos. 634 and 637
Overprinted **HAWAII 1778 - 1928**

SCOTT 647-648

A194

A195

A196

A197

A198

A199

A200

A201

A202

A203

A204

A205

HOW TO USE THIS BOOK

The number in the first column is its Scott number or identifying number.
The letter and number that come next (A41) indicate the design and refer to
the illustration so designated. Following that is the denomination of the stamp
and its color. Finally, the value, unused and used is shown.

Scott No.	Illus No.		Description	Unused Value	Used Value	//////
1929, Perf. 11						
680	A199	2c	carmine rose	65	65	☐☐☐☐☐
681	A200	2c	carmine rose	50	50	☐☐☐☐☐
1930, Perf. 11						
682	A201	2c	carmine rose	50	38	☐☐☐☐☐
683	A202	2c	carmine rose	1.00	90	☐☐☐☐☐
1930, Perf. 11x10½, Rotary Press Printing						
684	A203	1½c	brown	25	15	☐☐☐☐☐
685	A204	4c	brown	75	15	☐☐☐☐☐
Coil Stamps, Perf. 10 Vertically						
686	A203	1½c	brown	1.50	15	☐☐☐☐☐
687	A204	4c	brown	2.75	38	☐☐☐☐☐
1930, Perf. 11						
688	A205	2c	carmine rose	85	75	☐☐☐☐☐
689	A206	2c	carmine rose	45	45	☐☐☐☐☐
a.			Imperf., pair	2,500.		☐☐☐☐☐
1931, Perf. 11						
690	A207	2c	carmine rose	20	15	☐☐☐☐☐
1931, Perf. 11x10½, Rotary Press Printing						
692	A166	11c	light blue	2.00	15	☐☐☐☐☐
693	A167	12c	brown violet	4.00	15	☐☐☐☐☐
694	A186	13c	yellow green	1.75	15	☐☐☐☐☐
695	A168	14c	dark blue	2.75	22	☐☐☐☐☐
696	A169	15c	gray	6.50	15	☐☐☐☐☐
Perf. 10½x11						
697	A187	17c	black	3.50	15	☐☐☐☐☐
698	A170	20c	carmine rose	7.75	15	☐☐☐☐☐
699	A171	25c	blue green	7.25	15	☐☐☐☐☐
700	A172	30c	brown	11.50	15	☐☐☐☐☐
701	A173	50c	lilac	35.00	15	☐☐☐☐☐
1931, Perf. 11, Flat Plate						
702	A208	2c	black & red	15	15	☐☐☐☐☐
703	A209	2c	carmine rose & black	35	25	☐☐☐☐☐
a.		2c	lake & black	4.00	65	☐☐☐☐☐
b.		2c	dark lake & black	300.00		☐☐☐☐☐
c.			Horiz. pair, imperf. vert. ..	4,000.		☐☐☐☐☐
1932, Perf. 11x10½, Rotary Press Printings						
704	A210	½c	olive brown	15	15	☐☐☐☐☐
705	A211	1c	green	15	15	☐☐☐☐☐

51

A206

A207

A208

A209

A210

A211

A212

A213

A214

A215

A216

A217

A218

A219

A220

A221

A222

A223

A224

A225

A226

A227

A228

Scott No.	Illus No.		Description	Unused Value	Used Value	//////
706	A212	1½c	brown	32	15	
707	A213	2c	carmine rose	15	15	
708	A214	3c	deep violet	40	15	
709	A215	4c	light brown	22	15	
710	A216	5c	blue	1.40	15	
711	A217	6c	red orange	2.75	15	
712	A218	7c	black	22	15	
713	A219	8c	olive bister	2.50	50	
714	A220	9c	pale red	2.00	15	
715	A221	10c	orange yellow	8.50	15	

Perf. 11

716	A222	2c	carmine rose	35	16	

Perf. 11x10½, Rotary Press Printing

717	A223	2c	carmine rose	15	15	

Perf. 11x10½

718	A224	3c	violet	1.25	15	
719	A225	5c	blue	2.00	20	
720	A226	3c	deep violet	15	15	
b.			Booklet pane of 6	27.50	5.00	
c.			Vert. pair, imperf. btwn.	300.00		

Coil Stamps, Perf. 10 Vertically, Rotary Press Printing

721	A226	3c	deep violet	2.25	15	

Perf. 10 Horizontally

722	A226	3c	deep violet	1.25	30	

Perf. 10 Vertically

723	A161	6c	deep orange	8.50	25	

1932-33, Perf. 11

724	A227	3c	violet	25	15	
a.			Vert. pair, imperf. horiz.	—		
725	A228	3c	violet	30	24	
726	A229	3c	violet	25	18	

1933, Perf. 10½x11, Rotary Press Printing

727	A230	3c	violet	15	15	
728	A231	1c	yellow green	15	15	
729	A232	3c	violet	15	15	

1933, Imperf., Flat Plate Printing

730			Sheet of 25	24.00	24.00	
a.	A231	1c	deep yellow green	65	35	

A229

A230

A231

A232

A233

A234

A235

A236

A237

A238

Scott No.	Illus No.		Description	Unused Value	Used Value	//////
731			Sheet of 25	22.50	22.50	☐☐☐☐☐
a.	A232	3c	deep violet	50	35	☐☐☐☐☐
732	A233	3c	violet	15	15	☐☐☐☐☐
733	A234	3c	dark blue	40	48	☐☐☐☐☐
734	A235	5c	blue	50	22	☐☐☐☐☐
a.			Horiz. pair, imperf. vert. ..	*2,000.*		☐☐☐☐☐

1934, Imperf.

Scott No.	Illus No.		Description	Unused Value	Used Value	//////
735			Sheet of 6	12.50	10.00	☐☐☐☐☐
a.	A234	3c	dark blue	2.00	1.65	☐☐☐☐☐
736	A236	3c	carmine rose	15	15	☐☐☐☐☐

Perf. 11x10½

Scott No.	Illus No.		Description	Unused Value	Used Value	//////
737	A237	3c	deep violet	15	15	☐☐☐☐☐

Perf. 11

Scott No.	Illus No.		Description	Unused Value	Used Value	//////
738	A237	3c	deep violet	15	15	☐☐☐☐☐
739	A238	3c	deep violet	15	15	☐☐☐☐☐
a.			Vert. pair, imperf. horiz. ..	250.00		☐☐☐☐☐
b.			Horiz. pair, imperf. vert. ..	325.00		☐☐☐☐☐
740	A239	1c	green	15	15	☐☐☐☐☐
a.			Vert. pair, imperf. horiz., with gum	*450.00*		☐☐☐☐☐
741	A240	2c	red	15	15	☐☐☐☐☐
a.			Vert. pair, imperf. horiz., with gum	*300.00*		☐☐☐☐☐
b.			Horiz. pair, imperf. vert., with gum	*300.00*		☐☐☐☐☐
742	A241	3c	deep violet	15	15	☐☐☐☐☐
a.			Vert. pair, imperf. horiz., with gum	*350.00*		☐☐☐☐☐
743	A242	4c	brown	35	32	☐☐☐☐☐
a.			Vert. pair, imperf. horiz., with gum	*500.00*		☐☐☐☐☐
744	A243	5c	blue	60	55	☐☐☐☐☐
a.			Horiz. pair, imperf. vert., with gum	*400.00*		☐☐☐☐☐
745	A244	6c	dark blue	1.00	75	☐☐☐☐☐
746	A245	7c	black	55	65	☐☐☐☐☐
a.			Horiz. pair, imperf. vert., with gum	*550.00*		☐☐☐☐☐
747	A246	8c	sage green	1.40	1.65	☐☐☐☐☐
748	A247	9c	red orange	1.50	55	☐☐☐☐☐
749	A248	10c	gray black	2.75	90	☐☐☐☐☐

A240

A239

A241

A242

A243

A244

A245

A246

A247

A249

A248

A250

A252

A253

Scott No.	Illus No.		Description	Unused Value	Used Value	// / / /
Imperf.						
750			Sheet of 6	27.50	25.00	☐☐☐☐☐
a.	A241	3c	deep violet	3.25	3.00	☐☐☐☐☐
751			Sheet of 6	12.00	12.00	☐☐☐☐☐
a.	A239	1c	green	1.35	1.50	☐☐☐☐☐

1935, Perf. 10½x11, Rotary Press Printing
752	A230	3c	violet	15	15	☐☐☐☐☐

Perf. 11, Flat Plate Printing
753	A234	3c	dark blue	40	40	☐☐☐☐☐

Scott No.	Illus No.		Description	Unused Value	Used Value	
Imperf.						
754	A237	3c	deep violet	50	50	☐☐☐☐☐
755	A238	3c	deep violet	50	50	☐☐☐☐☐
756	A239	1c	green	20	20	☐☐☐☐☐
757	A240	2c	red	22	22	☐☐☐☐☐
758	A241	3c	deep violet	45	40	☐☐☐☐☐
759	A242	4c	brown	90	90	☐☐☐☐☐
760	A243	5c	blue	1.40	1.25	☐☐☐☐☐
761	A244	6c	dark blue	2.25	2.00	☐☐☐☐☐
762	A245	7c	black	1.40	1.25	☐☐☐☐☐
763	A246	8c	sage green	1.50	1.40	☐☐☐☐☐
764	A247	9c	red orange	1.75	1.50	☐☐☐☐☐
765	A248	10c	gray black	3.50	3.00	☐☐☐☐☐
766			Pane of 25	24.00	24.00	☐☐☐☐☐
a.	A231	1c	yellow green	65	55	☐☐☐☐☐
767			Pane of 25	22.50	22.50	☐☐☐☐☐
a.	A232	3c	violet	50	35	☐☐☐☐☐
768			Pane of 6	18.00	12.50	☐☐☐☐☐
a.	A234	3c	dark blue	2.50	2.00	☐☐☐☐☐
769			Pane of 6	12.00	9.00	☐☐☐☐☐
a.	A239	1c	green	1.75	1.50	☐☐☐☐☐
770			Pane of 6	27.50	22.50	☐☐☐☐☐
a.	A241	3c	deep violet	3.00	3.00	☐☐☐☐☐
771	APSD1	16c	dark blue	2.00	2.00	☐☐☐☐☐

1935, Perf. 11x10½, 11
772	A249	3c	violet	15	15	☐☐☐☐☐
773	A250	3c	purple	15	15	☐☐☐☐☐
774	A251	3c	purple	15	15	☐☐☐☐☐
775	A252	3c	purple	15	15	☐☐☐☐☐

1936
776	A253	3c	purple	15	15	☐☐☐☐☐
777	A254	3c	purple	15	15	☐☐☐☐☐

A251   A255   A254

A256   A257   A258

A259   A260

A261   A262

A263   A264

A265

A266

A267

A268

A269a

A270

A269

A272

A273

A274

A275

A276

A271

A277

A278

Thomas Jefferson	James Madison	White House	James Monroe
A279	A280	A281	A282

John Q. Adams	Andrew Jackson	Martin Van Buren	William H. Harrison
A283	A284	A285	A286

John Tyler	James K. Polk	Zachary Taylor	Millard Fillmore
A287	A288	A289	A290

Franklin Pierce	James Buchanan	Abraham Lincoln	Andrew Johnson
A291	A292	A293	A294

Ulysses S. Grant	Rutherford B. Hayes	James A. Garfield	Chester A. Arthur
A295	A296	A297	A298

Grover Cleveland	Benjamin Harrison	William McKinley	Theodore Roosevelt
A299	A300	A301	A302

Scott No.	Illus No.		Description	Unused Value	Used Value	//////
778	A254a		Sheet of 4	1.75	1.75	☐☐☐☐☐
a.	A249	3c	violet	40	30	☐☐☐☐☐
b.	A250	3c	violet	40	30	☐☐☐☐☐
c.	A252	3c	violet	40	30	☐☐☐☐☐
d.	A253	3c	violet	40	30	☐☐☐☐☐
782	A255	3c	purple	15	15	☐☐☐☐☐
783	A256	3c	purple	15	15	☐☐☐☐☐
784	A257	3c	dark violet	15	15	☐☐☐☐☐

1936-37

785	A258	1c	green	15	15	☐☐☐☐☐
786	A259	2c	carmine	15	15	☐☐☐☐☐
787	A260	3c	purple	15	15	☐☐☐☐☐
788	A261	4c	gray	30	15	☐☐☐☐☐
789	A262	5c	ultra	60	15	☐☐☐☐☐
790	A263	1c	green	15	15	☐☐☐☐☐
791	A264	2c	carmine	15	15	☐☐☐☐☐
792	A265	3c	purple	15	15	☐☐☐☐☐
793	A266	4c	gray	30	15	☐☐☐☐☐
794	A267	5c	ultra	60	15	☐☐☐☐☐

1937

795	A268	3c	red violet	15	15	☐☐☐☐☐
796	A269	5c	gray blue	20	18	☐☐☐☐☐
797	A269a	10c	blue green	60	40	☐☐☐☐☐
798	A270	3c	bright red violet	15	15	☐☐☐☐☐
799	A271	3c	violet	15	15	☐☐☐☐☐
800	A272	3c	violet	15	15	☐☐☐☐☐
801	A273	3c	bright violet	15	15	☐☐☐☐☐
802	A274	3c	light violet	15	15	☐☐☐☐☐

1938-54, Perf. 11x10½, 11

803	A275	½c	deep orange	15	15	☐☐☐☐☐
804	A276	1c	green	15	15	☐☐☐☐☐
b.			Booklet pane of 6	1.50	*20*	☐☐☐☐☐
805	A277	1½c	bister brown	15	15	☐☐☐☐☐
b.			Horiz. pair, imperf. btwn.	150.00	25.00	☐☐☐☐☐
806	A278	2c	rose carmine	15	15	☐☐☐☐☐
b.			Booklet pane of 6	3.25	*50*	☐☐☐☐☐
807	A279	3c	deep violet	15	15	☐☐☐☐☐
a.			Booklet pane of 6	6.50	*50*	☐☐☐☐☐
b.			Horiz. pair, imperf. btwn.	650.00	—	☐☐☐☐☐
c.			Imperf., pair	*2,500.*		☐☐☐☐☐
808	A280	4c	red violet	80	15	☐☐☐☐☐
809	A281	4½c	dark gray	15	15	☐☐☐☐☐
810	A282	5c	bright blue	22	15	☐☐☐☐☐
811	A283	6c	red orange	25	15	☐☐☐☐☐
812	A284	7c	sepia	28	15	☐☐☐☐☐

William
Howard Taft
A303

Woodrow
Wilson
A304

Warren G.
Harding
A305

Calvin
Coolidge
A306

A308

A307

A309

A311

A310

A312

A313

A314

A315

A316

A317

Scott No.	Illus No.		Description	Unused Value	Used Value	//////
813	A285	8c	olive green	30	15	
814	A286	9c	rose pink	38	15	
815	A287	10c	brown red	28	15	
816	A288	11c	ultra	65	15	
817	A289	12c	bright violet	1.10	15	
818	A290	13c	blue green	1.50	15	
819	A291	14c	blue	90	15	
820	A292	15c	blue gray	50	15	
821	A293	16c	black	90	25	
822	A294	17c	rose red	85	15	
823	A295	18c	brown carmine	1.50	15	
824	A296	19c	bright violet	1.25	35	
825	A297	20c	brt blue green	70	15	
826	A298	21c	dull blue	1.50	15	
827	A299	22c	vermilion	1.25	40	
828	A300	24c	gray black	3.50	18	
829	A301	25c	deep red lilac	80	15	
830	A302	30c	deep ultra	4.25	15	
831	A303	50c	light red violet	7.00	15	
832	A304	$1	purple & black	7.00	15	
a.			Vert. pair, imperf. horiz.	1,750.		
b.			Wmkd. USIR	300.00	70.00	
c.		$1	red violet & black	6.00	15	
d.			As "c," vert. pair, imperf. horiz.	1,000.		
e.			Vert. pair, imperf. btwn.	2,500.		
f.			As "c," vert. pair, imperf. btwn.	7,000.		
833	A305	$2	yellow green & black	21.00	3.75	
834	A306	$5	carmine & black	95.00	3.00	
a.		$5	red brown & black	2,000.	1,250.	

1938

835	A307	3c	deep violet	22	15	
836	A308	3c	red violet	15	15	
837	A309	3c	bright violet	15	15	
838	A310	3c	violet	15	15	

1939, Coil Stamps, Perf. 10 Vertically

839	A276	1c	green	20	15	
840	A277	1½c	bister brown	24	15	
841	A278	2c	rose carmine	24	15	
842	A279	3c	deep violet	42	15	
843	A280	4c	red violet	6.75	35	
844	A281	4½c	dark gray	50	35	
845	A282	5c	bright blue	4.50	30	
846	A283	6c	red orange	1.10	15	
847	A287	10c	brown red	10.00	40	

Washington
Irving
A318

James Fenimore
Cooper
A319

Ralph Waldo
Emerson
A320

Louisa May
Alcott
A321

Samuel L. Clemens (Mark Twain)
A322

Henry W.
Longfellow
A323

John Greenleaf
Whittier
A324

James Russell
Lowell
A325

Walt
Whitman
A326

James Whitcomb Riley
A327

Horace Mann
A328

Mark Hopkins
A329

Charles W.
Eliot
A330

Frances E.
Willard
A331

Booker T. Washington
A332

Scott No.	Illus No.		Description	Unused Value	Used Value	/ / / / / /
Perf. 10 Horizontally						
848	A276	1c	green	55	15	☐☐☐☐☐
849	A277	1½c	bister brown	1.10	30	☐☐☐☐☐
850	A278	2c	rose carmine	2.00	40	☐☐☐☐☐
851	A279	3c	deep violet	1.90	35	☐☐☐☐☐
1939						
852	A311	3c	bright purple	15	15	☐☐☐☐☐
853	A312	3c	deep purple	15	15	☐☐☐☐☐
854	A313	3c	bright red violet	40	15	☐☐☐☐☐
855	A314	3c	violet	1.10	15	☐☐☐☐☐
856	A315	3c	deep red violet	18	15	☐☐☐☐☐
857	A316	3c	violet	15	15	☐☐☐☐☐
858	A317	3c	rose violet	15	15	☐☐☐☐☐
1940						
859	A318	1c	bright blue green	15	15	☐☐☐☐☐
860	A319	2c	rose carmine	15	15	☐☐☐☐☐
861	A320	3c	bright red violet	15	15	☐☐☐☐☐
862	A321	5c	ultra	28	20	☐☐☐☐☐
863	A322	10c	dark brown	1.50	1.35	☐☐☐☐☐
864	A323	1c	bright blue green	15	15	☐☐☐☐☐
865	A324	2c	rose carmine	15	15	☐☐☐☐☐
866	A325	3c	bright red violet	15	15	☐☐☐☐☐
867	A326	5c	ultra	32	18	☐☐☐☐☐
868	A327	10c	dark brown	1.65	1.40	☐☐☐☐☐
869	A328	1c	bright blue green	15	15	☐☐☐☐☐
870	A329	2c	rose carmine	15	15	☐☐☐☐☐
871	A330	3c	bright red violet	15	15	☐☐☐☐☐
872	A331	5c	ultra	38	25	☐☐☐☐☐
873	A332	10c	dark brown	1.10	1.25	☐☐☐☐☐
874	A333	1c	bright blue green	15	15	☐☐☐☐☐
875	A334	2c	rose carmine	15	15	☐☐☐☐☐
876	A335	3c	bright red violet	15	15	☐☐☐☐☐
877	A336	5c	ultra	25	15	☐☐☐☐☐
878	A337	10c	dark brown	1.00	95	☐☐☐☐☐
879	A338	1c	bright blue green	15	15	☐☐☐☐☐
880	A339	2c	rose carmine	15	15	☐☐☐☐☐
881	A340	3c	bright red violet	15	15	☐☐☐☐☐
882	A341	5c	ultra	40	22	☐☐☐☐☐
883	A342	10c	dark brown	3.50	1.35	☐☐☐☐☐
884	A343	1c	bright blue green	15	15	☐☐☐☐☐
885	A344	2c	rose carmine	15	15	☐☐☐☐☐
886	A345	3c	bright red violet	15	15	☐☐☐☐☐
887	A346	5c	ultra	48	22	☐☐☐☐☐
888	A347	10c	dark brown	1.75	1.40	☐☐☐☐☐
889	A348	1c	bright blue green	15	15	☐☐☐☐☐
890	A349	2c	rose carmine	15	15	☐☐☐☐☐

John James
Audubon
A333

Dr. Crawford
W. Long
A334

Luther Burbank
A335

Dr. Walter Reed
A336

Jane Addams
A337

Stephen Collins
Foster
A338

John Philip
Sousa
A339

Victor
Herbert
A340

Edward
MacDowell
A341

Ethelbert Nevin
A342

Gilbert Charles
Stuart
A343

James A. McNeill
Whistler
A344

Augustus
Saint-Gaudens
A345

Daniel Chester
French
A346

Frederic Remington— **A347**

66

Scott No.	Illus No.		Description	Unused Value	Used Value	//////
891	A350	3c	bright red violet	25	15	☐☐☐☐☐
892	A351	5c	ultra	1.00	32	☐☐☐☐☐
893	A352	10c	dark brown	10.00	2.25	☐☐☐☐☐
894	A353	3c	henna brown	25	15	☐☐☐☐☐
895	A354	3c	light violet	20	15	☐☐☐☐☐
896	A355	3c	bright violet	15	15	☐☐☐☐☐
897	A356	3c	brown violet	15	15	☐☐☐☐☐
898	A357	3c	violet	15	15	☐☐☐☐☐
899	A358	1c	bright blue green	15	15	☐☐☐☐☐
a.			Vert. pair, imperf. btwn. ..	500.00	—	☐☐☐☐☐
b.			Horiz. pair, imperf. btwn.	40.00	—	☐☐☐☐☐
900	A359	2c	rose carmine	15	15	☐☐☐☐☐
a.			Horiz. pair, imperf. btwn.	40.00	—	☐☐☐☐☐
901	A360	3c	bright violet	15	15	☐☐☐☐☐
a.			Horiz. pair, imperf. btwn.	30.00	—	☐☐☐☐☐
902	A361	3c	deep violet	16	15	☐☐☐☐☐

1941

903	A362	3c	light violet	15	15	☐☐☐☐☐

1942

904	A363	3c	violet	15	15	☐☐☐☐☐
905	A364	3c	violet	15	15	☐☐☐☐☐
b.		3c	purple	20.00	8.00	☐☐☐☐☐
906	A365	5c	bright blue	18	16	☐☐☐☐☐

1943

907	A366	2c	rose carmine	15	15	☐☐☐☐☐
908	A367	1c	bright blue green	15	15	☐☐☐☐☐

1943-44

909	A368	5c	Poland	18	15	☐☐☐☐☐
910	A368	5c	Czechoslovakia	18	15	☐☐☐☐☐
911	A368	5c	Norway	15	15	☐☐☐☐☐
912	A368	5c	Luxembourg	15	15	☐☐☐☐☐
913	A368	5c	Netherlands	15	15	☐☐☐☐☐
914	A368	5c	Belgium	15	15	☐☐☐☐☐
915	A368	5c	France	15	15	☐☐☐☐☐
916	A368	5c	Greece	38	25	☐☐☐☐☐
917	A368	5c	Yugoslavia	28	15	☐☐☐☐☐
918	A368	5c	Albania	18	15	☐☐☐☐☐
919	A368	5c	Austria	18	15	☐☐☐☐☐
920	A368	5c	Denmark	18	15	☐☐☐☐☐
921	A368	5c	Korea	15	15	☐☐☐☐☐

1944

922	A369	3c	violet	18	15	☐☐☐☐☐
923	A370	3c	violet	15	15	☐☐☐☐☐

Eli Whitney
A348

Samuel F. B. Morse
A349

Cyrus Hall
McCormick
A350

Elias Howe
A351

A353

A352

A355

A356

A354

A361

A358

A357

A359

A362

A360

A363

A364

A366

A367

A365

A368

A369

A370

A371

A372

A373

A374

A375

A377

A376

A378

A379

A380

A381

A382

A383

A384   A385   A386   A387

A388   A389   A390

A391   A392   A393

A394

A399

A395

A396   A397   A398

A401   A400   A402

Scott No.	Illus No.	Description	Unused Value	Used Value	//////
924	A371	3c bright red violet	15	15	☐☐☐☐☐
925	A372	3c deep violet	15	15	☐☐☐☐☐
926	A373	3c deep violet	15	15	☐☐☐☐☐

1945

927	A374	3c bright red violet	15	15	☐☐☐☐☐
928	A375	5c ultramarine	15	15	☐☐☐☐☐
929	A376	3c yellow green	15	15	☐☐☐☐☐

1945-46

930	A377	1c blue green	15	15	☐☐☐☐☐
931	A378	2c carmine rose	15	15	☐☐☐☐☐
932	A379	3c purple	15	15	☐☐☐☐☐
933	A380	5c bright blue	15	15	☐☐☐☐☐

1945

934	A381	3c olive................................	15	15	☐☐☐☐☐
935	A382	3c blue.................................	15	15	☐☐☐☐☐
936	A383	3c bright blue green	15	15	☐☐☐☐☐
937	A384	3c purple	15	15	☐☐☐☐☐
938	A385	3c dark blue	15	15	☐☐☐☐☐

1946

939	A386	3c blue green	15	15	☐☐☐☐☐
940	A387	3c dark violet	15	15	☐☐☐☐☐
941	A388	3c dark violet	15	15	☐☐☐☐☐
942	A389	3c deep blue	15	15	☐☐☐☐☐
943	A390	3c violet brown	15	15	☐☐☐☐☐
944	A391	3c brown violet	15	15	☐☐☐☐☐

1947

945	A392	3c bright red violet	15	15	☐☐☐☐☐
946	A393	3c purple	15	15	☐☐☐☐☐
947	A394	3c deep blue	15	15	☐☐☐☐☐
948	A395	Sheet of 2	60	50	☐☐☐☐☐
a.	A1	5c blue	30	25	☐☐☐☐☐
b.	A2	10c brown orange	30	25	☐☐☐☐☐
949	A396	3c brown violet	15	15	☐☐☐☐☐
950	A397	3c dark violet	15	15	☐☐☐☐☐
951	A398	3c blue green	15	15	☐☐☐☐☐
952	A399	3c bright green	15	15	☐☐☐☐☐

1948

953	A400	3c bright red violet	15	15	☐☐☐☐☐
954	A401	3c dark violet	15	15	☐☐☐☐☐
955	A402	3c brown violet	15	15	☐☐☐☐☐
956	A403	3c gray black	15	15	☐☐☐☐☐
957	A404	3c dark violet	15	15	☐☐☐☐☐

A403

A404

A405

A406

A407

A408

A409

A410

A411

A412

A413

A414

A416

A415

A417

A418

A419

A420

A421

72

Scott No.	Illus No.	Description	Unused Value	Used Value	//////
958	A405	5c deep blue	15	15	☐☐☐☐☐
959	A406	3c dark violet	15	15	☐☐☐☐☐
960	A407	3c bright red violet	15	15	☐☐☐☐☐
961	A408	3c blue	15	15	☐☐☐☐☐
962	A409	3c rose pink	15	15	☐☐☐☐☐
963	A410	3c deep blue	15	15	☐☐☐☐☐
964	A411	3c brown red	15	15	☐☐☐☐☐
965	A412	3c bright red violet	15	15	☐☐☐☐☐
966	A413	3c blue	15	15	☐☐☐☐☐
a.		Vert. pair, imperf btwn.	550.00		☐☐☐☐☐
967	A414	3c rose pink	15	15	☐☐☐☐☐
968	A415	3c sepia	15	15	☐☐☐☐☐
969	A416	3c orange yellow	15	15	☐☐☐☐☐
970	A417	3c violet	15	15	☐☐☐☐☐
971	A418	3c bright rose carmine	15	15	☐☐☐☐☐
972	A419	3c dark brown	15	15	☐☐☐☐☐
973	A420	3c violet brown	15	15	☐☐☐☐☐
974	A421	3c blue green	15	15	☐☐☐☐☐
975	A422	3c bright red violet	15	15	☐☐☐☐☐
976	A423	3c henna brown	15	15	☐☐☐☐☐
977	A424	3c rose pink	15	15	☐☐☐☐☐
978	A425	3c bright blue	15	15	☐☐☐☐☐
979	A426	3c carmine	15	15	☐☐☐☐☐
980	A427	3c bright red violet	15	15	☐☐☐☐☐
1949					
981	A428	3c blue green	15	15	☐☐☐☐☐
982	A429	3c ultramarine	15	15	☐☐☐☐☐
983	A430	3c green	15	15	☐☐☐☐☐
984	A431	3c aquamarine	15	15	☐☐☐☐☐
985	A432	3c bright rose carmine	15	15	☐☐☐☐☐
986	A433	3c bright red violet	15	15	☐☐☐☐☐
1950					
987	A434	3c yellow green	15	15	☐☐☐☐☐
988	A435	3c bright red violet	15	15	☐☐☐☐☐
989	A436	3c bright blue	15	15	☐☐☐☐☐
990	A437	3c deep green	15	15	☐☐☐☐☐
991	A438	3c light violet	15	15	☐☐☐☐☐
992	A439	3c bright red violet	15	15	☐☐☐☐☐
993	A440	3c violet brown	15	15	☐☐☐☐☐
994	A441	3c violet	15	15	☐☐☐☐☐
995	A442	3c sepia	15	15	☐☐☐☐☐
996	A443	3c bright blue	15	15	☐☐☐☐☐
997	A444	3c yellow orange	15	15	☐☐☐☐☐
1951					
998	A445	3c gray	15	15	☐☐☐☐☐

A422

A423

A424

A425

A426

A427

A428

A429

A430

A432

A433

A431

A434

A435

A436

74

Scott No.	Illus No.	Description	Unused Value	Used Value	/ / / / / /
999	A446	3c light olive green	15	15	☐☐☐☐☐
1000	A447	3c blue	15	15	☐☐☐☐☐
1001	A448	3c blue violet	15	15	☐☐☐☐☐
1002	A449	3c violet brown	15	15	☐☐☐☐☐
1003	A450	3c violet	15	15	☐☐☐☐☐

1952

Scott No.	Illus No.	Description	Unused Value	Used Value	/ / / / / /
1004	A451	3c carmine rose	15	15	☐☐☐☐☐
1005	A452	3c blue green	15	15	☐☐☐☐☐
1006	A453	3c bright blue	15	15	☐☐☐☐☐
1007	A454	3c deep blue	15	15	☐☐☐☐☐
1008	A455	3c deep violet	15	15	☐☐☐☐☐
1009	A456	3c blue green	15	15	☐☐☐☐☐
1010	A457	3c bright blue	15	15	☐☐☐☐☐
1011	A458	3c blue green	15	15	☐☐☐☐☐
1012	A459	3c violet blue	15	15	☐☐☐☐☐
1013	A460	3c deep blue	15	15	☐☐☐☐☐
1014	A461	3c violet	15	15	☐☐☐☐☐
1015	A462	3c violet	15	15	☐☐☐☐☐
1016	A463	3c deep blue & carmine	15	15	☐☐☐☐☐

1953

Scott No.	Illus No.	Description	Unused Value	Used Value	/ / / / / /
1017	A464	3c bright blue	15	15	☐☐☐☐☐
1018	A465	3c chocolate	15	15	☐☐☐☐☐
1019	A466	3c green	15	15	☐☐☐☐☐
1020	A467	3c violet brown	15	15	☐☐☐☐☐
1021	A468	5c green	15	15	☐☐☐☐☐
1022	A469	3c rose violet	15	15	☐☐☐☐☐
1023	A470	3c yellow green	15	15	☐☐☐☐☐
1024	A471	3c deep blue	15	15	☐☐☐☐☐
1025	A472	3c violet	15	15	☐☐☐☐☐
1026	A473	3c blue violet	15	15	☐☐☐☐☐
1027	A474	3c bright red violet	15	15	☐☐☐☐☐
1028	A475	3c copper brown	15	15	☐☐☐☐☐

1954

Scott No.	Illus No.	Description	Unused Value	Used Value	/ / / / / /
1029	A476	3c blue	15	15	☐☐☐☐☐

1954-68, Perf. 11x10½, 10½x11, 11

Scott No.	Illus No.	Description	Unused Value	Used Value	/ / / / / /
1030	A477	½c red orange	15	15	☐☐☐☐☐
1031	A478	1c dark green	15	15	☐☐☐☐☐
1031A	A478a	1¼c turquoise	15	15	☐☐☐☐☐
1032	A479	1½c brown carmine	15	15	☐☐☐☐☐
1033	A480	2c carmine rose	15	15	☐☐☐☐☐
1034	A481	2½c gray blue	15	15	☐☐☐☐☐

A437

A438

A439

A440

A441

A442

A443

A444

A445

A446

A447

A448

A449

A450

A451

A452

A453

A454

A455

A456

A457

A458

A459

A460

A461

A462

A463

A464

A465

A466

A467

A468

A469

A470

A471

A472

A473

A474

A475

A476

A477

A478

A478a

A479

A480

A481

A482

A483

A484

A485

A486

A487

A488

A489

A489a

A490

A491

Scott No.	Illus No.		Description	Unused Value	Used Value	//////
1035	A482	3c	deep violet	15	15	□□□□□
a.			Booklet pane of 6	4.50	*50*	□□□□□
b.			Tagged.............................	25	25	□□□□□
c.			Vert. pair, imperf.	*1,500.*		□□□□□
d.			Horiz. pair, imperf. btwn.	—		□□□□□
g.			As "a," vert. imperf. btwn.	*5,000.*		□□□□□
1036	A483	4c	red violet	15	15	□□□□□
a.			Booklet pane of 6	2.25	*50*	□□□□□
b.			Tagged.............................	50	40	□□□□□
d.			As "a," vert. imperf. horiz.	—		□□□□□
1037	A484	4½c	blue green	15	15	□□□□□
1038	A485	5c	deep blue	15	15	□□□□□
1039	A486	6c	carmine	25	15	□□□□□
1040	A487	7c	rose carmine	20	15	□□□□□

Perf. 11, Flat Plate or Rotary Press Printing

Scott No.	Illus No.		Description	Unused Value	Used Value	//////
1041	A488	8c	dark violet blue & carmine	24	15	□□□□□
a.			Double impression of carmine	*650.00*		□□□□□
1042	A489	8c	dark vio bl & car rose	20	15	□□□□□
1042A	A489a	8c	brown	22	15	□□□□□
1043	A490	9c	rose lilac	28	15	□□□□□
1044	A491	10c	rose lake	22	15	□□□□□
b.			Tagged.............................	2.00	50	□□□□□
1044A	A491a	11c	carmine & dark violet blue	28	15	□□□□□
c.			Tagged.............................	2.00	1.60	□□□□□
1045	A492	12c	red	32	15	□□□□□
a.			Tagged.............................	45	15	□□□□□
1046	A493	15c	rose lake	90	15	□□□□□
a.			Tagged.............................	1.00	35	□□□□□
1047	A494	20c	ultra	45	15	□□□□□
1048	A495	25c	green	1.40	15	□□□□□
1049	A496	30c	black	90	15	□□□□□
1050	A497	40c	brown red	1.90	15	□□□□□
1051	A498	50c	bright purple	1.50	15	□□□□□
1052	A499	$1	purple	5.00	15	□□□□□
1053	A500	$5	black	75.00	6.75	□□□□□

1954-73, Perf. 10 Vertically, Horizontally

Scott No.	Illus No.		Description	Unused Value	Used Value	//////
1054	A478	1c	dark green	18	15	□□□□□
b.			Imperf., pair...................	*2,000.*	—	□□□□□
1054A	A478a	1¼c	turquoise	15	15	□□□□□

A491a

A492

A493

A494

A495

A496

A497

A498

A499

A500

A507

A509

A508

A510

A511

A512

A513

A514

80

A516

A515

A517

A518

A519

A520

A521

Souvenir Sheet.

A523

A522

A524   A525   A526

A527

A528

81

A529

A530

A531

A532

A534

A533

A535

A537

A536

A538

A539

A540

A541

A542

A543

A544

82

Scott No.	Illus No.		Description	Unused Value	Used Value	
1055	A480	2c	rose carmine	15	15	☐☐☐☐☐
a.			Tagged	15	15	☐☐☐☐☐
b.			Imperf., pair (Bureau precanceled)		450.00	☐☐☐☐☐
c.			As "a," imperf. pair	525.00		☐☐☐☐☐
1056	A481	2½c	gray blue	25	25	☐☐☐☐☐
1057	A482	3c	deep violet	15	15	☐☐☐☐☐
a.			Imperf., pair	1,150.	—	☐☐☐☐☐
b.			Tagged	50	50	☐☐☐☐☐
1058	A483	4c	red violet	15	15	☐☐☐☐☐
a.			Imperf., pair	90.00	70.00	☐☐☐☐☐
1059	A484	4½c	blue green	1.50	1.20	☐☐☐☐☐
1059A	A495	25c	green	50	30	☐☐☐☐☐
b.			Tagged	55	20	☐☐☐☐☐
c.			Imperf., pair	40.00		☐☐☐☐☐

1954

1060	A507	3c	violet	15	15	☐☐☐☐☐
1061	A508	3c	brown orange	15	15	☐☐☐☐☐
1062	A509	3c	violet brown	15	15	☐☐☐☐☐
1063	A510	3c	violet brown	15	15	☐☐☐☐☐

1955

1064	A511	3c	violet brown	15	15	☐☐☐☐☐
1065	A512	3c	green	15	15	☐☐☐☐☐
1066	A513	8c	deep blue	16	15	☐☐☐☐☐
1067	A514	3c	purple	15	15	☐☐☐☐☐
1068	A515	3c	green	15	15	☐☐☐☐☐
1069	A516	3c	blue	15	15	☐☐☐☐☐
1070	A517	3c	deep blue	15	15	☐☐☐☐☐
1071	A518	3c	light brown	15	15	☐☐☐☐☐
1072	A519	3c	rose carmine	15	15	☐☐☐☐☐

1956

1073	A520	3c	bright carmine	15	15	☐☐☐☐☐
1074	A521	3c	deep blue	15	15	☐☐☐☐☐
1075	A522		Sheet of 2	2.25	2.00	☐☐☐☐☐
a.	A482	3c	deep violet	90	80	☐☐☐☐☐
b.	A488	8c	dark violet blue & carmine	1.25	1.00	☐☐☐☐☐
1076	A523	3c	deep violet	15	15	☐☐☐☐☐
1077	A524	3c	rose lake	15	15	☐☐☐☐☐
1078	A525	3c	brown	15	15	☐☐☐☐☐
1079	A526	3c	blue green	15	15	☐☐☐☐☐
1080	A527	3c	dark blue green	15	15	☐☐☐☐☐
1081	A528	3c	black brown	15	15	☐☐☐☐☐
1082	A529	3c	deep blue	15	15	☐☐☐☐☐
1083	A530	3c	black, *orange*	15	15	☐☐☐☐☐

A545

A546

A547

A551

A552

A553

A554

A555

A556

A557

A558

A561

A559

A560

A562

A564

A563

Scott No.	Illus No.	Description	Unused Value	Used Value	//////
1084	A531	3c violet	15	15	☐☐☐☐☐
1085	A532	3c dark blue	15	15	☐☐☐☐☐

1957

Scott No.	Illus No.	Description	Unused Value	Used Value	//////
1086	A533	3c rose red	15	15	☐☐☐☐☐
1087	A534	3c red lilac	15	15	☐☐☐☐☐
1088	A535	3c dark blue	15	15	☐☐☐☐☐
1089	A536	3c red lilac	15	15	☐☐☐☐☐
1090	A537	3c bright ultra	15	15	☐☐☐☐☐
1091	A538	3c blue green	15	15	☐☐☐☐☐
1092	A539	3c dark blue	15	15	☐☐☐☐☐
1093	A540	3c rose lake	15	15	☐☐☐☐☐
1094	A541	4c dark blue & deep carmine	15	15	☐☐☐☐☐
1095	A542	3c deep violet	15	15	☐☐☐☐☐
1096	A543	8c carmine, ultra & ocher	16	15	☐☐☐☐☐
1097	A544	3c rose lake	15	15	☐☐☐☐☐
1098	A545	3c blue, ocher & green	15	15	☐☐☐☐☐
1099	A546	3c black	15	15	☐☐☐☐☐

1958

Scott No.	Illus No.	Description	Unused Value	Used Value	//////
1100	A547	3c green	15	15	☐☐☐☐☐
1104	A551	3c deep claret	15	15	☐☐☐☐☐
1105	A552	3c purple	15	15	☐☐☐☐☐
1106	A553	3c green	15	15	☐☐☐☐☐
1107	A554	3c black & red orange	15	15	☐☐☐☐☐
1108	A555	3c light green	15	15	☐☐☐☐☐
1109	A556	3c bright greenish blue	15	15	☐☐☐☐☐
1110	A557	4c olive bister	15	15	☐☐☐☐☐
1111	A557	8c carmine, ultra & ocher	16	15	☐☐☐☐☐
1112	A558	4c reddish purple	15	15	☐☐☐☐☐

1958-59

Scott No.	Illus No.	Description	Unused Value	Used Value	//////
1113	A559	1c green	15	15	☐☐☐☐☐
1114	A560	3c purple	15	15	☐☐☐☐☐
1115	A561	4c sepia	15	15	☐☐☐☐☐
1116	A562	4c dark blue	15	15	☐☐☐☐☐

1958

Scott No.	Illus No.	Description	Unused Value	Used Value	//////
1117	A563	4c green	15	15	☐☐☐☐☐
1118	A563	8c carmine, ultra & ocher	16	15	☐☐☐☐☐
1119	A564	4c black	15	15	☐☐☐☐☐
1120	A565	4c crimson rose	15	15	☐☐☐☐☐
1121	A566	4c dark carmine rose	15	15	☐☐☐☐☐
1122	A567	4c green, yellow & brown	15	15	☐☐☐☐☐
1123	A568	4c blue	15	15	☐☐☐☐☐

A565

A566

A568

A567

A569

A570

A572

A571

A573

A574

A578

A575

A577

A576

A580

A579

A581

Scott No.	Illus No.		Description	Unused Value	Used Value	/ / / / / /
1959						
1124	A569	4c	blue green	15	15	
1125	A570	4c	blue................................	15	15	
a.			Horiz. pair, imperf. btwn.	1,250.		
1126	A570	8c	carmine, ultra & ocher	16	15	
1127	A571	4c	blue................................	15	15	
1128	A572	4c	bright greenish blue	15	15	
1129	A573	8c	rose lake	16	15	
1130	A574	4c	black	15	15	
1131	A575	4c	red & dark blue	15	15	
1132	A576	4c	ocher, dark blue & deep carmine	15	15	
1133	A577	4c	blue, green & ocher	15	15	
1134	A578	4c	brown	15	15	
1135	A579	4c	green	15	15	
1136	A580	4c	gray	15	15	
1137	A580	8c	carmine, ultra & ocher	16	15	
1138	A581	4c	rose lake	15	15	
a.			Vert. pair, imperf. btwn. ..	400.00		
b.			Vert. pair, imperf. horiz. ..	300.00		
1960-61						
1139	A582	4c	dark violet blue & carmine	15	15	
1140	A583	4c	olive bister & green	15	15	
1141	A584	4c	gray & vermilion	15	15	
1142	A585	4c	carmine & dark blue	15	15	
1143	A586	4c	magenta & green	15	15	
1144	A587	4c	green & brown.................	15	15	
1960						
1145	A588	4c	red, dark blue & dark bister	15	15	
1146	A589	4c	dull blue	15	15	
1147	A590	4c	blue................................	15	15	
a.			Vert. pair, imperf. btwn. ..	3,250.		
1148	A590	8c	carmine, ultra & ocher	16	15	
a.			Horiz. pair, imperf. btwn.	—		
1149	A591	4c	gray black	15	15	
1150	A592	4c	dark blue, brown orange & green	15	15	
1151	A593	4c	blue................................	15	15	
a.			Vert. pair, imperf. btwn. ..	150.00		
1152	A594	4c	deep violet	15	15	
1153	A595	4c	dark blue & red...............	15	15	
1154	A596	4c	sepia	15	15	
1155	A597	4c	dark blue.........................	15	15	
1156	A598	4c	green	15	15	

A582

A583

A584

A589

A585

A586

A587

A588

A590

A591

A592

A593

A594

A595

A596

A597

A598

A599

A600

A604

A608

A603

A601

A613

A605

A606

A602

A609

A610

A611

A612

A607

A614

A616

A615

A617

A618

A619

A621

A622

A620

A623

A624

A625

A626

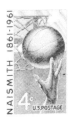
A627

A628

A629

A631

A630

Scott No.	Illus No.		Description	Unused Value	Used Value	//////
1157	A599	4c	green & rose red	15	15	☐☐☐☐☐
1158	A600	4c	blue & pink	15	15	☐☐☐☐☐
1159	A601	4c	blue	15	15	☐☐☐☐☐
1160	A601	8c	carmine, ultra & ocher	16	15	☐☐☐☐☐
1161	A602	4c	dull violet	15	15	☐☐☐☐☐
1162	A603	4c	dark blue	15	15	☐☐☐☐☐
1163	A604	4c	indigo, slate & rose red ...	15	15	☐☐☐☐☐
1164	A605	4c	dark blue & carmine	15	15	☐☐☐☐☐
1165	A606	4c	blue	15	15	☐☐☐☐☐
1166	A606	8c	carmine, ultra & ocher	16	15	☐☐☐☐☐
1167	A607	4c	dark blue & bright red	15	15	☐☐☐☐☐
1168	A608	4c	green	15	15	☐☐☐☐☐
1169	A608	8c	carmine, ultra & ocher	16	15	☐☐☐☐☐
1170	A609	4c	dull violet	15	15	☐☐☐☐☐
1171	A610	4c	deep claret	15	15	☐☐☐☐☐
1172	A611	4c	dull violet	15	15	☐☐☐☐☐
1173	A612	4c	deep violet	18	15	☐☐☐☐☐

1961

1174	A613	4c	red orange	15	15	☐☐☐☐☐
1175	A613	8c	carmine, ultra & ocher	16	15	☐☐☐☐☐
1176	A614	4c	blue, slate & brown orange	15	15	☐☐☐☐☐
1177	A615	4c	dull violet	15	15	☐☐☐☐☐

1961-65

1178	A616	4c	light green	16	15	☐☐☐☐☐
1179	A617	4c	black, *peach blossom*.......	15	15	☐☐☐☐☐
1180	A618	5c	gray & blue	15	15	☐☐☐☐☐
1181	A619	5c	dark red & black	15	15	☐☐☐☐☐
1182	A620	5c	Prus blue & black	25	15	☐☐☐☐☐
a.			Horiz. pair, imperf. vert. ..	*4,500.*		☐☐☐☐☐

1961

1183	A621	4c	brown, dark red & green, *yellow*...........................	15	15	☐☐☐☐☐
1184	A622	4c	blue green	15	15	☐☐☐☐☐
1185	A623	4c	blue	15	15	☐☐☐☐☐
1186	A624	4c	ultra, *grayish*	15	15	☐☐☐☐☐
1187	A625	4c	multicolored	15	15	☐☐☐☐☐
1188	A626	4c	blue	15	15	☐☐☐☐☐
1189	A627	4c	brown	15	15	☐☐☐☐☐
1190	A628	4c	blue, green, orange & black	15	15	☐☐☐☐☐

1962

1191	A629	4c	light blue, maroon & bister	15	15	☐☐☐☐☐
1192	A630	4c	carmine, violet blue & green	15	15	☐☐☐☐☐

A633

A632

A634

A637

A636

A640

A638

A635

A639

A642

A645

A663

A646

A650

A644

A643

A641

A662

A664

A665

Scott No.	Illus No.		Description	Unused Value	Used Value	//////
1193	A631	4c	dark blue & yellow	15	15	☐☐☐☐☐
1194	A632	4c	blue & bister	15	15	☐☐☐☐☐
1195	A633	4c	black, *buff*	15	15	☐☐☐☐☐
1196	A634	4c	red & dark blue	15	15	☐☐☐☐☐
1197	A635	4c	blue, dark slate grn & red	15	15	☐☐☐☐☐
1198	A636	4c	slate	15	15	☐☐☐☐☐
1199	A637	4c	rose red	15	15	☐☐☐☐☐
1200	A638	4c	violet	15	15	☐☐☐☐☐
1201	A639	4c	black, *yellow bister*	15	15	☐☐☐☐☐
1202	A640	4c	dark blue & red brown ...	15	15	☐☐☐☐☐
1203	A641	4c	black, brown & yellow	15	15	☐☐☐☐☐
1204	A641	4c	blk, brown & yel (yellow inverted)	15	15	☐☐☐☐☐
1205	A642	4c	green & red	15	15	☐☐☐☐☐
1206	A643	4c	blue green & black	15	15	☐☐☐☐☐
1207	A644	4c	multicolored	15	15	☐☐☐☐☐
a.			Horiz. pair, imperf. btwn.	*4,500.*		☐☐☐☐☐
1963-66						
1208	A645	5c	blue & red	25	15	☐☐☐☐☐
a.			Tagged	16	15	☐☐☐☐☐
b.			Horiz. pair, imperf. btwn.	*1,250.*		☐☐☐☐☐
1962-66, Perf. 11x10½						
1209	A646	1c	green	15	15	☐☐☐☐☐
a.			Tagged	15	15	☐☐☐☐☐
1213	A650	5c	dark blue gray	15	15	☐☐☐☐☐
a.			Booklet pane 5 + label	2.50	*1.50*	☐☐☐☐☐
b.			Tagged	50	22	☐☐☐☐☐
c.			As "a," tagged	1.90	*1.50*	☐☐☐☐☐
Coil stamps, Perf. 10 Vertically						
1225	A646	1c	green	15	15	☐☐☐☐☐
a.			Tagged	15	15	☐☐☐☐☐
1229	A650	5c	dark blue gray	1.00	15	☐☐☐☐☐
a.			Tagged	1.25	15	☐☐☐☐☐
b.			Imperf., pair	*375.00*		☐☐☐☐☐
1963						
1230	A662	5c	dark carmine & brown	15	15	☐☐☐☐☐
1231	A663	5c	green, buff & red	15	15	☐☐☐☐☐
1232	A664	5c	green, red & blk	15	15	☐☐☐☐☐
1233	A665	5c	dark blue, black & red	15	15	☐☐☐☐☐
1234	A666	5c	ultra & green	15	15	☐☐☐☐☐
1235	A667	5c	blue green	15	15	☐☐☐☐☐
1236	A668	5c	bright purple	15	15	☐☐☐☐☐
1237	A669	5c	Prussian blue & black	15	15	☐☐☐☐☐
1238	A670	5c	gray, dark blue & red	15	15	☐☐☐☐☐

93

A666

A667

A668

A669

A667

A671

A675

A670

A676

A680

A672

A678

A679

A673

A677

A674

A681

A682

94

Scott No.	Illus No.		Description	Unused Value	Used Value	/ / / / / /
1239	A671	5c	bluish black & red	15	15	☐☐☐☐☐
1240	A672	5c	dark blue, bluish black & red	15	15	☐☐☐☐☐
a.			Tagged............................	65	40	☐☐☐☐☐
1241	A673	5c	dark blue & multi	15	15	☐☐☐☐☐

1964

Scott No.	Illus No.		Description	Unused Value	Used Value	/ / / / / /
1242	A674	5c	black	15	15	☐☐☐☐☐
1243	A675	5c	indigo, red brown & olive	15	15	☐☐☐☐☐
1244	A676	5c	blue green	15	15	☐☐☐☐☐
1245	A677	5c	brown, grn, yel grn & olive	15	15	☐☐☐☐☐
1246	A678	5c	blue gray	15	15	☐☐☐☐☐
1247	A679	5c	bright ultra	15	15	☐☐☐☐☐
1248	A680	5c	red, yellow & blue	15	15	☐☐☐☐☐
1249	A681	5c	dark blue & red	15	15	☐☐☐☐☐
1250	A682	5c	black brown, *tan*	15	15	☐☐☐☐☐
1251	A683	5c	green	15	15	☐☐☐☐☐
1252	A684	5c	red, black & blue	15	15	☐☐☐☐☐
a.			Blue omitted	*1,250.*		☐☐☐☐☐
1253	A685	5c	multicolored	15	15	☐☐☐☐☐
1254	A686	5c	green, carmine & black ...	30	15	☐☐☐☐☐
a.			Tagged............................	75	40	☐☐☐☐☐
1255	A687	5c	carmine, green & black ...	30	15	☐☐☐☐☐
a.			Tagged............................	75	40	☐☐☐☐☐
1256	A688	5c	carmine, green & black ...	30	15	☐☐☐☐☐
a.			Tagged............................	75	40	☐☐☐☐☐
1257	A689	5c	black, green & carmine ...	30	15	☐☐☐☐☐
a.			Tagged............................	75	40	☐☐☐☐☐
b.			Block of 4, #1254-1257 ...	1.25	1.00	☐☐☐☐☐
c.			Block of 4, #1254a-1257a	4.25	2.00	☐☐☐☐☐
1258	A690	5c	blue green	15	15	☐☐☐☐☐
1259	A691	5c	ultra, black & dull red	15	15	☐☐☐☐☐
1260	A692	5c	red lilac	15	15	☐☐☐☐☐

1965

Scott No.	Illus No.		Description	Unused Value	Used Value	/ / / / / /
1261	A693	5c	deep carmine, violet blue & gray	15	15	☐☐☐☐☐
1262	A694	5c	maroon & black	15	15	☐☐☐☐☐
1263	A695	5c	black, purple & red orange	15	15	☐☐☐☐☐
1264	A696	5c	black	15	15	☐☐☐☐☐
1265	A697	5c	black, yellow ocher & red lilac	15	15	☐☐☐☐☐
1266	A698	5c	dull blue & black	15	15	☐☐☐☐☐
1267	A699	5c	red, black & dark blue	15	15	☐☐☐☐☐
1268	A700	5c	maroon, *tan*	15	15	☐☐☐☐☐

A684

A683

A685

A686

A687

A688

A689

A690

A691

A692

A696

A694

A695

A697

A693

A698

96

Scott No.	Illus No.		Description	Unused Value	Used Value	//////
1269	A701	5c	rose red	15	15	☐☐☐☐☐
1270	A702	5c	black & blue	15	15	☐☐☐☐☐
1271	A703	5c	red, yellow & black	15	15	☐☐☐☐☐
a.			Yellow omitted	550.00		☐☐☐☐☐
1272	A704	5c	emerald, black & red	15	15	☐☐☐☐☐
1273	A705	5c	black, brown & olive	15	15	☐☐☐☐☐
1274	A706	11c	black, carmine & bister ...	32	16	☐☐☐☐☐
1275	A707	5c	pale blue, blk, car & vio blue	15	15	☐☐☐☐☐
1276	A708	5c	car, dk olive grn & bister	15	15	☐☐☐☐☐
a.			Tagged	75	25	☐☐☐☐☐

1965-78, Perf. 11x10½, 10½x11

Scott No.	Illus No.		Description	Unused Value	Used Value	//////
1278	A710	1c	green, tagged	15	15	☐☐☐☐☐
a.			Booklet pane of 8	1.00	25	☐☐☐☐☐
b.			Booklet pane of 4 + 2 labels	75	20	☐☐☐☐☐
c.			Untagged (Bureau precanceled)		15	☐☐☐☐☐
1279	A711	1¼c	light green	15	15	☐☐☐☐☐
1280	A712	2c	dark blue gray, tagged	15	15	☐☐☐☐☐
a.			Booklet pane of 5 + label	1.20	40	☐☐☐☐☐
b.			Untagged (Bureau precanceled)		15	☐☐☐☐☐
c.			Booklet pane of 6	1.00	35	☐☐☐☐☐
1281	A713	3c	violet, tagged	15	15	☐☐☐☐☐
a.			Untagged (Bureau precanceled)		15	☐☐☐☐☐
1282	A714	4c	black	15	15	☐☐☐☐☐
a.			Tagged	15	15	☐☐☐☐☐
1283	A715	5c	blue	15	15	☐☐☐☐☐
a.			Tagged	15	15	☐☐☐☐☐
1283B	A715a	5c	blue, tagged	15	15	☐☐☐☐☐
d.			Untagged (Bureau precanceled)		15	☐☐☐☐☐
1284	A716	6c	gray brown	15	15	☐☐☐☐☐
a.			Tagged	15	15	☐☐☐☐☐
b.			Booklet pane of 8	1.50	50	☐☐☐☐☐
c.			Booklet pane of 5 + label	1.25	50	☐☐☐☐☐
1285	A717	8c	violet	20	15	☐☐☐☐☐
a.			Tagged	20	15	☐☐☐☐☐
1286	A718	10c	lilac, tagged	20	15	☐☐☐☐☐
b.			Untagged (Bureau precanceled)		20	☐☐☐☐☐
1286A	A718a	12c	black, tagged	25	15	☐☐☐☐☐
c.			Untagged (Bureau precanceled)		25	☐☐☐☐☐

A700

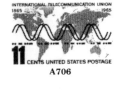

A706

A701

A703

A702

A705

A704

A708

A707

A699

A710

A711

A712

A713

A714

A715

A715a
Redrawn

A716

A717

98

Scott No.	Illus No.		Description	Unused Value	Used Value	//////
1287	A719	13c	brown, tagged	25	15	□□□□□
a.			Untagged (Bureau precanceled)		25	□□□□□
1288	A720	15c	rose claret, tagged	30	15	□□□□□
a.			Untagged (Bureau precanceled)		30	□□□□□
d.			Type II	55	15	□□□□□

Perf. 10

Scott No.	Illus No.		Description	Unused Value	Used Value	//////
1288B	A720	15c	dk rose claret (from bklt. pane)	28	15	□□□□□
c.			Booklet pane of 8	2.25	1.25	□□□□□
e.			As "c," vert. imperf. btwn.	—		□□□□□

Perf. 11x10½, 10½x11

Scott No.	Illus No.		Description	Unused Value	Used Value	//////
1289	A721	20c	deep olive	45	15	□□□□□
a.			Tagged	45	15	□□□□□
1290	A722	25c	rose lake	55	15	□□□□□
a.			Tagged	55	15	□□□□□
b.		25c	maroon	—		□□□□□
1291	A723	30c	red lilac	65	15	□□□□□
a.			Tagged	60	15	□□□□□
1292	A724	40c	blue black	85	15	□□□□□
a.			Tagged	80	15	□□□□□
1293	A725	50c	rose magenta	1.00	15	□□□□□
a.			Tagged	85	15	□□□□□
1294	A726	$1	dull purple	2.50	15	□□□□□
a.			Tagged	2.00	15	□□□□□
1295	A727	$5	gray black	13.50	2.00	□□□□□
a.			Tagged	8.50	2.00	□□□□□

1966-81, Coil stamps, Tagged, Perf. 10 Horizontally

Scott No.	Illus No.		Description	Unused Value	Used Value	//////
1297	A713	3c	violet	15	15	□□□□□
a.			Imperf., pair	30.00		□□□□□
b.			Untagged (Bureau precanceled)		15	□□□□□
c.			As "b," imperf. pair		6.00	□□□□□
1298	A716	6c	gray brown	15	15	□□□□□
a.			Imperf., pair	2,500.		□□□□□

Perf. 10 Vertically

Scott No.	Illus No.		Description	Unused Value	Used Value	//////
1299	A710	1c	green	15	15	□□□□□
a.			Untagged (Bureau precanceled)		15	□□□□□
b.			Imperf., pair	30.00	—	□□□□□

A718

A718a

A719

A720

A721

A723

A722

A724

A725

A726

A727

A727a

U.S. POSTAGE

A730

A732

A731

A728

A729

A734

A733

A735

100

Scott No.	Illus No.		Description	Unused Value	Used Value	//////
1303	A714	4c	black	15	15	☐☐☐☐☐
a.			Untagged (Bureau precanceled)		15	☐☐☐☐☐
b.			Imperf., pair	675.00		☐☐☐☐☐
1304	A715	5c	blue	15	15	☐☐☐☐☐
a.			Untagged (Bureau precanceled)		15	☐☐☐☐☐
b.			Imperf., pair	200.00		☐☐☐☐☐
e.			As "a," imperf. pair		450.00	☐☐☐☐☐
1304C	A715a	5c	blue	15	15	☐☐☐☐☐
d.			Imperf., pair	—		☐☐☐☐☐
1305	A727a	6c	gray brown	15	15	☐☐☐☐☐
a.			Imperf., pair	65.00		☐☐☐☐☐
b.			Untagged (Bureau precanceled)		20	☐☐☐☐☐
1305E	A720	15c	rose claret	25	15	☐☐☐☐☐
f.			Untagged (Bureau precanceled)		30	☐☐☐☐☐
g.			Imperf., pair	30.00		☐☐☐☐☐
h.			Pair, imperf. between	200.00		☐☐☐☐☐
i.			Type II	35	15	☐☐☐☐☐
j.			Imperf., pair, type II	80.00		☐☐☐☐☐
1305C	A726	$1	dull purple	1.50	20	☐☐☐☐☐
d.			Imperf., pair	2,250.		☐☐☐☐☐

1966

Scott No.	Illus No.		Description	Unused Value	Used Value	//////
1306	A728	5c	blk, crimson & dark blue	15	15	☐☐☐☐☐
1307	A729	5c	orange brown & black	15	15	☐☐☐☐☐
1308	A730	5c	yellow, ocher & violet blue	15	15	☐☐☐☐☐
1309	A731	5c	multicolored	15	15	☐☐☐☐☐
1310	A732	5c	multicolored	15	15	☐☐☐☐☐
1311	A733	5c	multicolored	15	15	☐☐☐☐☐
1312	A734	5c	carmine, dark & light blue	15	15	☐☐☐☐☐
1313	A735	5c	red	15	15	☐☐☐☐☐
1314	A736	5c	yellow, black & green	15	15	☐☐☐☐☐
a.			Tagged	30	20	☐☐☐☐☐
1315	A737	5c	black, bister, red & ultra ..	15	15	☐☐☐☐☐
a.			Tagged	30	20	☐☐☐☐☐
b.			Black & bister (engr.) omitted	—		☐☐☐☐☐
1316	A738	5c	black, pink & blue	15	15	☐☐☐☐☐
a.			Tagged	30	20	☐☐☐☐☐
1317	A739	5c	green, red & black	15	15	☐☐☐☐☐
a.			Tagged	30	20	☐☐☐☐☐

A737

A736

A739

A738

A741

A743

A745

A740

A747

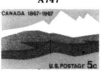

A744

A742

A746

A749

A748

A751

A750

A752

Scott No.	Illus No.		Description	Unused Value	Used Value					
1318	A740	5c	emerald, pink & black	15	15					
a.			Tagged............................	30	20					
1319	A741	5c	ver, yellow, blue & green	15	15					
a.			Tagged............................	30	20					
1320	A742	5c	red, dark & light blue, black	15	15					
b.			Tagged............................	30	20					
b.			Red, dark blue & black omitted	4,500.						
c.			Dark blue (engr.) omitted	4,000.						
1321	A743	5c	multicolored	15	15					
a.			Tagged............................	30	20					
1322	A744	5c	multicolored	15	15					
a.			Tagged............................	30	20					

1967

Scott No.	Illus No.		Description	Unused Value	Used Value					
1323	A745	5c	multicolored	15	15					
1324	A746	5c	multicolored	15	15					
1325	A747	5c	multicolored	15	15					
1326	A748	5c	blue, red & black	15	15					
1327	A749	5c	red, black & green	15	15					
1328	A750	5c	dk red brown, lemon & yellow	15	15					
1329	A751	5c	red, blue, black & carmine	15	15					
1330	A752	5c	green, black & yellow	15	15					
a.			Vert. pair, imperf. btwn. ..	—						
b.			Green (engr.) omitted	—						
c.			Black & green (engr.) omitted	—						
d.			Yellow & green (litho.) omitted	—						
1331	A753	5c	multicolored	50	15					
a.			Pair, #1331-1332	1.10	1.25					
1332	A754	5c	multicolored	50	15					
1333	A755	5c	dark & light blue, black ...	15	15					
1333	A755	5c	dark blue, light blue & black	15	15					
1334	A756	5c	blue	15	15					
1335	A757	5c	gold & multicolored	15	15					
1336	A758	5c	multicolored	15	15					
1337	A759	5c	brt grnsh blue, green & red brown	15	15					

1968-71, Perf. 11

Scott No.	Illus No.		Description	Unused Value	Used Value					
1338	A760	6c	dark blue, red & green	15	15					
k.			Vert. pair, imperf. btwn. ..	600.00						

A753   A754

A755

A757

A756

A758

A759

A760

A761

A764

A762

A765

A763

A766

A769

104

Scott No.	Illus No.		Description	Unused Value	Used Value	//////
Coil stamp, Perf. 10 Vertically						
1338A	A760	6c	dark blue, red & green	15	15	
b.			Imperf., pair	450.00		
Perf. 11x10½						
1338D	A760	6c	dark blue, red & green	15	15	
e.			Horiz. pair, imperf. btwn.	110.00		
1338F	A760	8c	multicolored	16	15	
i.			Vert. pair, imperf.	45.00		
j.			Horiz. pair, imperf. btwn.	40.00		
p.			Slate green omitted	—		
Coil stamp, Perf. 10 Vertically						
1338G	A760	8c	multicolored	18	15	
h.			Imperf., pair	55.00		
1968						
1339	A761	6c	multicolored	15	15	
1340	A762	6c	blue, rose red & white	15	15	
a.			White omitted	1,500.		
1341	A763	$1	sepia, dk blue, ocher & brn red	2.50	1.25	
1342	A764	6c	ultra & orange red	15	15	
1343	A765	6c	chalky blue, black & red ..	15	15	
1344	A766	6c	black, yellow & orange ...	15	15	
1345	A767	6c	dark blue	50	25	
1346	A768	6c	dark blue & red	35	25	
1347	A769	6c	dark blue & olive green ...	30	25	
1348	A770	6c	dark blue & red	30	25	
1349	A771	6c	dark blue, yellow & red ...	30	25	
1350	A772	6c	dark blue & red	30	25	
1351	A773	6c	dark bl, olive grn & red ...	30	25	
1352	A774	6c	dark blue & red	30	25	
1353	A775	6c	dark blue, yellow & red ...	30	25	
1354	A776	6c	dark blue, red & yellow ...	30	25	
a.			Strip of 10, #1345-1354 ..	3.25	3.00	
1355	A777	6c	multicolored	16	15	
a.			Ocher (Walt Disney, 6c, etc.) omitted	800.00	—	
b.			Vert. pair, imperf. horiz. ..	825.00		
c.			Imperf., pair	850.00		
d.			Black omitted	2,000.		
e.			Horiz. pair, imperf. btwn.	3,250.		
f.			Blue omitted	2,000.		
1356	A778	6c	black, apple green & org brn	15	15	
1357	A779	6c	yel, dp yel, maroon & blk	15	15	
1358	A780	6c	brt blue, dk blue & blk ...	15	15	
1359	A781	6c	light gray brown & blk brn	15	15	

A767

A768

A770

A771

A772

A773

A774

A775

A776

A777

A778

A779

A781

A783

A780

A785

A782

A786

A784

106

Scott No.	Illus No.		Description	Unused Value	Used Value	//////
1360	A782	6c	brown	15	15	
1361	A783	6c	multicolored	15	15	
1362	A784	6c	black & multi	15	15	
a.			Vert. pair, imperf. btwn.	550.00		
b.			Red & dark blue omitted	1,400.		
1363	A785	6c	multicolored	15	15	
a.			Untagged	15	15	
b.			Imperf., pair, tagged	275.00		
c.			Light yellow omitted	125.00		
d.			Imperf., pair, untagged	400.00		
1364	A786	6c	black & multi	16	15	

1969

1365	A787	6c	multicolored	40	15	
1366	A788	6c	multicolored	40	15	
1367	A789	6c	multicolored	40	15	
1368	A790	6c	multicolored	40	15	
a.			Block of 4, #1365-1368	1.70	1.25	
1369	A791	6c	red, blue & black	15	15	
1370	A792	6c	multicolored	15	15	
a.			Horiz. pair, imperf. btwn.	275.00		
b.			Black and Prus blue omitted	950.00		
1371	A793	6c	black, blue & ocher	15	15	
1372	A794	6c	multicolored	15	15	
1373	A795	6c	multicolored	15	15	
1374	A796	6c	multicolored	15	15	
1375	A797	6c	multicolored	15	15	
1376	A798	6c	multicolored	75	15	
1377	A799	6c	multicolored	75	15	
1378	A800	6c	multicolored	75	15	
1379	A801	6c	multicolored	75	15	
a.			Block of 4, #1376-1379	3.00	3.00	
1380	A802	6c	green	15	15	
1381	A803	6c	yellow, red, black & green	75	15	
a.			Black (1869-1969, United States, 6c, Professional Baseball) omitted	1,250.		
1382	A804	6c	red & green	15	15	
1383	A805	6c	blue, black & red	15	15	
1384	A806	6c	dark green & multi	15	15	
			Precanceled	50	15	
b.			Imperf., pair	1,250.		
c.			Light green omitted	25.00		
d.			Lt grn, red yellow omitted	1,000.	—	
e.			Yellow omitted	—		

PLANT for more BEAUTIFUL CITIES

A787

PLANT for more BEAUTIFUL PARKS

A788

PLANT for more BEAUTIFUL HIGHWAYS

A789

PLANT for more BEAUTIFUL STREETS

A790

CALIFORNIA 1769 1969
United States 6 cents

A795

The American Legion
50 years
Veterans as Citizens
U.S. POSTAGE 6 CENTS

A791

Grandma Moses
6c U.S. Postage

A792

In the beginning God...
APOLLO 8
SIX CENTS · UNITED STATES

A793

JOHN WESLEY POWELL
1869 EXPEDITION
6c U.S. POSTAGE

A796

Father of the Blues
6¢ UNITED STATES

A794

ALABAMA 1819 1969
UNITED STATES

A797

Pseudotsuga menziesii
XI INTERNATIONAL BOTANICAL CONGRESS
6¢ UNITED STATES
BOTANICAL

A798

6¢ UNITED STATES
Cypripedium reginae

A799

Pinus splendens
XI INTERNATIONAL BOTANICAL CONGRESS
6¢ UNITED STATES
BOTANICAL

A800

6¢ UNITED STATES
Franklinia alatamaha

A801

Scott No.	Illus No.		Description	Unused Value	Used Value	/ / / / / /
1385	A807	6c	multicolored	15	15	☐☐☐☐☐
1386	A808	6c	multicolored	15	15	☐☐☐☐☐

1970

1387	A809	6c	multicolored	15	15	☐☐☐☐☐
1388	A810	6c	multicolored	15	15	☐☐☐☐☐
1389	A811	6c	multicolored	15	15	☐☐☐☐☐
1390	A812	6c	multicolored	15	15	☐☐☐☐☐
a.			Block of 4, #1387-1390 ...	50	50	☐☐☐☐☐
1391	A813	6c	black & multi	15	15	☐☐☐☐☐
1392	A814	6c	black, *light brown*...........	15	15	☐☐☐☐☐

1970-74, Tagged, Perf. 11x10½, 10½x11, 11 (#1394)

1393	A815	6c	dark blue gray	15	15	☐☐☐☐☐
a.			Booklet pane of 8	1.25	*50*	☐☐☐☐☐
b.			Booklet pane of 5 + label	1.25	*50*	☐☐☐☐☐
c.			Untagged (Bureau precanceled)		15	☐☐☐☐☐
1393D	A816	7c	bright blue	15	15	☐☐☐☐☐
e.			Untagged (Bureau precanceled)		15	☐☐☐☐☐
1394	A815a	8c	black, red & blue gray	16	15	☐☐☐☐☐
1395	A815	8c	deep claret	18	15	☐☐☐☐☐
a.			Booklet pane of 8	1.80	*1.25*	☐☐☐☐☐
b.			Booklet pane of 6	1.25	*75*	☐☐☐☐☐
c.			Booklet pane of 4 + 2 labels	1.65	*50*	☐☐☐☐☐
d.			Booklet pane of 7 + label	1.75	*1.00*	☐☐☐☐☐
1396	A817	8c	multicolored	15	15	☐☐☐☐☐
1397	A817a	14c	gray brown	25	15	☐☐☐☐☐
a.			Untagged (Bureau precanceled)		25	☐☐☐☐☐
1398	A818	16c	brown	28	15	☐☐☐☐☐
a.			Untagged (Bureau precanceled)		35	☐☐☐☐☐
1399	A818a	18c	violet	32	15	☐☐☐☐☐
1400	A818b	21c	green	32	15	☐☐☐☐☐

Coil stamps, Perf. 10 Vertically

1401	A815	6c	dark blue gray	15	15	☐☐☐☐☐
a.			Untagged (Bureau precanceled)		15	☐☐☐☐☐
b.			Imperf., pair	*1,500.*		☐☐☐☐☐
1402	A815	8c	deep claret	15	15	☐☐☐☐☐
a.			Imperf., pair	45.00		☐☐☐☐☐
b.			Untagged (Bureau precanceled)		15	☐☐☐☐☐
c.			Pair, imperf. btwn.	*6,250.*		☐☐☐☐☐

A802

A803

A807

U.S. 6¢ POSTAGE

DWIGHT D.
EISENHOWER

A805

A806

A804

A808

AMERICAN BALD EAGLE

A809

AFRICAN ELEPHANT HERD

A810

HAIDA CEREMONIAL CANOE

A811

THE AGE OF REPTILES

A812

A813

A814

EISENHOWER·USA 6¢
Dot between ''R''
and ''U''

A815

EISENHOWER USA 8¢
No dot between
''R'' and ''U''

A815a

US 7¢

A816

UNITED STATES POSTAL SERVICE
U.S. MAIL
8 cents

A817

US
LaGuardia 14¢

A817a

Ernie Pyle
Journalist 16¢

A818

ELIZABETH BLACKWELL FIRST WOMAN PHYSICIAN
US POSTAGE 18¢

A818a

GIANNINI
AMADEO P.
US.A 21¢

A818b

WOMAN SUFFRAGE
1920-1970
50ᵀᴴ ANNIVERSARY 6¢

A820

EDGAR LEE
MASTERS
AMERICAN POET
UNITED STATES 6¢

A819

SOUTH CAROLINA
1670 1970
6¢

A821

Stone Mountain Memorial
UNITED STATES 6 CENTS

A822

GREAT NORTHWEST
1820 FORT SNELLING 1970
US 6¢

A823

SAVE OUR SOIL
UNITED STATES · SIX CENTS

A824

SAVE OUR CITIES
UNITED STATES · SIX CENTS

A825

SAVE OUR WATER
UNITED STATES · SIX CENTS

A826

SAVE OUR AIR
UNITED STATES · SIX CENTS

A827

Christmas 6us

A828

Christmas 6u.s.

A829

Christmas 6u.s.

A830

Christmas 6u.s.

A831

Christmas 6u.s.

A832

50 years of service

DISABLED AMERICAN VETERANS

UNITED 6c STATES

A835

HONORING U.S. SERVICEMEN

PRISONERS OF WAR

MISSING AND KILLED IN ACTION

UNITED 6c STATES

A836

UNITED STATES POSTAGE 6 CENTS

UN

United Nations 25ᵗʰ Anniversary

A833

1620 THE LANDING OF THE PILGRIMS

U.S. POSTAGE 6 CENTS

A834

UNITED STATES

AMERICA'S WOOL

A837

6c US

DOUGLAS MacARTHUR

A838

giving BLOOD saves lives

United States Postage 6

A839

Missouri 1821-1971 United States 8c

A840

Scott No.	Illus No.		Description	Unused Value	Used Value	//////
1970						
1405	A819	6c	black & olive bister	15	15	☐☐☐☐☐☐
1406	A820	6c	blue	15	15	☐☐☐☐☐☐
1407	A821	6c	bister, black & red	15	15	☐☐☐☐☐☐
1408	A822	6c	gray	15	15	☐☐☐☐☐☐
1409	A823	6c	yellow & multi	15	15	☐☐☐☐☐☐
1410	A824	6c	multicolored	22	15	☐☐☐☐☐☐
1411	A825	6c	multicolored	22	15	☐☐☐☐☐☐
1412	A826	6c	multicolored	22	15	☐☐☐☐☐☐
1413	A827	6c	multicolored	22	15	☐☐☐☐☐☐
a.			Block of 4, #1410-1413 ...	1.00	1.00	☐☐☐☐☐☐
1414	A828	6c	multicolored	15	15	☐☐☐☐☐☐
a.			Precanceled	15	15	☐☐☐☐☐☐
b.			Black omitted	*650.00*		☐☐☐☐☐☐
c.			As "a," blue omitted	*2,000.*		☐☐☐☐☐☐
1415	A829	6c	multicolored	40	15	☐☐☐☐☐☐
a.			Precanceled	90	15	☐☐☐☐☐☐
b.			Black omitted	*1,500.*		☐☐☐☐☐☐
1416	A830	6c	multicolored	40	15	☐☐☐☐☐☐
a.			Precanceled	90	15	☐☐☐☐☐☐
b.			Black omitted	*1,500.*		☐☐☐☐☐☐
c.			Imperf., pair (#1416, 1418)		*4,000.*	☐☐☐☐☐☐
1417	A831	6c	multicolored	40	15	☐☐☐☐☐☐
a.			Precanceled	90	15	☐☐☐☐☐☐
b.			Black omitted	*1,500.*		☐☐☐☐☐☐
1418	A832	6c	multicolored	40	15	☐☐☐☐☐☐
a.			Precanceled	90	15	☐☐☐☐☐☐
b.			Block of 4, #1415-1418 ...	1.90	1.75	☐☐☐☐☐☐
c.			As "b," precanceled	3.75	3.50	☐☐☐☐☐☐
d.			Black omitted	*1,500.*		☐☐☐☐☐☐
1419	A833	6c	black, vermilion & ultra ..	15	15	☐☐☐☐☐☐
1420	A834	6c	black, org, yel, brn, mag & blue	15	15	☐☐☐☐☐☐
a.			Orange & yellow omitted	*1,200.*		☐☐☐☐☐☐
1421	A835	6c	multicolored	15	15	☐☐☐☐☐☐
a.			Pair, #1421-1422	25	25	☐☐☐☐☐☐
1422	A836	6c	dark blue, black & red	15	15	☐☐☐☐☐☐
1971						
1423	A837	6c	multicolored	15	15	☐☐☐☐☐☐
1424	A838	6c	black, red & dark blue	15	15	☐☐☐☐☐☐
1425	A839	6c	light blue, scarlet & indigo	15	15	☐☐☐☐☐☐
1426	A840	8c	multicolored	15	15	☐☐☐☐☐☐
1427	A841	8c	multicolored	16	15	☐☐☐☐☐☐
1428	A842	8c	multicolored	16	15	☐☐☐☐☐☐
1429	A843	8c	multicolored	16	15	☐☐☐☐☐☐

A841

A842

A843

A844

A845

A847

A846

A848   **A849**

A850

A851

A852

A853

Scott No.	Illus No.		Description	Unused Value	Used Value	//////
1430	A844	8c	multicolored	16	15	☐☐☐☐☐
a.			Block of 4, #1427-1430 ...	65	65	☐☐☐☐☐
b.			As "a," lt grn & dk grn omitted from #1427-1428	3,500.		☐☐☐☐☐
c.			As "a," red omitted from #1427, 1429-1430	9,000.		☐☐☐☐☐
1431	A845	8c	red & dark blue	16	15	☐☐☐☐☐
1432	A846	8c	red, blue, gray & black	16	15	☐☐☐☐☐
a.			Gray & black omitted	650.00		☐☐☐☐☐
b.			Gray (U.S. Postage 8c) omitted	1,100.		☐☐☐☐☐
1433	A847	8c	multicolored	15	15	☐☐☐☐☐
1434	A848	8c	blkac, blue, yellow & red	15	15	☐☐☐☐☐
a.			Pair, #1434-1435	30	25	☐☐☐☐☐
b.			As "a," blue & red (litho.) omitted	1,500.		☐☐☐☐☐
1435	A849	8c	black, blue, yellow & red	15	15	☐☐☐☐☐
1436	A850	8c	multi, *greenish*	15	15	☐☐☐☐☐
a.			Black & olive (engr.) omitted	950.00		☐☐☐☐☐
b.			Pale rose omitted	7,500.		☐☐☐☐☐
1437	A851	8c	multicolored	15	15	☐☐☐☐☐
1438	A852	8c	blue, deep blue & black ...	15	15	☐☐☐☐☐
1439	A853	8c	multicolored	15	15	☐☐☐☐☐
a.			Black omitted	4,500.		☐☐☐☐☐
1440	A854	8c	black brown & ocher	16	15	☐☐☐☐☐
1441	A855	8c	black brown & ocher	16	15	☐☐☐☐☐
1442	A856	8c	black brown & ocher	16	15	☐☐☐☐☐
1443	A857	8c	black brown & ocher	16	15	☐☐☐☐☐
a.			Block of 4, #1440-1443 ...	65	65	☐☐☐☐☐
b.			As "a," black brown omitted	2,400.		☐☐☐☐☐
c.			As "a," ocher omitted	—		☐☐☐☐☐
1444	A858	8c	gold & multi	15	15	☐☐☐☐☐
a.			Gold omitted	500.00		☐☐☐☐☐
1445	A859	8c	multicolored	15	15	☐☐☐☐☐

1972

Scott No.	Illus No.		Description	Unused Value	Used Value	//////
1446	A860	8c	black, brown & light blue	15	15	☐☐☐☐☐
1447	A861	8c	dark blue, light blue & red	15	15	☐☐☐☐☐
1448	A862	2c	black & multi	15	15	☐☐☐☐☐
1449	A863	2c	black & multi	15	15	☐☐☐☐☐
1450	A864	2c	black & multi	15	15	☐☐☐☐☐
1451	A865	2c	black & multi	15	15	☐☐☐☐☐
a.			Block of 4, #1448-1451 ...	20	20	☐☐☐☐☐
b.			As "a," black (litho.) omitted	2,500.		☐☐☐☐☐

A854

A855

A856

A857

A862

A863

A864

A865

A858

A860

A867

A859

A861

A866

A868

Scott No.	Illus No.		Description	Unused Value	Used Value	//////
1452	A866	6c	black & multi	15	15	□□□□□
1453	A867	8c	black, blue, brown & multi	15	15	□□□□□
1454	A868	15c	black & multi..................	30	18	□□□□□
1455	A869	8c	black & multi	15	15	□□□□□
a.			Yellow omitted..............	—		□□□□□
b.			Dark brown & olive			
			omitted........................	—		□□□□□
c.			Dark brown omitted	—		□□□□□
1456	A870	8c	deep brown	16	15	□□□□□
1457	A871	8c	deep brown	16	15	□□□□□
1458	A872	8c	deep brown	16	15	□□□□□
1459	A873	8c	deep brown	16	15	□□□□□
a.			Block of 4, #1456-1459 ...	65	65	□□□□□
1460	A874	6c	multicolored	15	15	□□□□□
1461	A875	8c	multicolored	15	15	□□□□□
1462	A876	15c	multicolored	28	18	□□□□□
1463	A877	8c	yellow & black	15	15	□□□□□
1464	A878	8c	multicolored	16	15	□□□□□
1465	A879	8c	multicolored	16	15	□□□□□
1466	A880	8c	multicolored	16	15	□□□□□
1467	A881	8c	multicolored	16	15	□□□□□
a.			Block of 4, #1464-1467 ...	65	65	□□□□□
b.			As "a," brown omitted	*3,750.*		□□□□□
c.			As "a," green & blue			
			omitted........................	—		□□□□□
d.			As "a," red & brown			
			omitted........................	*4,250.*		□□□□□
1468	A882	8c	multicolored	15	15	□□□□□
1469	A883	8c	yellow, orange & dark			
			brown..........................	15	15	□□□□□
1470	A884	8c	black & multi	15	15	□□□□□
a.			Horiz. pair, imperf. btwn.	*4,500.*		□□□□□
b.			Red & black (engr.)			
			omitted........................	*1,500.*		□□□□□
c.			Yellow & tan (litho.)			
			omitted........................	*1,800.*		□□□□□
1471	A885	8c	multicolored	15	15	□□□□□
a.			Pink omitted	250.00		□□□□□
b.			Black omitted	*3,750.*		□□□□□
1472	A886	8c	multicolored	15	15	□□□□□
1473	A887	8c	black & multi	16	15	□□□□□
a.			Blue & orange omitted	*1,000.*		□□□□□
b.			Blue omitted	*2,000.*		□□□□□
c.			Orange omitted	*2,000.*		□□□□□
1474	A888	8c	dark blue green, black &			
			brown..........................	15	15	□□□□□
a.			Black (litho.) omitted	*1,100.*		□□□□□

Family Planning

UNITED STATES 8¢

A869

A870

A871

A872

A873

A874

A875

A876

A877

A878

A879

A880

A881

A883

A882

A884

A885

A887

A886

A888

A889

A890

A891

A892

A893

A894

A895

A896

A897

A898

A899

A900

A901

A902

HOW TO USE THIS BOOK

The number in the first column is its Scott number or identifying number. The letter and number that come next (A41) indicate the design and refer to the illustration so designated. Following that is the denomination of the stamp and its color. Finally, the value, unused and used is shown.

Scott No.	Illus No.		Description	Unused Value	Used Value	/ / / / / /
1973						
1475	A889	8c	red, emerald & violet blue	15	15	
1476	A890	8c	ultra, greenish black & red	15	15	
1477	A891	8c	black, vermilion & ultra .	15	15	
1478	A892	8c	multicolored	15	15	
1479	A893	8c	multicolored	15	15	
1480	A894	8c	black & multi	15	15	
1481	A895	8c	black & multi	15	15	
1482	A896	8c	black & multi	15	15	
1483	A897	8c	black & multi	15	15	
a.			Block of 4, #1480-1483 ...	65	45	
b.			As "a," black (engr.) omitted	*1,750.*		
c.			As "a," black (litho.) omitted	*1,650.*		
1484	A898	8c	deep green & multi	15	15	
a.			Vert. pair, imperf. horiz. ..	*250.00*		
1485	A899	8c	Prussian blue & multi	15	15	
a.			Vert. pair, imperf. horiz. ..	*300.00*		
1486	A900	8c	yellow brown & multi	15	15	
1487	A901	8c	deep brown & multi	15	15	
a.			Vert. pair, imperf. horiz. ..	*350.00*		
1488	A902	8c	black & orange	15	15	
a.			Orange omitted	*1,100.*		
b.			Black (engraved) omitted	*1,600.*		
1489	A903	8c	multicolored	15	15	
1490	A904	8c	multicolored	15	15	
1491	A905	8c	multicolored	15	15	
1492	A906	8c	multicolored	15	15	
1493	A907	8c	multicolored	15	15	
1494	A908	8c	multicolored	15	15	
1495	A909	8c	multicolored	15	15	
1496	A910	8c	multicolored	15	15	
1497	A911	8c	multicolored	15	15	
1498	A912	8c	multicolored	15	15	
a.			Strip of 10, #1489-1498 ..	1.50	1.00	
1499	A913	8c	carmine rose, black & blue	15	15	
1500	A914	6c	lilac & multi	15	15	
1501	A915	8c	tan & multi	15	15	
a.			Black (inscriptions & U.S. 8c) omitted	*750.00*		
b.			Tan (background) & lilac omitted	*2,000.*		
1502	A916	15c	gray green & multi	28	15	
a.			Black (inscriptions . "U.S. 15c") omitted	*1,600.*		
1503	A917	15c	black & multicolored	15	15	
a.			Horiz. pair, imperf. vert. ..	*300.00*		

U.S. POSTAL SERVICE 8c

A903

U.S. POSTAL SERVICE 8c

A904

U.S. POSTAL SERVICE 8c

A905

U.S. POSTAL SERVICE 8c

A906

U.S. POSTAL SERVICE 8c

A907

U.S. POSTAL SERVICE 8c

A908

U.S. POSTAL SERVICE 8c

A909

U.S. POSTAL SERVICE 8c

A910

U.S. POSTAL SERVICE 8c

A911

U.S. POSTAL SERVICE 8c

A912

Harry S. Truman

U.S. Postage 8 cents **A913**

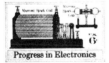

Progress in Electronics

A914

Progress in Electronics

A915

Progress in Electronics

A916

122

Scott No.	Illus No.		Description	Unused Value	Used Value	/////
1973-74						
1504	A918	8c	multicolored	15	15	☐☐☐☐☐
a.			Green & red brn omitted .	*1,150.*		☐☐☐☐☐
b.			Vert. pair, imperf. btwn ...		—	☐☐☐☐☐
1505	A919	10c	multicolored	18	15	☐☐☐☐☐
1506	A920	10c	multicolored	18	15	☐☐☐☐☐
a.			Black blue (engr.) omitted	*750.00*		☐☐☐☐☐
1973						
1507	A921	8c	tan & multi	15	15	☐☐☐☐☐
1508	A922	8c	green & multi	15	15	☐☐☐☐☐
a.			Vert. pair, imperf. btwn. ..	*500.00*		☐☐☐☐☐

1973-74, Tagged, Perf. 11x10½

1509	A923	10c	red & blue	18	15	☐☐☐☐☐
a.			Horiz. pair, imperf. btwn.	*50.00*	—	☐☐☐☐☐
b.			Blue omitted	*150.00*		☐☐☐☐☐
c.			Vert. pair, imperf.	*1,150.*		☐☐☐☐☐
d.			Horiz. pair, imperf. vert. ..	—		☐☐☐☐☐
1510	A924	10c	blue	18	15	☐☐☐☐☐
a.			Untagged (Bureau precanceled)		18	☐☐☐☐☐
b.			Booklet pane of 5 + label	1.50	30	☐☐☐☐☐
c.			Booklet pane of 8	1.65	30	☐☐☐☐☐
d.			Booklet pane of 6	5.25	30	☐☐☐☐☐
e.			Vert. pair, imperf. horiz. ..	*250.00*		☐☐☐☐☐
f.			Vert. pair, imperf. btwn. ..	—		☐☐☐☐☐
1511	A925	10c	multicolored	18	15	☐☐☐☐☐
a.			Yellow omitted	*50.00*		☐☐☐☐☐

Coil Stamps, Perf. 10 Vertically

1518	A926	6.3c	brick red	15	15	☐☐☐☐☐
a.			Untagged (Bureau precanceled)		15	☐☐☐☐☐
b.			Imperf., pair	*250.00*		☐☐☐☐☐
c.			As "a," imperf. pair		*125.00*	☐☐☐☐☐
1519	A923	10c	red & blue	18	15	☐☐☐☐☐
a.			Imperf., pair	30.00		☐☐☐☐☐
1520	A924	10c	blue	18	15	☐☐☐☐☐
a.			Untagged (Bureau precanceled)		25	☐☐☐☐☐
b.			Imperf., pair	*40.00*		☐☐☐☐☐

1974						
1525	A928	10c	red & dark blue	18	15	☐☐☐☐☐
1526	A929	10c	black	18	15	☐☐☐☐☐

A917

A918

A919

A920

A921

A922

A923

A924

A925

A926

A928

A929

A930

A931

A932

Letters
mingle souls

A933

Universal
Postal Union
1874-1974

A934

Letters
mingle souls

A935

Universal
Postal Union
1874-1974

A936

Letters
mingle souls

A937

Universal
Postal Union
1874-1974

A938

Letters
mingle souls

A939

Universal
Postal Union
1874-1974

A940

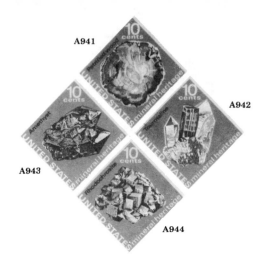

A941

A942

A943

A944

A946

A947

A948

A949

A945

A951

A950

126

Scott No.	Illus No.		Description	Unused Value	Used Value	//////
1527	A930	10c	multicolored	18	15	□□□□□
1528	A931	10c	yellow & multi	18	15	□□□□□
a.			Blue ("Horse Racing") omitted	1,000.		□□□□□
b.			Red ("U.S. postage 10 cents") omitted	—		□□□□□
1529	A932	10c	multicolored	18	15	□□□□□
a.			Vert. pair, imperf. btwn. ..	—		□□□□□
1530	A933	10c	multicolored	20	15	□□□□□
1531	A934	10c	multicolored	20	15	□□□□□
1532	A935	10c	multicolored	20	15	□□□□□
1533	A936	10c	multicolored	20	15	□□□□□
1534	A937	10c	multicolored	20	15	□□□□□
1535	A938	10c	multicolored	20	15	□□□□□
1536	A939	10c	multicolored	20	15	□□□□□
1537	A940	10c	multicolored	20	15	□□□□□
a.			Block or strip of 8, #1530-1537	1.60	1.50	□□□□□
b.			As "a" (block), imperf. vert.	7,500.		□□□□□
1538	A941	10c	light blue & multi	18	15	□□□□□
a.			Light blue & yellow omitted	—		□□□□□
1539	A942	10c	light blue & multi	18	15	□□□□□
a.			Light blue omitted	—		□□□□□
b.			Black & purple omitted ...	—		□□□□□
1540	A943	10c	light blue & multi	18	15	□□□□□
a.			Light blue & yellow omitted	—		□□□□□
1541	A944	10c	light blue & multi	18	15	□□□□□
a.			Block or strip of 4, #1538-1541	80	80	□□□□□
b.			As "a," lt bl & yel omitted	2,000.		□□□□□
c.			Light blue omitted	—		□□□□□
d.			Black & red omitted	—		□□□□□
1542	A945	10c	green & multi	18	15	□□□□□
a.			Dull black (litho.) omitted	1,000.		□□□□□
b.			Grn (engr. & litho.), blk (engr. & litho.), blue omitted	3,250.		□□□□□
c.			Green (engr.) omitted	—		□□□□□
d.			Green (engr.), black (litho.) omitted	—		□□□□□
1543	A946	10c	dark blue & red	18	15	□□□□□
1544	A947	10c	gray, dark blue & red	18	15	□□□□□
1545	A948	10c	gray, dark blue & red	18	15	□□□□□
1546	A949	10c	red & dark blue	18	15	□□□□□
a.			Block of 4, #1543-1546 ...	75	75	□□□□□

Retarded Children
Can Be Helped

A952

Christmas

A953

Currier and Ives

A954

Peace on Earth

Christmas

A955

Benjamin West

American artist
10 cents U.S. postage

A956

MOVIEMAKER US 10¢

D.W. GRIFFITH

A958

Paul Laurence
Dunbar

American poet

10 cents U.S. postage

A957

PIONEER ★ JUPITER

US 10¢

A959

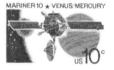

MARINER 10 ★ VENUS MERCURY

US 10¢

A960

Contributors
To The
Cause...

Sybil Ludington 🕊 *Youthful Heroine*

A962

Contributors
To The
Cause...

Salem Poor 🕊 *Gallant Soldier*

A963

Contributors
To The
Cause...

Haym Salomon 🕊 *Financial Hero*

A964

Contributors
To The
Cause...

Peter Francisco 🕊 *Fighter Extraordinary*

A965

Scott No.	Illus No.		Description	Unused Value	Used Value	//////
1547	A950	10c	multicolored	18	15	
a.			Blue & orange omitted	*800.00*		
b.			Orange & green omitted ..	*900.00*		
c.			Green omitted	*950.00*		
1548	A951	10c	dk blue, black, org & yellow	18	15	
1549	A952	10c	brown red & dark brown	18	15	
1550	A953	10c	multicolored	18	15	
1551	A954	10c	multicolored	18	15	
1552	A955	10c	multicolored	18	15	

1975

Scott No.	Illus No.		Description	Unused Value	Used Value	//////
1553	A956	10c	multicolored	18	15	
1554	A957	10c	multicolored	18	15	
a.			Imperf., pair	*1,250.*		
1555	A958	10c	multicolored	18	15	
a.			Brown (engr.) omitted	*700.00*		
1556	A959	10c	violet blue, yellow & red	18	15	
a.			Red (litho.) omitted	*1,500.*		
b.			Blue (engr.) omitted	*1,000.*		
1557	A960	10c	blk, red, ultra & bister	18	15	
a.			Red omitted	*750.00*		
b.			Ultra & bister omitted	*1,800.*		
1558	A961	10c	multicolored	18	15	
1559	A962	8c	multicolored	16	15	
a.			Back inscription omitted .	*275.00*		
1560	A963	10c	multicolored	18	15	
a.			Back inscription omitted .	*300.00*		
1561	A964	10c	multicolored	18	15	
a.			Back inscription omitted .	*350.00*		
b.			Red omitted	*250.00*		
1562	A965	18c	multicolored	35	20	
1563	A966	10c	multicolored	18	15	
a.			Vert. pair, imperf. horiz. ..	*500.00*		
1564	A967	10c	multicolored	18	15	
1565	A968	10c	multicolored	18	15	
1566	A969	10c	multicolored	18	15	
1567	A970	10c	multicolored	18	15	
1568	A971	10c	multicolored	18	15	
a.			Block of 4, #1565-1568 ...	75	75	
1569	A972	10c	multicolored	18	15	
a.			Pair, #1569-1570	40	25	
b.			As "a," vert. pair, imperf. horiz.	*1,650.*		
1570	A973	10c	multicolored	18	15	
1571	A974	10c	blue, orange & dark blue .	18	15	
1572	A975	10c	multicolored	18	15	
1573	A976	10c	multicolored	18	15	

A961

US Bicentennial 10cents

A966

US Bicentennial 10c

A967

A968

A969

A970

A971

A972

A973

130

A974

A979

A975

A976

A977

A978

A980

A981

A982

A983

A984

A985

A987

A988

A994

A995

A996

A997

A998

A999

A1001

A1002

A1003

A1004

A1005

A1006

A1007

A1008

A1009

A1010

132

Scott No.	Illus No.		Description	Unused Value	Used Value	//////
1574	A977	10c	multicolored	18	15	
1575	A978	10c	multicolored	18	15	
a.			Block of 4, #1572-1575 ...	80	80	
b.			As "a," red (10c) omitted	—		
1576	A979	10c	green, Prus blue & rose brn	18	15	
1577	A980	10c	multicolored	18	15	
a.			Pair, #1577-1578	40	20	
b.			As "a," brown blue (litho.) omitted	1,250.		
c.			As "a," brown, blue & yellow (litho.) omitted	—		
1578	A981	10c	multicolored	18	15	
1579	A982	(10c)	multicolored	18	15	
a.			Imperf., pair	110.00		
1580	A983	(10c)	multicolored	18	15	
a.			Imperf., pair	120.00		
b.			Perf. 10½x11	60	15	

1973-81, Perf. 11x10½

Scott No.	Illus No.		Description	Unused Value	Used Value	//////
1581	A984	1c	dark blue, *greenish*	15	15	
a.			Untagged (Bureau precanceled)		15	
1582	A985	2c	red brown, *greenish*	15	15	
a.			Untagged (Bureau precanceled)		15	
b.			Cream paper	15	15	
1584	A987	3c	olive, *greenish*	15	15	
a.			Untagged (Bureau precanceled)		15	
1585	A988	4c	rose magenta, *cream*	15	15	
a.			Untagged (Bureau precanceled)		1.25	
1590	A994	9c	slate green	50	20	
a.			Perf. 10	18.50	10.00	
1591	A994	9c	slate green, *gray*	16	15	
a.			Untagged (Bureau precanceled)		18	
1592	A995	10c	violet, *gray*	18	15	
a.			Untagged (Bureau precanceled)		25	
1593	A996	11c	orange, *gray*.....................	20	15	
1594	A997	12c	brown red, *beige*	22	15	
1595	A998	13c	brown	25	15	
a.			Booklet pane of 6	1.90	50	
b.			Booklet pane of 7 + label	1.75	50	
c.			Booklet pane of 8	2.00	50	
d.			Booklet pane of 5 + label	1.40	50	
e.			Vert. pair, imperf between	—		

133

A1011

A1012

A1013

A1014

A1015

A1016

A1019

A1020

A1021

A1022

HOW TO USE THIS BOOK

The number in the first column is its Scott number or identifying number. The letter and number that come next (A41) indicate the design and refer to the illustration so designated. Following that is the denomination of the stamp and its color. Finally, the value, unused and used is shown.

Scott No.	Illus No.		Description	Unused Value	Used Value	//////

Perf. 11

Scott No.	Illus No.		Description	Unused Value	Used Value	//////
1596	A999	13c	multicolored	26	15	☐☐☐☐☐
a.			Imperf., pair	50.00	—	☐☐☐☐☐
b.			Yellow omitted	225.00		☐☐☐☐☐
1597	A1001	15c	gray, dark blue & red	28	15	☐☐☐☐☐
a.			Vert. pair, imperf.	17.50		☐☐☐☐☐
b.			Gray omitted	250.00		☐☐☐☐☐
c.			Vert. strip of 3, imperf. btwn. & at top	—		☐☐☐☐☐

Perf. 11x10½

Scott No.	Illus No.		Description	Unused Value	Used Value	//////
1598	A1001	15c	gray, dark blue & red	30	15	☐☐☐☐☐
a.			Booklet pane of 8	3.50	60	☐☐☐☐☐
1599	A1002	16c	blue	34	15	☐☐☐☐☐
1603	A1003	24c	red, *blue*	45	15	☐☐☐☐☐
1604	A1004	28c	brown, *blue*	55	15	☐☐☐☐☐
1605	A1005	29c	blue, *blue*	55	15	☐☐☐☐☐
1606	A1006	30c	green, *blue*	55	15	☐☐☐☐☐

Perf. 11

Scott No.	Illus No.		Description	Unused Value	Used Value	//////
1608	A1007	50c	tan, black & orange	95	15	☐☐☐☐☐
a.			Black omitted	400.00		☐☐☐☐☐
b.			Vert. pair, imperf. horiz. ..	—		☐☐☐☐☐
1610	A1008	$1	tan, brown, orange & yellow	1.75	20	☐☐☐☐☐
a.			Brown (engraved) omitted	300.00		☐☐☐☐☐
b.			Tan, orange & yellow omitted	300.00		☐☐☐☐☐
c.			Brown inverted	12,500.		☐☐☐☐☐
1611	A1009	$2	tan, dark grn, org & yel ...	3.75	45	☐☐☐☐☐
1612	A1010	$5	tan, red brown, yel & org	9.00	1.50	☐☐☐☐☐

Coil stamp, Perf. 10 Vertically

Scott No.	Illus No.		Description	Unused Value	Used Value	//////
1613	A1011	3.1c	brown, *yellow*	15	15	☐☐☐☐☐
a.			Untagged (Bureau precanceled)		50	☐☐☐☐☐
b.			Imperf., pair	1,250.		☐☐☐☐☐
1614	A1012	7.7c	brown, *bright yellow*	18	15	☐☐☐☐☐
a.			Untagged (Bureau precanceled)		35	☐☐☐☐☐
b.			As "a," imperf., pair	1,400.		☐☐☐☐☐
1615	A1013	7.9c	carmine, *yellow*	15	15	☐☐☐☐☐
a.			Untagged (Bureau precanceled)		16	☐☐☐☐☐
b.			Imperf., pair	650.00		☐☐☐☐☐

Don't forget to update these Scott Albums with yearly supplements

Scott Minuteman Album
Scott National Album
Scott American Album

Published in March every year.

Scott No.	Illus No.		Description	Unused Value	Used Value	//////
1615C	A1014	8.4c	dark blue, *yellow*	22	15	☐☐☐☐☐
d.			Untagged (Bureau precanceled)		16	☐☐☐☐☐
e.			As "d," pair, imperf. between		60.00	☐☐☐☐☐
f.			As "d," imperf., pair		15.00	☐☐☐☐☐
1616	A994	9c	slate green, *gray*	20	15	☐☐☐☐☐
a.			Imperf., pair	*125.00*		☐☐☐☐☐
b.			Untagged (Bureau precanceled)		28	☐☐☐☐☐
c.			As "b," imperf., pair		*190.00*	☐☐☐☐☐
1617	A995	10c	violet, *gray*	24	15	☐☐☐☐☐
a.			Untagged (Bureau precanceled)		25	☐☐☐☐☐
b.			Imperf., pair	*60.00*		☐☐☐☐☐
1618	A998	13c	brown	25	15	☐☐☐☐☐
a.			Untagged (Bureau precanceled)		45	☐☐☐☐☐
b.			Imperf., pair	25.00		☐☐☐☐☐
g.			Pair, imperf. between	—		☐☐☐☐☐
h.			As "a," imperf., pair		—	☐☐☐☐☐
1618C	A1001	15c	gray, dark blue & red	40	15	☐☐☐☐☐
d.			Imperf., pair	20.00		☐☐☐☐☐
e.			Pair, imperf. between	*150.00*		☐☐☐☐☐
f.			Gray omitted	*40.00*		☐☐☐☐☐
1619	A1002	16c	blue	32	15	☐☐☐☐☐
a.			Huck press printing	50	15	☐☐☐☐☐

1975-77, Perf. 11x10½

1622	A1018	13c	dark blue & red	24	15	☐☐☐☐☐
a.			Horiz. pair, imperf. btwn.	50.00		☐☐☐☐☐
b.			Vert. pair, imperf.	*1,250.*		☐☐☐☐☐
c.			Perf. 11	65	15	☐☐☐☐☐
d.			As "c," vert. pair, imperf.	200.00		☐☐☐☐☐
e.			Horiz. pair, imperf. vert. ..	—		☐☐☐☐☐
1623	A1016	13c	blue & red	22	15	☐☐☐☐☐
a.			Booklet pane of 8, #1590, & 7 #1623	2.50	*60*	☐☐☐☐☐
b.			Perf. 10	1.00	1.00	☐☐☐☐☐
c.			Booklet pane of 8, #1590a & #1623b	30.00	—	☐☐☐☐☐
d.			Pair, #1590 & 1623	75	—	☐☐☐☐☐
e.			Pair, #1590a & 1623b	20.00	—	☐☐☐☐☐

Coil stamp, Perf. 10 Vertically

1625	A1015	13c	dark blue & red	30	15	☐☐☐☐☐
a.			Imperf., pair	22.50		☐☐☐☐☐

State Flags A1023-A1072

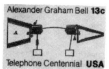

A1073

Commercial Aviation

A1074

A1075

138

Scott No.	Illus No.	Description	Unused Value	Used Value	//////
1976					
1629	A1019	13c multicolored	25	15	
1630	A1020	13c multicolored	25	15	
1631	A1021	13c multicolored	25	15	
a.		Strip of 3, #1629-1631	75	60	
b.		As "a," imperf.	1,200.		
c.		Vert. pair, imperf.	800.00		
1632	A1022	13c dark blue, red & ultra	24	15	
1633	A1023	13c Delaware	25	20	
1634	A1024	13c Pennsylvania	25	20	
1635	A1025	13c New Jersey	25	20	
1636	A1026	13c Georgia	25	20	
1637	A1027	13c Connecticut	25	20	
1638	A1028	13c Massachusetts	25	20	
1639	A1029	13c Maryland	25	20	
1640	A1030	13c South Carolina	25	20	
1641	A1031	13c New Hampshire	25	20	
1642	A1032	13c Virginia	25	20	
1643	A1033	13c New York	25	20	
1644	A1034	13c North Carolina	25	20	
1645	A1035	13c Rhode Island	25	20	
1646	A1036	13c Vermont	25	20	
1647	A1037	13c Kentucky	25	20	
1648	A1038	13c Tennessee	25	20	
1649	A1039	13c Ohio	25	20	
1650	A1040	13c Louisiana	25	20	
1651	A1041	13c Indiana	25	20	
1652	A1042	13c Mississippi	25	20	
1653	A1043	13c Illinois	25	20	
1654	A1044	13c Alabama	25	20	
1655	A1045	13c Maine	25	20	
1656	A1046	13c Missouri	25	20	
1657	A1047	13c Arkansas	25	20	
1658	A1048	13c Michigan	25	20	
1659	A1049	13c Florida	25	20	
1660	A1050	13c Texas	25	20	
1661	A1051	13c Iowa	25	20	
1662	A1052	13c Wisconsin	25	20	
1663	A1053	13c California	25	20	
1664	A1054	13c Minnesota	25	20	
1665	A1055	13c Oregon	25	20	
1666	A1056	13c Kansas	25	20	
1667	A1057	13c West Virginia	25	20	
1668	A1058	13c Nevada	25	20	
1669	A1059	13c Nebraska	25	20	
1670	A1060	13c Colorado	25	20	
1671	A1061	13c North Dakota	25	20	
1672	A1062	13c South Dakota	25	20	

Surrender of Cornwallis at Yorktown, by John Trumbull– **A1076**

Declaration of Independence, by John Trumbull— **A1077**

Scott No.	Illus No.		Description	Unused Value	Used Value	//////
1673	A1063	13c	Montana	25	20	
1674	A1064	13c	Washington	25	20	
1675	A1065	13c	Idaho	25	20	
1676	A1066	13c	Wyoming	25	20	
1677	A1067	13c	Utah	25	20	
1678	A1068	13c	Oklahoma	25	20	
1679	A1069	13c	New Mexico	25	20	
1680	A1070	13c	Arizona	25	20	
1681	A1071	13c	Alaska	25	20	
1682	A1072	13c	Hawaii	25	20	
a.			Pane of 50	13.00	—	
1683	A1073	13c	black, purple & red, *tan* ...	24	15	
1684	A1074	13c	blue & multi	24	15	
1685	A1075	13c	multicolored	24	15	
1686	A1076		Sheet of 5	3.50	—	
a.-e.		13c	multi, any single	45	40	
f.			USA 13c omitted on b, c & d, imperf., untagged	—	*1,500.*	
g.			USA 13c omitted on a & e	*450.00*	—	
h.			Imperf., untagged		*1,750.*	
i.			USA 13c omitted on b, c & d	*450.00*		
j.			USA 13c double on b	—		
k.			USA 13c omitted on c & d	—		
l.			USA 13c omitted on e	*500.00*		
m.			USA 13c omitted, imperf., untagged	—	—	
1687	A1077	7c	Sheet of 5	4.50	—	
a.-e.		18c	multi, any single	55	55	
f.			Design marginal inscriptions omitted	*4,750.*		
g.			USA 18c omitted on a & c	—		
h.			USA 18c omitted on b, d & e	*500.00*		
i.			USA 18c omitted on d	*500.00*		
j.			Black omitted in design ...	*1,200.*		
k.			USA 18c omitted, imperf., untagged	*2,250.*		
m.			USA 18c omitted on b & e	*500.00*		
n.			USA 18c omitted on b & d	—		

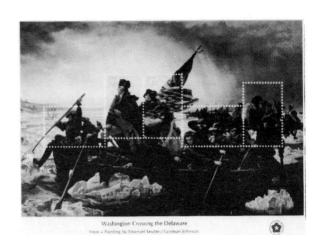

Washington Crossing the Delaware
From a Painting by Emanuel Leutze/Eastman Johnson

Washington Crossing the Delaware, by
Emanuel Leutze/Eastman Johnson— **A1078**

Washington Reviewing His Ragged Army at Valley Forge
From a Painting by William T. Trego

Washington Reviewing Army at Valley Forge,
by William T. Trego— **A1079**

A1080

142

Scott No.	Illus No.		Description	Unused Value	Used Value	//////
1688	A1078	8c	Sheet of 5	5.50	—	☐☐☐☐☐
a.-e.		24c	multi, any single	70	70	☐☐☐☐☐
f.			USA 24c omitted, imperf., untagged......................	2,850.		☐☐☐☐☐
g.			USA 24c omitted on d & e	—	450.00	☐☐☐☐☐
h.			Design & marginal inscriptions omitted.....	2,250.		☐☐☐☐☐
i.			USA 24c omitted on a, b & c	—	—	☐☐☐☐☐
j.			Imperf., untagged	2,250.		☐☐☐☐☐
k.			USA 24c of d & e inverted	—		☐☐☐☐☐
1689	A1079	9c	Sheet of 5	6.50	—	☐☐☐☐☐
a.-e.		31c	multi, any single	85	85	☐☐☐☐☐
f.			USA 31c omitted, imperf., untagged......................	2,100.		☐☐☐☐☐
g.			USA 31c omitted on a & c	—		☐☐☐☐☐
h.			USA 31c omitted on b, d & e	—	—	☐☐☐☐☐
i.			USA 31c omitted on e	600.00		☐☐☐☐☐
j.			Black omitted in design ...	1,350.		☐☐☐☐☐
k.			Imperf., untagged		2,000.	☐☐☐☐☐
l.			USA 31c omitted on b & d	—		☐☐☐☐☐
m.			USA 31c omitted on a, c & e	—		☐☐☐☐☐
n.			As "m," imperf., untagged......................	—		☐☐☐☐☐
p.			As "h," imperf., untagged		2,400.	☐☐☐☐☐
q.			As "g," imperf., untagged	2,500.		☐☐☐☐☐
1690	A1080	13c	ultra & multi	20	15	☐☐☐☐☐
a.			Light blue omitted	400.00		☐☐☐☐☐
1691	A1081	13c	multicolored	22	15	☐☐☐☐☐
1692	A1082	13c	multicolored	22	15	☐☐☐☐☐
1693	A1083	13c	multicolored	22	15	☐☐☐☐☐
1694	A1084	13c	multicolored	22	15	☐☐☐☐☐
a.			Strip of 4, #1691-1694	95	75	☐☐☐☐☐
1695	A1085	13c	multicolored	28	15	☐☐☐☐☐
1696	A1086	13c	multicolored	28	15	☐☐☐☐☐
1697	A1087	13c	multicolored	28	15	☐☐☐☐☐
1698	A1088	13c	multicolored	28	15	☐☐☐☐☐
a.			Block of 4, #1695-1698 ...	1.15	85	☐☐☐☐☐
b.			As "a," imperf.	750.00		☐☐☐☐☐
1699	A1089	13c	multicolored	26	15	☐☐☐☐☐
a.			Horiz. pair, imperf. vert. ..	400.00		☐☐☐☐☐
1700	A1090	13c	black & gray	24	15	☐☐☐☐☐

JULY 4,1776: JULY 4,1776: JULY 4,1776: JULY 4,1776

Declaration of Independence, by John Trumbull

A1081   **A1082**   **A1083**   **A1084**

A1085

A1086

A1089

A1087

A1088

A1090

A1091

A1092   **A1093**

A1094

Scott No.	Illus No.	Description	Unused Value	Used Value	//////
1701	A1091	13c multicolored	24	15	
a.		Imperf., pair	110.00		
1702	A1092	13c multicolored	24	15	
a.		Imperf., pair	120.00		
1703	A1092	13c multicolored	24	15	
a.		Imperf., pair	140.00		
b.		Vert. pair, imperf. btwn. ..	—		
1977					
1704	A1093	13c multicolored	24	15	
a.		Horiz. pair, imperf. vert. ..	450.00		
1705	A1094	13c black & multi	24	15	
1706	A1095	13c multicolored	24	15	
1707	A1096	13c multicolored	24	15	
1708	A1097	13c multicolored	24	15	
1709	A1098	13c multicolored	24	15	
a.		Block or strip of 4	1.00	60	
b.		As "a," imperf. vert.	2,500.		
1710	A1099	13c multicolored	24	15	
a.		Imperf., pair	1,250.		
1711	A1100	13c multicolored	24	15	
a.		Horiz. pair, imperf. btwn.	500.00		
b.		Horiz. pair, imperf. vert. ..	800.00		
1712	A1101	13c tan & multi	24	15	
1713	A1102	13c tan & multi	24	15	
1714	A1103	13c tan & multi	24	15	
1715	A1104	13c tan & multi	24	15	
a.		Block of 4, #1712-1715 ...	1.00	60	
b.		As "a," imperf. horiz.	—		
1716	A1105	13c blue, black & red	24	15	
1717	A1106	13c multicolored	24	15	
1718	A1107	13c multicolored	24	15	
1719	A1108	13c multicolored	24	15	
1720	A1109	13c multicolored	24	15	
a.		Block of 4, #1717-1720 ...	1.00	80	
1721	A1110	13c blue	24	15	
1722	A1111	13c multicolored	24	15	
1723	A1112	13c multicolored	24	15	
a.		Pair, #1723-1724	50	40	
1724	A1113	13c multicolored	24	15	
1725	A1114	13c black & multi	24	15	
1726	A1115	13c red & brown, *cream*	24	15	
1727	A1116	13c multicolored	24	15	
1728	A1117	13c multicolored	24	15	
1729	A1118	13c multicolored	24	15	
a.		Imperf., pair	75.00		
1730	A1119	13c multicolored	24	15	
a.		Imperf., pair	275.00		

Zia: Museum of New Mexico
Pueblo Art USA 13c
A1095

San Ildefonso: Denver Art Museum
Pueblo Art USA 13c
A1096

Hopi: Heard Museum Phoenix
Pueblo Art USA 13c
A1097

Acoma: School of American Research
Pueblo Art USA 13c
A1098

COLORADO

Lafayette

A1099

A1100

US Bicentennial 13c
A1105

A1101

A1102

A1103

A1104

146

A1106

A1107

A1108

A1109

A1110

A1112

A1111

A1114

A1113

A1115

A1116

A1117

A1118

A1120

A1119

147

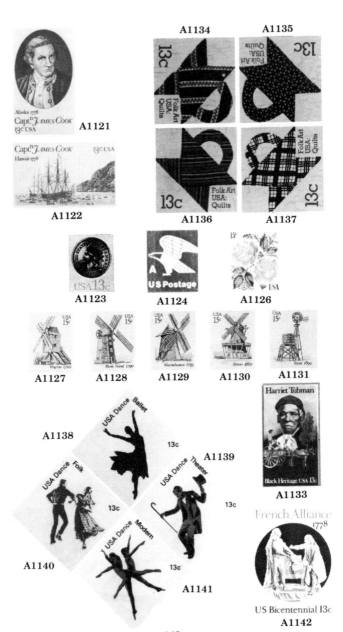

A1121

A1122

A1134

A1135

A1136

A1137

A1123

A1124

A1126

A1127

A1128

A1129

A1130

A1131

A1138

A1139

A1140

A1141

A1133

A1142

148

1978

Scott No.	Illus No.		Description	Unused Value	Used Value	
1731	A1120	13c	black & brown	24	15	☐☐☐☐☐
1732	A1121	13c	dark blue	24	15	☐☐☐☐☐
a.			Pair, #1732-1733	50	30	☐☐☐☐☐
b.			As "a," imperf. between ..	*4,500.*		☐☐☐☐☐
1733	A1122	13c	green	24	15	☐☐☐☐☐
a.			Vert. pair, imperf. horiz. ..	—		☐☐☐☐☐

1978-80

Scott No.	Illus No.		Description	Unused Value	Used Value	
1734	A1123	13c	brown & blue green, *bister*	24	15	☐☐☐☐☐
a.			Horiz. pair, imperf. vert. ..	*300.00*		☐☐☐☐☐
1735	A1124	(15c)	orange	24	15	☐☐☐☐☐
a.			Imperf., vert. pair...........	*80.00*		☐☐☐☐☐
b.			Vert. pair, imperf. horiz. ..	*300.00*		☐☐☐☐☐
1736	A1124	(15c)	orange	25	15	☐☐☐☐☐
a.			Booklet pane of 8	2.25	*60*	☐☐☐☐☐
1737	A1126	15c	multicolored	25	15	☐☐☐☐☐
a.			Booklet pane of 8	2.25	*60*	☐☐☐☐☐
b.			As "a," imperf.	—		☐☐☐☐☐
1738	A1127	15c	sepia, *yellow*	30	15	☐☐☐☐☐
1739	A1128	15c	sepia, *yellow*	30	15	☐☐☐☐☐
1740	A1129	15c	sepia, *yellow*	30	15	☐☐☐☐☐
1741	A1130	15c	sepia, *yellow*	30	15	☐☐☐☐☐
1742	A1131	15c	sepia, *yellow*	30	15	☐☐☐☐☐
a.			Bklt. pane, 2 each #1738-1742	3.60	*60*	☐☐☐☐☐
b.			Strip of 5, #1738-1742	1.50	—	☐☐☐☐☐

Coil stamp, Perf. 10 Vertically

Scott No.	Illus No.		Description	Unused Value	Used Value	
1743	A1124	(15c)	orange	25	15	☐☐☐☐☐
a.			Imperf., pair	*100.00*		☐☐☐☐☐

1978

Scott No.	Illus No.		Description	Unused Value	Used Value	
1744	A1133	13c	multicolored	24	15	☐☐☐☐☐
1745	A1134	13c	multicolored	24	15	☐☐☐☐☐
1746	A1135	13c	multicolored	24	15	☐☐☐☐☐
1747	A1136	13c	multicolored	24	15	☐☐☐☐☐
1748	A1137	13c	multicolored	24	15	☐☐☐☐☐
a.			Block of 4, #1745-1748 ...	1.00	60	☐☐☐☐☐
1749	A1138	13c	multicolored	24	15	☐☐☐☐☐
1750	A1139	13c	multicolored	24	15	☐☐☐☐☐
1751	A1140	13c	multicolored	24	15	☐☐☐☐☐
1752	A1141	13c	multicolored	24	15	☐☐☐☐☐
a.			Block of 4, #1749-1752 ...	1.00	60	☐☐☐☐☐
1753	A1142	13c	blue, black & red	24	15	☐☐☐☐☐
1754	A1143	13c	brown	24	15	☐☐☐☐☐
1755	A1144	13c	multicolored	24	15	☐☐☐☐☐

AI143

A1146

A1144

A1149

A1150

A1145

A1151

A1152

A1147

A1153

A1154

A1155

A1156

150

Scott No.	Illus No.		Description	Unused Value	Used Value	//////
1756	A1145	15c	multicolored	28	15	☐☐☐☐☐
1757	A1146		Block of 8	1.65	1.65	☐☐☐☐☐
a.		13c	Cardinal	20	15	☐☐☐☐☐
b.		13c	Mallard	20	15	☐☐☐☐☐
c.		13c	Canada goose	20	15	☐☐☐☐☐
d.		13c	Blue jay	20	15	☐☐☐☐☐
e.		13c	Moose	20	15	☐☐☐☐☐
f.		13c	Chipmunk	20	15	☐☐☐☐☐
g.		13c	Red fox	20	15	☐☐☐☐☐
h.		13c	Raccoon	20	15	☐☐☐☐☐
i.			Yel, grn, red, brn, bl, blk (litho.) omitted	3,500.		☐☐☐☐☐
1758	A1147	15c	multicolored	26	15	☐☐☐☐☐
1759	A1148	15c	multicolored	28	15	☐☐☐☐☐
1760	A1149	15c	multicolored	28	15	☐☐☐☐☐
1761	A1150	15c	multicolored	28	15	☐☐☐☐☐
1762	A1151	15c	multicolored	28	15	☐☐☐☐☐
1763	A1152	15c	multicolored	28	15	☐☐☐☐☐
a.			Block of 4, #1760-1763	1.15	85	☐☐☐☐☐
1764	A1153	15c	multicolored	28	15	☐☐☐☐☐
1765	A1154	15c	multicolored	28	15	☐☐☐☐☐
1766	A1155	15c	multicolored	28	15	☐☐☐☐☐
1767	A1156	15c	multicolored	28	15	☐☐☐☐☐
a.			Block of 4, #1764-1767	1.15	85	☐☐☐☐☐
b.			As "a," imperf. horiz.	12,500.		☐☐☐☐☐
1768	A1157	15c	blue & multi	28	15	☐☐☐☐☐
a.			Imperf., pair	90.00		☐☐☐☐☐
1769	A1158	15c	red & multi	28	15	☐☐☐☐☐
a.			Imperf., pair	100.00		☐☐☐☐☐
b.			Vert. pair, imperf. horiz.	1,750.		☐☐☐☐☐

1979

Scott No.	Illus No.		Description	Unused Value	Used Value	//////
1770	A1159	15c	blue	28	15	☐☐☐☐☐
1771	A1160	15c	multicolored	28	15	☐☐☐☐☐
a.			Imperf., pair	—		☐☐☐☐☐
1772	A1161	15c	orange red	28	15	☐☐☐☐☐
1773	A1162	15c	dark blue	28	15	☐☐☐☐☐
1774	A1163	15c	chocolate	28	15	☐☐☐☐☐
1775	A1164	15c	multicolored	28	15	☐☐☐☐☐
1776	A1165	15c	multicolored	28	15	☐☐☐☐☐
1777	A1166	15c	multicolored	28	15	☐☐☐☐☐
1778	A1167	15c	multicolored	28	15	☐☐☐☐☐
a.			Block of 4, #1775-1778	1.15	85	☐☐☐☐☐
b.			As "a," imperf. horiz.	3,750.		☐☐☐☐☐
1779	A1168	15c	black & brick red	30	15	☐☐☐☐☐
1780	A1169	15c	black & brick red	30	15	☐☐☐☐☐
1781	A1170	15c	black & brick red	30	15	☐☐☐☐☐

151

A1148

A1157

A1158

A1159

A1161

A1160

A1162

A1163

A1164

A1165

A1166

A1167

Scott No.	Illus No.		Description	Unused Value	Used Value	//////
1782	A1171	15c	black & brick red	30	15	
a.			Block of 4, #1779-1782 ...	1.25	85	
1783	A1172	15c	multicolored	28	15	
1784	A1173	15c	multicolored	28	15	
1785	A1174	15c	multicolored	28	15	
1786	A1175	15c	multicolored	28	15	
a.			Block of 4, #1783-1786 ...	1.25	85	
b.			As "a," imperf.	600.00		
1787	A1176	15c	multicolored	28	15	
a.			Imperf., pair	400.00		
1788	A1177	15c	multicolored	28	15	
1789	A1178	15c	multicolored	28	15	
a.			Perf. 11	30	15	
b.			Perf. 12	2,000.	1,000.	
c.			Vert. pair, imperf. horiz. ..	200.00		
d.			As "a," vert. pair, imperf horiz.	160.00		

1979-80

1790	A1179	10c	multicolored	20	20	
1791	A1180	15c	multicolored	28	15	
1792	A1181	15c	multicolored	28	15	
1793	A1182	15c	multicolored	28	15	
1794	A1183	15c	multicolored	28	15	
a.			Block of 4, #1791-1794 ...	1.15	85	
b.			As "a," imperf.	1,400.		
1795	A1184	15c	multicolored	50	15	
a.			Perf. 11	1.05	—	
1796	A1185	15c	multicolored	50	15	
a.			Perf. 11	1.05	—	
1797	A1186	15c	multicolored	50	15	
a.			Perf. 11	1.05	—	
1798	A1187	15c	multicolored	50	15	
a.			Perf. 11	1.05	—	
b.			Block of 4, #1795-1798 ...	2.00	1.00	
c.			Block of 4, #1795a-1798a	4.25	—	

1979

1799	A1188	15c	multicolored	28	15	
a.			Imperf., pair	100.00		
b.			Vert. pair, imperf. horiz. ..	700.00		
c.			Vert. pair, imperf. btwn. ..	—		
1800	A1189	15c	multicolored	28	15	
a.			Green & yellow omitted .	800.00		
b.			Green, yellow & tan omitted	850.00		
1801	A1190	15c	multicolored	28	15	
a.			Imperf., pair	250.00		

153

A1168 Jefferson Did 1826 Virginia Rotunda

Architecture USA 15c

A1169 Latrobe Did 1820 Baltimore Cathedral

Architecture USA 15c

A1170 Bulfinch Did 1844 Boston State House

Architecture USA 15c

A1171 Strickland 1788-1854 Philadelphia Exchange

Architecture USA 15c

Endangered Flora

15c USA

PERSISTENT TRILLIUM

A1172

Endangered Flora

15c USA

HAWAIIAN WILD BROADBEAN

A1173

Endangered Flora

15c USA

CONTRA COSTA WALLFLOWER

A1174

Endangered Flora

15c USA

ANTIOCH DUNES EVENING PRIMROSE

A1175

USA 15c

Seeing For Me

A1176

Special Olympics

Skill · Sharing · Joy
USA 15c

A1177

I have not yet begun to fight

John Paul Jones
US Bicentennial 15c

A1178

A1179

A1180

A1181

A1184

A1185

A1182

A1183

A1186

A1187

A1188

A1191

A1189

155

A1190

A1192

A1193

A1194

A1195

A1196

A1197

A1199

A1209

A1208

A1210

A1211

A1212

A1213

156

Scott No.	Illus No.		Description	Unused Value	Used Value	//////
1802	A1191	15c	multicolored	28	15	☐☐☐☐☐

1980

1803	A1192	15c	multicolored	28	15	☐☐☐☐☐
1804	A1193	15c	multicolored	28	15	☐☐☐☐☐
a.			Horiz. pair, imperf. vert. ..	800.00		☐☐☐☐☐
1805	A1194	15c	multicolored	28	15	☐☐☐☐☐
1806	A1195	15c	claret & multi	28	15	☐☐☐☐☐
1807	A1196	15c	multicolored	28	15	☐☐☐☐☐
1808	A1195	15c	green & multi	28	15	☐☐☐☐☐
1809	A1197	15c	multicolored	28	15	☐☐☐☐☐
1810	A1195	15c	red & multi	28	15	☐☐☐☐☐
a.			Vert. strip of 6 #1805- 1810	1.75	1.50	☐☐☐☐☐

1980-81, Coil stamps, Perf. 10 Vertically

1811	A984	1c	dark blue, *greenish*	15	15	☐☐☐☐☐
a.			Imperf., pair	175.00		☐☐☐☐☐
1813	A1199	3.5c	purple, *yellow*	15	15	☐☐☐☐☐
a.			Untagged (Bureau precanceled, lines only)		15	☐☐☐☐☐
b.			Imperf., pair	225.00		☐☐☐☐☐
1816	A997	12c	brown red, *beige*	24	15	☐☐☐☐☐
a.			Untagged (Bureau precanceled)		25	☐☐☐☐☐
b.			Imperf., pair	225.00		☐☐☐☐☐

1981

1818	A1207	(18c)	violet	32	15	☐☐☐☐☐
1819	A1207	(18c)	violet	40	15	☐☐☐☐☐
a.			Booklet pane of 8	3.50	1.50	☐☐☐☐☐

Coil stamp, Perf. 10 Vertically

1820	A1207	(18c)	violet	40	15	☐☐☐☐☐
a.			Imperf., pair	90.00		☐☐☐☐☐

1980

1821	A1208	15c	Prussian blue	28	15	☐☐☐☐☐
1822	A1209	15c	red brown & sepia	28	15	☐☐☐☐☐
1823	A1210	15c	black & red	28	15	☐☐☐☐☐
a.			Vert. pair, imperf. horiz. ..	250.00		☐☐☐☐☐
1824	A1211	15c	multicolored	28	15	☐☐☐☐☐
1825	A1212	15c	carmine & violet bl	28	15	☐☐☐☐☐
a.			Horiz. pair, imperf. vert. ..	500.00		☐☐☐☐☐

A1214 — Coral Reefs USA 15c, Brain Coral: U.S. Virgin Islands

A1215 — Coral Reefs USA 15c, Elkhorn Coral: Florida

A1218 — Organized Labor Proud and Free USA 15c

A1219 — Edith Wharton, USA 15c

A1216 — Coral Reefs USA 15c, Chalice Coral: American Samoa

A1217 — Coral Reefs USA 15c, Finger Coral: Hawaii

A1220 — Learning never ends, USA 15c

A1221

A1222 — Chilkat Tlingit, Indian Art USA 15c

Heiltsuk, Bella Bella, Indian Art USA 15c

A1223 — Tlingit, Indian Art USA 15c

A1224 — Bella Coola, Indian Art USA 15c

HOW TO USE THIS BOOK

The number in the first column is its Scott number or identifying number. The letter and number that come next (A41) indicate the design and refer to the illustration so designated. Following that is the denomination of the stamp and its color. Finally, the value, unused and used is shown.

Scott No.	Illus No.		Description	Unused Value	Used Value	/ / / / / /
1826	A1213	15c	multicolored	28	15	☐☐☐☐☐
a.			Red, brown & blue (engr.) omitted	800.00		☐☐☐☐☐
b.			Red, brn, bl (engr.), bl & yel (litho.) omitted	1,400.		☐☐☐☐☐
1827	A1214	15c	multicolored	30	15	☐☐☐☐☐
1828	A1215	15c	multicolored	30	15	☐☐☐☐☐
1829	A1216	15c	multicolored	30	15	☐☐☐☐☐
1830	A1217	15c	multicolored	30	15	☐☐☐☐☐
a.			Block of 4, #1827-1830 ...	1.20	85	☐☐☐☐☐
b.			As "a," imperf.	1,250.		☐☐☐☐☐
c.			As "a," imperf. btwn., vert.	—		☐☐☐☐☐
d.			As "a," imperf. vert.	3,000.		☐☐☐☐☐
1831	A1218	15c	multicolored	28	15	☐☐☐☐☐
a.			Imperf., pair	400.00		☐☐☐☐☐
1832	A1219	15c	purple	28	15	☐☐☐☐☐
1833	A1220	15c	multicolored	28	15	☐☐☐☐☐
a.			Horiz. pair, imperf. btwn.	250.00		☐☐☐☐☐
1834	A1221	15c	multicolored	30	15	☐☐☐☐☐
1835	A1222	15c	multicolored	30	15	☐☐☐☐☐
1836	A1223	15c	multicolored	30	15	☐☐☐☐☐
1837	A1224	15c	multicolored	30	15	☐☐☐☐☐
a.			Block of 4, #1834-1837 ...	1.25	85	☐☐☐☐☐
1838	A1225	15c	black & brick red	30	15	☐☐☐☐☐
1839	A1226	15c	black & brick red	30	15	☐☐☐☐☐
1840	A1227	15c	black & brick red	30	15	☐☐☐☐☐
1841	A1228	15c	black & brick red	30	15	☐☐☐☐☐
a.			Block of 4, #1838-1841 ...	1.25	85	☐☐☐☐☐
1842	A1229	15c	multicolored	28	15	☐☐☐☐☐
a.			Imperf., pair	100.00		☐☐☐☐☐
1843	A1230	15c	multicolored	28	15	☐☐☐☐☐
a.			Imperf., pair	100.00		☐☐☐☐☐
b.			Buff omitted	—		☐☐☐☐☐

1980-85

Scott No.	Illus No.		Description	Unused Value	Used Value	/ / / / / /
1844	A1231	1c	black	15	15	☐☐☐☐☐
a.			Imperf. pair	350.00		☐☐☐☐☐
b.			Vert. pair, imperf. btwn. ..	—		☐☐☐☐☐
1845	A1232	2c	brown black	15	15	☐☐☐☐☐
1846	A1233	3c	olive green	15	15	☐☐☐☐☐
1847	A1234	4c	violet	15	15	☐☐☐☐☐
1848	A1235	5c	henna brown	15	15	☐☐☐☐☐
1849	A1236	6c	orange vermilion	15	15	☐☐☐☐☐
a.			Vert. pair, imperf. btwn. ..	2,300.		☐☐☐☐☐
1850	A1237	7c	brt carmine	15	15	☐☐☐☐☐
1851	A1238	8c	olive black	15	15	☐☐☐☐☐
1852	A1239	9c	dark green	16	15	☐☐☐☐☐

Brunswick 1838-1895 Smithsonian, Washington
Architecture USA 15c

A1225

Richardson 1838-1886 Trinity Church, Boston
Architecture USA 15c

A1226

Furness 1839-1912 Penn Academy, Philadelphia
Architecture USA 15c

A1227

A.J. Davis 1803-1892 Lyndhurst, Tarrytown, NY
Architecture USA 15c

A1228

Christmas USA 15c

A1229

USA 15c
Season's Greetings

A1230

USA 15c
Everett Dirksen

A1261

Whitney Moore Young

Black Heritage USA 15c

A1262

A1263

Rose USA 18c

Camellia USA 18c

A1264

A1265

Dahlia USA 18c

Lily USA 18c

A1266

160

Scott No.	Illus No.		Description	Unused Value	Used Value	//////
1853	A1240	10c	Prussian blue	18	15	☐☐☐☐☐
a.			Vert. pair, imperf. btwn. ..	1,100.		☐☐☐☐☐
b.			Horiz. pair, imperf. btwn.	—		☐☐☐☐☐
1854	A1241	11c	dark blue	20	15	☐☐☐☐☐
1855	A1242	13c	light maroon	24	15	☐☐☐☐☐
1856	A1243	14c	slate green	25	15	☐☐☐☐☐
a.			Vert. pair, imperf. horiz. ..	*150.00*		☐☐☐☐☐
b.			Horiz. pair, imperf. btwn.	8.50		☐☐☐☐☐
c.			Vert. pair, imperf. btwn. ..	*2,000.*		☐☐☐☐☐
1857	A1244	17c	green	32	15	☐☐☐☐☐
1858	A1245	18c	dark blue	32	15	☐☐☐☐☐
1859	A1246	19c	brown	35	15	☐☐☐☐☐
1860	A1247	20c	claret	40	15	☐☐☐☐☐
1861	A1248	20c	green	38	15	☐☐☐☐☐
1862	A1249	20c	black	38	15	☐☐☐☐☐
1863	A1250	22c	dark chalky blue	40	15	☐☐☐☐☐
a.			Vert. pair, imperf. horiz. ..	*2,500.*		☐☐☐☐☐
b.			Vert. pair, imperf. btwn. ..	—		☐☐☐☐☐
c.			Horiz. pair, imperf. btwn.	—		☐☐☐☐☐
1864	A1251	30c	olive gray	55	15	☐☐☐☐☐
1865	A1252	35c	gray	65	15	☐☐☐☐☐
1866	A1253	37c	blue	70	15	☐☐☐☐☐
1867	A1254	39c	rose lilac	70	15	☐☐☐☐☐
a.			Vert. pair, imperf. horiz. ..	*600.00*		☐☐☐☐☐
b.			Vert. pair, imperf. btwn. ..	*1,250.*		☐☐☐☐☐
1868	A1255	40c	dark green	70	15	☐☐☐☐☐
1869	A1256	50c	brown	90	15	☐☐☐☐☐
1981						
1874	A1261	15c	gray	28	15	☐☐☐☐☐
1875	A1262	15c	multicolored	28	15	☐☐☐☐☐
1876	A1263	18c	multicolored	35	15	☐☐☐☐☐
1877	A1264	18c	multicolored	35	15	☐☐☐☐☐
1878	A1265	18c	multicolored	35	15	☐☐☐☐☐
1879	A1266	18c	multicolored	35	15	☐☐☐☐☐
a.			Block of 4, #1876-1879 ...	1.40	85	☐☐☐☐☐
1880	A1267	18c	Bighorn	35	15	☐☐☐☐☐
1881	A1268	18c	Puma	35	15	☐☐☐☐☐
1882	A1269	18c	Harbor seal	35	15	☐☐☐☐☐
1883	A1270	18c	Bison	35	15	☐☐☐☐☐
1884	A1271	18c	Brown bear	35	15	☐☐☐☐☐
1885	A1272	18c	Polar bear	35	15	☐☐☐☐☐
1886	A1273	18c	Elk (wapiti)	35	15	☐☐☐☐☐
1887	A1274	18c	Moose	35	15	☐☐☐☐☐
1888	A1275	18c	White-tailed deer	35	15	☐☐☐☐☐
1889	A1276	18c	Pronghorn	35	15	☐☐☐☐☐
a.			Bklt. pane of 10, #1880-1889	9.00	—	☐☐☐☐☐

A1231

A1232

A1233

A1234

A1235

A1236

A1237

A1238

A1239

A1240

A1241

A1242

A1243

A1244

A1245

A1246

A1247

A1248

A1249

A1250

A1251

A1252

A1253

A1254

A1255

A1256

Scott No.	Illus No.		Description	Unused Value	Used Value	//////
1890	A1277	18c	multicolored	32	15	☐☐☐☐☐
a.			Imperf., pair	100.00		☐☐☐☐☐
b.			Vert. pair, imperf. horiz. ..	—		☐☐☐☐☐

Coil stamp, Perf. 10 Vertically

1891	A1278	18c	multicolored	36	15	☐☐☐☐☐
a.			Imperf., pair	20.00		☐☐☐☐☐
b.			Pair, imperf. btwn.	—		☐☐☐☐☐
1892	A1279	6c	multicolored	55	15	☐☐☐☐☐
1893	A1280	18c	multicolored	32	15	☐☐☐☐☐
a.			Booklet pane of 8 (2 #1892, 6 #1893)	3.25	—	☐☐☐☐☐
b.			As "a," vert. imperf. btwn.	*80.00*		☐☐☐☐☐
c.			Pair, #1892, 1893	90	—	☐☐☐☐☐
1894	A1281	20c	black, dark blue & red	35	15	☐☐☐☐☐
a.			Vert. pair, imperf.	40.00		☐☐☐☐☐
b.			Vert. pair, imperf. horiz. ..	*650.00*		☐☐☐☐☐
c.			Dark blue omitted	*100.00*		☐☐☐☐☐
d.			Black omitted	*300.00*		☐☐☐☐☐

Coil stamp, Perf. 10 Vertically

1895	A1281	20c	black, dark blue & red	35	15	☐☐☐☐☐
a.			Imperf., pair	10.00		☐☐☐☐☐
b.			Black omitted	40.00		☐☐☐☐☐
c.			Dark blue omitted	—		☐☐☐☐☐
d.			Pair, imperf. btwn.	—		☐☐☐☐☐
e.			Untagged (Bureau precanceled)	50	50	☐☐☐☐☐
1896	A1281	20c	black, dark blue & red	35	15	☐☐☐☐☐
a.			Booklet pane of 6	2.25	—	☐☐☐☐☐
b.			Booklet pane of 10	4.00	—	☐☐☐☐☐

1981-84, Coil stamps, Perf. 10 Vertically

1897	A1282	1c	violet	15	15	☐☐☐☐☐
b.			Imperf., pair	*800.00*		☐☐☐☐☐
1897A	A1283	2c	black	15	15	☐☐☐☐☐
e.			Imperf., pair	*70.00*		☐☐☐☐☐
1898	A1284	3c	dark green	15	15	☐☐☐☐☐
1898A	A1285	4c	reddish brown	15	15	☐☐☐☐☐
b.			Untagged (Bureau precanceled)	15	15	☐☐☐☐☐
c.			As "b," imperf., pair	*750.00*		☐☐☐☐☐
d.			No. 1898A, imperf., pair .	*950.00*	—	☐☐☐☐☐
1899	A1286	5c	gray green	15	15	☐☐☐☐☐
a.			Imperf., pair	—		☐☐☐☐☐
1900	A1287	5.2c	carmine	15	15	☐☐☐☐☐
a.			Untagged (Bureau precanceled)	15	15	☐☐☐☐☐

Omnibus 1880s
USA 1c

A1282

Locomotive 1870s
USA 2c

A1283

Handcar 1880s
USA 3c

A1284

Stagecoach 1890s
USA 4c

A1285

Motorcycle
1913
USA 5c

A1286

Sleigh 1880s
USA 5.2c
Auth
Nonprofit
Org

A1287

Bicycle 1870s
USA 5.9c
Auth
Nonprofit
Org

A1288

Baby Buggy 1880s
USA 7.4c

A1289

Mail Wagon 1880s
USA 9.3c
Bulk
Rate

A1290

Hansom Cab 1890s
USA 10.9c
Bulk
Rate

A1291

RR Caboose 1890s
USA 11c
Bulk Rate

A1292

Electric Auto 1917
USA 17c

A1293

Surrey 1890s
USA 18c

A1294

Fire Pumper
1860s
USA 20c

A1295

USA $9.35

A1296

Scott No.	Illus No.		Description	Unused Value	Used Value	//////
1901	A1288	5.9c	blue	18	15	☐☐☐☐☐
a.			Untagged (Bureau precanceled, lines only)	18	18	☐☐☐☐☐
b.			As "a," imperf., pair	225.00		☐☐☐☐☐
1902	A1289	7.4c	brown	18	15	☐☐☐☐☐
a.			Untagged (Bureau precanceled)	20	20	☐☐☐☐☐
1903	A1290	9.3c	carmine rose	25	15	☐☐☐☐☐
a.			Untagged (Bureau precanceled, lines only)	22	22	☐☐☐☐☐
b.			As "a," imperf., pair	140.00		☐☐☐☐☐
1904	A1291	10.9c	purple	24	15	☐☐☐☐☐
a.			Untagged (Bureau precanceled, lines only)	24	24	☐☐☐☐☐
b.			As "a," imperf., pair	200.00		☐☐☐☐☐
1905	A1292	11c	red	24	15	☐☐☐☐☐
a.			Untagged	24	15	☐☐☐☐☐
1906	A1293	17c	ultra	32	15	☐☐☐☐☐
a.			Untagged (Bureau precanceled, Presorted First Class)	35	35	☐☐☐☐☐
b.			Imperf., pair	165.00		☐☐☐☐☐
c.			As "a," imperf., pair	650.00		☐☐☐☐☐
1907	A1294	18c	dark brown	34	15	☐☐☐☐☐
a.			Imperf., pair	120.00		☐☐☐☐☐
1908	A1295	20c	vermilion	32	15	☐☐☐☐☐
a.			Imperf., pair	100.00		☐☐☐☐☐

1983, Booklet stamp, Perf. 10 Vertically

1909	A1296	$9.35	multicolored	22.50	14.00	☐☐☐☐☐
a.			Booklet pane of 3	62.50	—	☐☐☐☐☐

1981

1910	A1297	18c	multicolored	32	15	☐☐☐☐☐
1911	A1298	18c	multicolored	32	15	☐☐☐☐☐
1912	A1299	18c	multicolored	32	15	☐☐☐☐☐
1913	A1300	18c	multicolored	32	15	☐☐☐☐☐
1914	A1301	18c	multicolored	32	15	☐☐☐☐☐
1915	A1302	18c	multicolored	32	15	☐☐☐☐☐
1916	A1303	18c	multicolored	32	15	☐☐☐☐☐
1917	A1304	18c	multicolored	32	15	☐☐☐☐☐
1918	A1305	18c	multicolored	32	15	☐☐☐☐☐
1919	A1306	18c	multicolored	32	15	☐☐☐☐☐
a.			Block of 8, #1912-1919 ...	3.00	2.75	☐☐☐☐☐
b.			As "a," imperf.	8,000.		☐☐☐☐☐

A1207   A1281

A1267   A1268

A1269   A1270

A1271   A1272

A1273   A1274

A1275   A1276

A1277   A1278   A1279   A1280

A1332   A1333   A1334   A1390

Scott No.	Illus No.		Description	Unused Value	Used Value	//////
1920	A1307	18c	blue & black	32	15	☐☐☐☐☐
1921	A1308	18c	multicolored	35	15	☐☐☐☐☐
1922	A1309	18c	multicolored	35	15	☐☐☐☐☐
1923	A1310	18c	multicolored	35	15	☐☐☐☐☐
1924	A1311	18c	multicolored	35	15	☐☐☐☐☐
a.			Block of 4, #1921-1924 ...	1.40	1.00	☐☐☐☐☐
1925	A1312	18c	multicolored	32	15	☐☐☐☐☐
a.			Vert. pair, imperf. horiz. ..	2,750.		☐☐☐☐☐
1926	A1313	18c	multicolored	32	15	☐☐☐☐☐
a.			Black (engr., inscriptions) omitted	500.00	—	☐☐☐☐☐
1927	A1314	18c	blue & black	42	15	☐☐☐☐☐
a.			Imperf., pair	350.00		☐☐☐☐☐
b.			Vert. pair, imperf. horiz. ..	—		☐☐☐☐☐
1928	A1315	18c	black & red	42	15	☐☐☐☐☐
1929	A1316	18c	black & red	42	15	☐☐☐☐☐
1930	A1317	18c	black & red	42	15	☐☐☐☐☐
1931	A1318	18c	black & red	42	15	☐☐☐☐☐
a.			Block of 4, #1928-1931 ...	1.75	1.00	☐☐☐☐☐
1932	A1319	18c	purple	32	15	☐☐☐☐☐
1933	A1320	18c	green	32	15	☐☐☐☐☐
1934	A1321	18c	gray, green & brown	32	15	☐☐☐☐☐
a.			Vert. pair, imperf. btwn. ..	250.00		☐☐☐☐☐
b.			Brown omitted	525.00		☐☐☐☐☐
1935	A1322	18c	multicolored	32	16	☐☐☐☐☐
1936	A1322	20c	multicolored	35	15	☐☐☐☐☐
1937	A1323	18c	multicolored	35	15	☐☐☐☐☐
1938	A1324	18c	multicolored	35	15	☐☐☐☐☐
a.			Pair, #1937-1938	80	15	☐☐☐☐☐
b.			As "a," black (engr., inscriptions) omitted	550.00		☐☐☐☐☐
1939	A1325	(20c)	multicolored	38	15	☐☐☐☐☐
a.			Imperf., pair	110.00		☐☐☐☐☐
b.			Vert. pair, imperf. horiz. ..	1,650.		☐☐☐☐☐
1940	A1326	(20c)	multicolored	38	15	☐☐☐☐☐
a.			Imperf., pair	250.00		☐☐☐☐☐
b.			Vert. pair, imperf. horiz. ..	—		☐☐☐☐☐
1941	A1327	20c	multicolored	38	15	☐☐☐☐☐
1942	A1328	20c	multicolored	35	15	☐☐☐☐☐
1943	A1329	20c	multicolored	35	15	☐☐☐☐☐
1944	A1330	20c	multicolored	35	15	☐☐☐☐☐
1945	A1331	20c	multicolored	35	15	☐☐☐☐☐
a.			Block of 4, #1942-1945 ...	1.50	15	☐☐☐☐☐
b.			As "a," deep brown omitted	7,500.		☐☐☐☐☐
c.			#1945, imperf., vert. pair	5,250.		☐☐☐☐☐

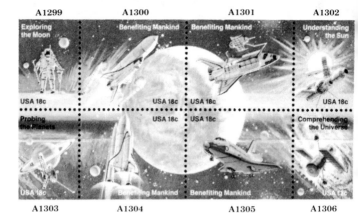

A1299   A1300   A1301   A1302

Exploring the Moon

Benefiting Mankind

Benefiting Mankind

Understanding the Sun

USA 18c

USA 18c   USA 18c

USA 18c

Probing the Planets

USA 18c   USA 18c

Comprehending the Universe

USA 18c

Benefiting Mankind

Benefiting Mankind

USA 18c

A1303   A1304   A1305   A1306

The Gift of Self

USA 18c

American Red Cross
1881-1981

A1297

Save Wetland Habitats

USA 18c

A1308

Save Grassland Habitats

USA 18c

A1309

USA 18c

USA 18c

Save Mountain Habitats
A1310

Save Woodland Habitats
A1311

USA 18c

A1298

Scott No.	Illus No.		Description	Unused Value	Used Value	//////
1946	A1332	(20c)	brown	38	15	☐☐☐☐☐

Coil stamp, Perf. 10 Vertically

1947	A1332	(20c)	brown	60	15	☐☐☐☐☐
a.			Imperf., pair	2,000.		☐☐☐☐☐
1948	A1333	(20c)	brown	38	15	☐☐☐☐☐
a.			Booklet pane of 10	4.50	—	☐☐☐☐☐

1982

1949	A1334	20c	dark blue (from bklt. pane)	50	15	☐☐☐☐☐
a.			Booklet pane of 10	5.00	—	☐☐☐☐☐
b.			As "a," vert. imperf. btwn.	100.00		☐☐☐☐☐
c.			Type II	50	15	☐☐☐☐☐
d.			As "c," booklet pane of 10	5.00	—	☐☐☐☐☐
1950	A1335	20c	blue	38	15	☐☐☐☐☐
1951	A1336	20c	multicolored	38	15	☐☐☐☐☐
a.			Perf. 11	48	15	☐☐☐☐☐
b.			Imperf., pair	275.00		☐☐☐☐☐
c.			Blue omitted	200.00		☐☐☐☐☐
1952	A1337	20c	multicolored	38	15	☐☐☐☐☐
1953	A1338	20c	Alabama	40	25	☐☐☐☐☐
1954	A1339	20c	Alaska	40	25	☐☐☐☐☐
1955	A1340	20c	Arizona	40	25	☐☐☐☐☐
1956	A1341	20c	Arkansas	40	25	☐☐☐☐☐
1957	A1342	20c	California	40	25	☐☐☐☐☐
1958	A1343	20c	Colorado	40	25	☐☐☐☐☐
1959	A1344	20c	Connecticut	40	25	☐☐☐☐☐
1960	A1345	20c	Delaware	40	25	☐☐☐☐☐
1961	A1346	20c	Florida	40	25	☐☐☐☐☐
1962	A1347	20c	Georgia	40	25	☐☐☐☐☐
1963	A1348	20c	Hawaii	40	25	☐☐☐☐☐
1964	A1349	20c	Idaho	40	25	☐☐☐☐☐
1965	A1350	20c	Illinois	40	25	☐☐☐☐☐
1966	A1351	20c	Indiana	40	25	☐☐☐☐☐
1967	A1352	20c	Iowa	40	25	☐☐☐☐☐
1968	A1353	20c	Kansas	40	25	☐☐☐☐☐
1969	A1354	20c	Kentucky	40	25	☐☐☐☐☐
1970	A1355	20c	Louisiana	40	25	☐☐☐☐☐
1971	A1356	20c	Maine	40	25	☐☐☐☐☐
1972	A1357	20c	Maryland	40	25	☐☐☐☐☐
1973	A1358	20c	Massachusetts	40	25	☐☐☐☐☐
1974	A1359	20c	Michigan	40	25	☐☐☐☐☐
1975	A1360	20c	Minnesota	40	25	☐☐☐☐☐
1976	A1361	20c	Mississippi	40	25	☐☐☐☐☐
1977	A1362	20c	Missouri	40	25	☐☐☐☐☐
1978	A1363	20c	Montana	40	25	☐☐☐☐☐
1979	A1364	20c	Nebraska	40	25	☐☐☐☐☐

A1307

 A1312

A1313

A1314

A1327

A1315

A1316

A1317

A1318

A1319

A1321

A1322

A1320

A1323   A1324

A1325   A1326

A1329

A1328   A1330   A1331

A1335   A1336   A1337

A1338–A1387—State Birds and Flowers

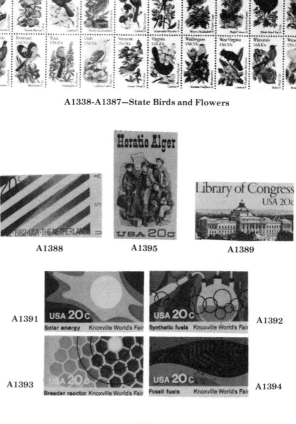

A1388   A1395   A1389

A1391

A1392

A1393

A1394

Scott No.	Illus No.		Description	Unused Value	Used Value	//////
1980	A1365	20c	Nevada	40	25	☐☐☐☐☐
1981	A1366	20c	New Hampshire	40	25	☐☐☐☐☐
1982	A1367	20c	New Jersey	40	25	☐☐☐☐☐
1983	A1368	20c	New Mexico	40	25	☐☐☐☐☐
1984	A1369	20c	New York	40	25	☐☐☐☐☐
1985	A1370	20c	North Carolina	40	25	☐☐☐☐☐
1986	A1371	20c	North Dakota	40	25	☐☐☐☐☐
1987	A1372	20c	Ohio	40	25	☐☐☐☐☐
1988	A1373	20c	Oklahoma	40	25	☐☐☐☐☐
1989	A1374	20c	Oregon	40	25	☐☐☐☐☐
1990	A1375	20c	Pennsylvania	40	25	☐☐☐☐☐
1991	A1376	20c	Rhode Island	40	25	☐☐☐☐☐
1992	A1377	20c	South Carolina	40	25	☐☐☐☐☐
1993	A1378	20c	South Dakota	40	25	☐☐☐☐☐
1994	A1379	20c	Tennessee	40	25	☐☐☐☐☐
1995	A1380	20c	Texas	40	25	☐☐☐☐☐
1996	A1381	20c	Utah	40	25	☐☐☐☐☐
1997	A1382	20c	Vermont	40	25	☐☐☐☐☐
1998	A1383	20c	Virginia	40	25	☐☐☐☐☐
1999	A1384	20c	Washington	40	25	☐☐☐☐☐
2000	A1385	20c	West Virginia	40	25	☐☐☐☐☐
2001	A1386	20c	Wisconsin	40	25	☐☐☐☐☐
2002	A1387	20c	Wyoming	40	25	☐☐☐☐☐
			#1953a-2002a, any single, perf. 11	45	30	☐☐☐☐☐
b.			Pane of 50, perf. 10½x11	22.50	—	☐☐☐☐☐
c.			Pane of 50, perf. 11	25.00	—	☐☐☐☐☐
d.			Pane of 50, imperf.	—		☐☐☐☐☐
2003	A1388	20c	ver, brt blue & gray black	38	15	☐☐☐☐☐
a.			Imperf., pair	*425.00*		☐☐☐☐☐
2004	A1389	20c	red & black	38	15	☐☐☐☐☐

Coil stamp, Perf. 10 Vertically

2005	A1390	20c	sky blue	75	15	☐☐☐☐☐
a.			Imperf., pair	*125.00*		☐☐☐☐☐
2006	A1391	20c	multicolored	40	15	☐☐☐☐☐
2007	A1392	20c	multicolored	40	15	☐☐☐☐☐
2008	A1393	20c	multicolored	40	15	☐☐☐☐☐
2009	A1394	20c	multicolored	40	15	☐☐☐☐☐
a.			Block of 4, #2006-2009	1.75	1.00	☐☐☐☐☐
2010	A1395	20c	red & black, *tan*	38	15	☐☐☐☐☐
2011	A1396	20c	brown	38	15	☐☐☐☐☐
2012	A1397	20c	multicolored	38	15	☐☐☐☐☐
2013	A1398	20c	multicolored	38	15	☐☐☐☐☐
2014	A1399	20c	multicolored	38	15	☐☐☐☐☐
a.			Black & green (engr.) omitted	*225.00*		☐☐☐☐☐

A1396

A1399

A1397

A1398

A1400

A1401

A1402

A1403

A1404

A1405

A1406

A1407

Scott No.	Illus No.		Description	Unused Value	Used Value	//////
2015	A1400	20c	red & black	38	15	
a.			Vert. pair, imperf. horiz. ..	300.00		
2016	A1401	20c	multicolored	1.00	15	
2017	A1402	20c	multicolored	38	15	
a.			Imperf., pair	1,000.		
2018	A1403	20c	multicolored	38	15	
2019	A1404	20c	black & brown	38	15	
2020	A1405	20c	black & brown	38	15	
2021	A1406	20c	black & brown	38	15	
2022	A1407	20c	black & brown	38	15	
a.			Block of 4, #2019-2022 ...	1.90	1.00	
2023	A1408	20c	multicolored	38	15	
2024	A1409	20c	multicolored	38	15	
a.			Imperf., pair	700.00		
2025	A1410	13c	multicolored	26	15	
a.			Imperf., pair	500.00		
2026	A1411	20c	multicolored	38	15	
a.			Imperf., pair	150.00		
b.			Horiz. pair, imperf. vert. ..	—		
c.			Vert. pair, imperf. horiz. ..	—		
2027	A1412	20c	multicolored	55	15	
2028	A1413	20c	multicolored	55	15	
2029	A1414	20c	multicolored	55	15	
2030	A1415	20c	multicolored	55	15	
a.			Block of 4, #2027-2030 ...	2.35	1.00	
b.			As "a," imperf.	3,000.		
c.			As "a," imperf. horiz.	—		

1983

Scott No.	Illus No.		Description	Unused Value	Used Value	//////
2031	A1416	20c	multicolored	38	15	
a.			Black (engr.) omitted	1,400.		
2032	A1417	20c	multicolored	38	15	
2033	A1418	20c	multicolored	38	15	
2034	A1419	20c	multicolored	38	15	
2035	A1420	20c	multicolored	38	15	
a.			Block of 4, #2032-2035 ...	1.65	1.00	
b.			As "a," imperf.	3,500.		
2036	A1421	20c	multicolored	38	15	
2037	A1422	20c	multicolored	38	15	
a.			Imperf., pair	2,500.		
2038	A1423	20c	multicolored	38	15	
2039	A1424	20c	red & black	38	15	
a.			Imperf., pair	850.00		
2040	A1425	20c	brown	38	15	
2041	A1426	20c	blue	38	15	
2042	A1427	20c	multicolored	40	15	
2043	A1428	20c	multicolored	38	15	

175

A1408

A1409

A1411

A1410

A1416

A1412

A1413

A1414

A1415

A1421

A1422

Scott No.	Illus No.		Description	Unused Value	Used Value	/ / / / / /
2044	A1429	20c	multicolored	40	15	
a.			Imperf., pair	500.00		
2045	A1430	20c	multicolored	40	15	
a.			Red omitted	300.00		
2046	A1431	20c	blue	1.00	15	
2047	A1432	20c	multicolored	40	15	
2048	A1433	13c	multicolored	28	15	
2049	A1434	13c	multicolored	28	15	
2050	A1435	13c	multicolored	28	15	
2051	A1436	13c	multicolored	28	15	
a.			Block of 4, #2048-2051 ...	1.20	80	
2052	A1437	20c	multicolored	38	15	
2053	A1438	20c	buff, blue & red	40	15	
2054	A1439	20c	yellow & maroon	38	15	
2055	A1440	20c	multicolored	45	15	
2056	A1441	20c	multicolored	45	15	
2057	A1442	20c	multicolored	45	15	
2058	A1443	20c	multicolored	45	15	
a.			Block of 4, #2055-2058 ...	1.90	1.00	
b.			As "a," black omitted	450.00		
2059	A1444	20c	multicolored	40	15	
2060	A1445	20c	multicolored	40	15	
2061	A1446	20c	multicolored	40	15	
2062	A1447	20c	multicolored	40	15	
a.			Block of 4, #2059-2062 ...	1.70	1.00	
b.			As "a," black omitted	475.00		
c.			As "a," black omitted on #2059, 2061	—		
2063	A1448	20c	multicolored	38	15	
2064	A1449	20c	multicolored	38	15	
a.			Imperf., pair	165.00		
2065	A1450	20c	multicolored	38	15	

1984

Scott No.	Illus No.		Description	Unused Value	Used Value	/ / / / / /
2066	A1451	20c	multicolored	38	15	
2067	A1452	20c	multicolored	45	15	
2068	A1453	20c	multicolored	45	15	
2069	A1454	20c	multicolored	45	15	
2070	A1455	20c	multicolored	45	15	
a.			Block of 4, #2067-2070 ...	1.90	1.00	
2071	A1456	20c	multicolored	38	15	
2072	A1457	20c	multicolored	38	15	
a.			Horiz. pair, imperf. vert. ..	200.00		
2073	A1458	20c	multicolored	42	15	
a.			Horiz. pair, imperf. vert. ..	1,200.		
2074	A1459	20c	multicolored	38	15	
2075	A1460	20c	multicolored	38	15	
2076	A1461	20c	Wild pink	42	15	

A1418

A1417

A1419

A1420

A1423

A1429

A1431

A1432

A1424

A1425

A1426

A1427

A1428

USA 20c
Medal of Honor
A1430

CIVIL
SERVICE
1883
1983
USA20c
A1438

Treaty of Paris 1783
US Bicentennial 2O cents
A1437

A1433   **A1434**

Olympics 84
USA
13c

Olympics 84
USA
13c

USA
13c
Olympics 84

Olympics 84
USA
13c

A1435   **A1436**

A1440   **A1441**

USA
2O.   Charles Steinmetz

USA
2Oc   Edwin Armstrong

USA
Nikola Tesla   2O.

Philo T. Farnsworth   2Oc

A1442   **A1443**

A1439

A1448

A1449

A1444   **A1445**

A1446   **A1447**

A1450

A1452   **A1453**

A1451

A1456

A1454   **A1455**

A1457

A1458

A1461

A1462

A1459

A1460

A1463

A1464

A1466

A1467

A1468

Jim Thorpe

A1473

A1474

A1469

A1470

A1465

A1471

A1472

Scott No.	Illus No.		Description	Unused Value	Used Value	//////
2077	A1462	20c	Yellow ladys-slipper	42	15	□□□□□
2078	A1463	20c	Spreading pogonia	42	15	□□□□□
2079	A1464	20c	Pacific calypso	42	15	□□□□□
a.			Block of 4, #2076-2079 ...	1.80	1.00	□□□□□
2080	A1465	20c	multicolored	40	15	□□□□□
2081	A1466	20c	multicolored	40	15	□□□□□
2082	A1467	20c	multicolored	62	15	□□□□□
2083	A1468	20c	multicolored	62	15	□□□□□
2084	A1469	20c	multicolored	62	15	□□□□□
2085	A1470	20c	multicolored	62	15	□□□□□
a.			Block of 4, #2082-2085 ...	2.75	1.00	□□□□□
2086	A1471	20c	multicolored	38	15	□□□□□
2087	A1472	20c	multicolored	38	15	□□□□□
2088	A1473	20c	multicolored	38	15	□□□□□
2089	A1474	20c	dark brown	40	15	□□□□□
2090	A1475	20c	multicolored	40	15	□□□□□
2091	A1476	20c	multicolored	40	15	□□□□□
2092	A1477	20c	blue	60	15	□□□□□
a.			Horiz. pair, imperf. vert. ..	500.00		□□□□□
2093	A1478	20c	multicolored	40	15	□□□□□
2094	A1479	20c	sage green	38	15	□□□□□
2095	A1480	20c	orange & dark brown	45	15	□□□□□
2096	A1481	20c	multicolored	38	15	□□□□□
a.			Horiz. pair, imperf. btwn. ..	300.00		□□□□□
b.			Vert. pair, imperf. btwn. ..	200.00		□□□□□
c.			Block of 4, imperf. btwn, vert. and horiz.	3,500.		□□□□□
2097	A1482	20c	multicolored	1.00	15	□□□□□
a.			Horiz. pair, imperf. vert. ..	1,600.		□□□□□
2098	A1483	20c	multicolored	40	15	□□□□□
2099	A1484	20c	multicolored	40	15	□□□□□
2100	A1485	20c	multicolored	40	15	□□□□□
2101	A1486	20c	multicolored	40	15	□□□□□
a.			Block of 4, #2098-2101 ...	1.75	1.00	□□□□□
2102	A1487	20c	multicolored	38	15	□□□□□
2103	A1488	20c	multicolored	38	15	□□□□□
a.			Vert. pair, imperf. horiz. ..	1,500.		□□□□□
2104	A1489	20c	multicolored	40	15	□□□□□
a.			Horiz. pair, imperf. vert. ..	600.00		□□□□□
2105	A1490	20c	deep blue	38	15	□□□□□
2106	A1491	20c	brown & maroon	38	15	□□□□□
2107	A1492	20c	multicolored	40	15	□□□□□
2108	A1493	20c	multicolored	40	15	□□□□□
a.			Horiz. pair, imperf. vert. ..	1,250.		□□□□□
2109	A1494	20c	multicolored	40	15	□□□□□

1985

| 2110 | A1495 | 22c | multicolored .... | 40 | 15 | □□□□□ |

A1475

A1478

A1479

A1476

A1477

A1480

A1481

A1482

A1483

 **A1484**

A1485

 **A1486**

A1487

A1488

A1489

A1490

A1494

A1491

A1492

A1493

A1495

A1496

A1497

A1498

A1499

HOW TO USE THIS BOOK

The number in the first column is its Scott number or identifying number. The letter and number that come next (A41) indicate the design and refer to the illustration so designated. Following that is the denomination of the stamp and its color. Finally, the value, unused and used is shown.

A1500

A1501

A1502

A1503

A1505

A1504

A1506

A1507

A1508

A1509

A1510

A1511

A1512

A1513

A1514

A1515

A1516

A1517

A1518

A1519

Scott No.	Illus No.		Description	Unused Value	Used Value	//////
2111	A1496	(22c)	green	60	15	☐☐☐☐☐
a.			Vert. pair, imperf.	*75.00*		☐☐☐☐☐
b.			Vert. pair, imperf. horiz. ..	*1,350.*		☐☐☐☐☐

Coil stamp, Perf. 10 Vertically

2112	A1496	(22c)	green	60	15	☐☐☐☐☐
a.			Imperf., pair	50.00		☐☐☐☐☐
2113	A1497	(22c)	green	80	15	☐☐☐☐☐
a.			Booklet pane of 10	8.50		☐☐☐☐☐
b.			As "a," imperf. btwn.			
			horiz.	—		☐☐☐☐☐
2114	A1498	22c	blue, red & black	40	15	☐☐☐☐☐

Coil stamp, Perf. 10 Vertically

2115	A1498	22c	blue, red & black	40	15	☐☐☐☐☐
a.			Imperf., pair	12.50		☐☐☐☐☐
b.			Inscribed T at bottom	48	15	☐☐☐☐☐
c.			Black field of stars	—	—	☐☐☐☐☐
2116	A1499	22c	blue, red & black	48	15	☐☐☐☐☐
a.			Booklet pane of 5	2.50	—	☐☐☐☐☐
2117	A1500	22c	black & brown	40	15	☐☐☐☐☐
2118	A1501	22c	multicolored	40	15	☐☐☐☐☐
2119	A1502	22c	black & brown	40	15	☐☐☐☐☐
2120	A1503	22c	black & violet	40	15	☐☐☐☐☐
2121	A1504	22c	multicolored	40	15	☐☐☐☐☐
a.			Booklet pane of 10	4.00	—	☐☐☐☐☐
b.			As "a," violet omitted	*750.00*		☐☐☐☐☐
c.			As "a," vert. imperf. btwn.	*650.00*		☐☐☐☐☐
d.			As "a," imperf.	—		☐☐☐☐☐
e.			Strip of 5, #2117-2121	2.00		☐☐☐☐☐

Booklet stamp, Perf. 10 Vertically

2122	A1505	$10.75	multicolored	17.00	6.75	☐☐☐☐☐
a.			Booklet pane of 3	52.50	—	☐☐☐☐☐
b.			Type II	17.50	—	☐☐☐☐☐
c.			As "b," booklet pane of 3	52.50	—	☐☐☐☐☐

1985-87, Coil stamps, Perf. 10 Vertically

2123	A1506	3.4c	dark bluish green	15	15	☐☐☐☐☐
a.			Untagged (Bureau Precancel)	15	15	☐☐☐☐☐
2124	A1507	4.9c	brown black	15	15	☐☐☐☐☐
a.			Untagged (Bureau Precancel)	16	16	☐☐☐☐☐
2125	A1508	5.5c	deep magenta	15	15	☐☐☐☐☐
a.			Untagged (Bureau precancel)	15	15	☐☐☐☐☐
2126	A1509	6c	red brown	15	15	☐☐☐☐☐
a.			Untagged (Bureau Precancel)	15	15	☐☐☐☐☐
b.			As "a," imperf., pair	200.00		☐☐☐☐☐

A1520

A1527

A1526

A1521

A1522

A1523

A1524

A1525

A1528

A1530

A1529

A1535

188

Scott No.	Illus No.		Description	Unused Value	Used Value	//////
2127	A1510	7.1c	lake	15	15	
a.			Untagged (Bureau Precancel)	15	15	
2128	A1511	8.3c	green	18	15	
a.			Untagged (Bureau Precancel)	18	18	
2129	A1512	8.5c	dark Prussian green	16	15	
a.			Untagged (Bureau Precancel)	16	16	
2130	A1513	10.1c	slate blue	22	15	
a.			Untagged (Bureau Precancel)	22	22	
b.			As "a," imperf., pair	15.00		
2131	A1514	11c	dark green	22	15	
2132	A1515	12c	dark blue	24	15	
a.			Untagged (Bureau Precancel)	24	24	
b.			Type II, untagged (Bureau Precancel)	24	24	
2133	A1516	12.5c	olive green	25	15	
a.			Untagged (Bureau Precancel)	25	25	
b.			As "a," imperf., pair	50.00		
2134	A1517	14c	sky blue	28	15	
a.			Imperf., pair	80.00		
b.			Type II	28	15	
2135	A1518	17c	sky blue	30	15	
a.			Imperf., pair	600.00		
2136	A1519	25c	orange brown	45	15	
a.			Imperf., pair	12.50		
b.			Pair, imperf. between	—		

1985

Scott No.	Illus No.		Description	Unused Value	Used Value	//////
2137	A1520	22c	multicolored	42	15	
2138	A1521	22c	multicolored	60	15	
2139	A1522	22c	multicolored	60	15	
2140	A1523	22c	multicolored	60	15	
2141	A1524	22c	multicolored	60	15	
a.			Block of 4, #2138-2141 ...	2.65	1.00	
2142	A1525	22c	multicolored	40	15	
a.			Vert. pair, imperf. horiz. ..	750.00		
2143	A1526	22c	multicolored	40	15	
a.			Imperf., pair	1,750.		
2144	A1527	22c	multicolored	45	15	
2145	A1528	22c	multicolored	40	15	
a.			Red, black & blue omitted	225.00		
b.			Red & black omitted	1,250.		
c.			Red omitted	—		
2146	A1529	22c	multicolored	40	15	
a.			Imperf., pair	300.00		
2147	A1530	22c	multicolored	40	15	

A1532

A1536

A1533

A1537

A1538

A1539

A1540

A1541

A1543

A1544

A1545

A1546

Scott No.	Illus No.		Description	Unused Value	Used Value	放//////
Coil stamps, Perf. 10 Vertically						
2149	A1532	18c	multicolored	32	15	☐☐☐☐☐
a.			Untagged (Bureau Precancel)	35	35	☐☐☐☐☐
b.			Imperf., pair	950.00		☐☐☐☐☐
c.			As "a," imperf., pair	700.00		☐☐☐☐☐
2150	A1533	21.1c	multicolored	40	15	☐☐☐☐☐
a.			Untagged (Bureau Precancel)	38	38	☐☐☐☐☐
1985						
2152	A1535	22c	gray green & rose red	42	15	☐☐☐☐☐
2153	A1536	22c	deep blue & light blue	42	15	☐☐☐☐☐
2154	A1537	22c	gray green & rose red	45	15	☐☐☐☐☐
2155	A1538	22c	multicolored	75	15	☐☐☐☐☐
2156	A1539	22c	multicolored	75	15	☐☐☐☐☐
2157	A1540	22c	multicolored	75	15	☐☐☐☐☐
2158	A1541	22c	multicolored	75	15	☐☐☐☐☐
a.			Block of 4, #2155-2158 ...	3.40	1.00	☐☐☐☐☐
2159	A1542	22c	multicolored	42	15	☐☐☐☐☐
2160	A1543	22c	multicolored	50	15	☐☐☐☐☐
2161	A1544	22c	multicolored	50	15	☐☐☐☐☐
2162	A1545	22c	multicolored	50	15	☐☐☐☐☐
2163	A1546	22c	multicolored	50	15	☐☐☐☐☐
a.			Block of 4, #2160-2163 ...	2.35	1.00	☐☐☐☐☐
2164	A1547	22c	multicolored	42	15	☐☐☐☐☐
2165	A1548	22c	multicolored	40	15	☐☐☐☐☐
a.			Imperf., pair	110.00		☐☐☐☐☐
2166	A1549	22c	multicolored	40	15	☐☐☐☐☐
a.			Imperf., pair	130.00		☐☐☐☐☐
1986-93						
2167	A1550	22c	multicolored	42	15	☐☐☐☐☐
a.			Vert. pair, imperf. horiz. ..	—		☐☐☐☐☐
2168	A1551	1c	brownish vermilion	15	15	☐☐☐☐☐
2169	A1552	2c	bright blue	15	15	☐☐☐☐☐
2170	A1553	3c	bright blue	15	15	☐☐☐☐☐
2171	A1554	4c	blue violet	15	15	☐☐☐☐☐
a.			Untagged	15	15	☐☐☐☐☐
2172	A1555	5c	dark olive green	15	15	☐☐☐☐☐
2173	A1556	5c	carmine	15	15	☐☐☐☐☐
a.			Untagged	15	15	☐☐☐☐☐
2176	A1559	10c	lake	18	15	☐☐☐☐☐
b.			Untagged	20	15	☐☐☐☐☐
2177	A1560	14c	crimson	25	15	☐☐☐☐☐
2178	A1561	15c	claret	28	15	☐☐☐☐☐
2179	A1562	17c	dull blue green	30	15	☐☐☐☐☐
2180	A1563	21c	blue violet	38	15	☐☐☐☐☐
2182	A1565	23c	purple	42	15	☐☐☐☐☐

A1551   A1552   A1553   A1554

A1555   A1556   A1559

A1560   A1561   A1562   A1563

A1565   A1566   A1567   A1567a

A1567b   A1568   A1569   A1571

A1573   A1574   A1575   A1576

A1577   A1577a   A1578   A1579

Scott No.	Illus No.		Description	Unused Value	Used Value	//////
2183	A1566	25c	blue	45	15	
a.			Booklet pane of 10	4.50		
2184	A1567	28c	myrtle green	50	15	
2184A	A1567a	29c	blue	50	15	
2184B	A1567b	29c	Thomas Jefferson	50	15	
2185	A1568	35c	black	65	15	
2186	A1569	40c	dark blue	70	15	
2188	A1571	45c	bright blue	80	15	
2190	A1573	52c	purple	90	15	
2191	A1574	56c	scarlet	95	15	
2192	A1575	65c	dark blue	1.20	18	
2193	A1576	75c	deep magenta	1.50	20	
2194	A1577	$1	dark Prussian green	2.50	50	
2194A	A1577a	$1	deep blue	1.75	50	
2195	A1578	$2	bright violet	3.00	50	
2196	A1579	$5	copper red	7.00	1.00	
2197	A1566	25c	blue	45	15	
a.			Booklet pane of 6	2.65		

1986

Scott No.	Illus No.		Description	Unused Value	Used Value	//////
2198	A1581	22c	multicolored	45	15	
2199	A1582	22c	multicolored	45	15	
2200	A1583	22c	multicolored	45	15	
2201	A1584	22c	multicolored	45	15	
a.			Bklt. pane of 4, #2198-2201	2.00	—	
b.			As "a," black omitted on #2198, 2201	45.00		
c.			As "a," blue (litho.) omitted on #2198-2200	—		
d.			As "a," buff (litho.) omitted	—		
2202	A1585	22c	multicolored	40	15	
2203	A1586	22c	multicolored	40	15	
2204	A1587	22c	dk bl, dk red & grysh blk .	42	15	
a.			Horiz. pair, imperf. vert. ..	*1,000.*		
b.			Dark red omitted	*2,500.*		
2205	A1588	22c	multicolored	50	15	
2206	A1589	22c	multicolored	50	15	
2207	A1590	22c	multicolored	50	15	
2208	A1591	22c	multicolored	50	15	
2209	A1592	22c	multicolored	50	15	
a.			Bklt. pane of 5, #2205-2209	4.00	—	
2210	A1593	22c	multicolored	40	15	
a.			Vert. pair, imperf. horiz. ..	*350.00*		
b.			Horiz. pair, imperf. vert. ..	*1,000.*		

A1542

Help End Hunger USA 22

A1547

A1548

A1549

A1550

LOVE
USA 22

A1585

Sojourner Truth 22

Black Heritage USA

A1586

San Jacinto 1836
Republic of Texas

A1587

Duke Ellington
22 USA

A1594

A1588-1592

Public Hospitals USA 22

A1593

194

A1599a

A1599b

A1599c

A1599d

Scott No.	Illus No.	Description	Unused Value	Used Value	//////
2211	A1594	22c multicolored	42	15	☐☐☐☐☐
a.		Vert. pair, imperf. horiz. ..	1,100.	—	☐☐☐☐☐
2216		Sheet of 9	3.50		☐☐☐☐☐
a.-i.	A1599	22c any single	38	20	☐☐☐☐☐
j.		Blue omitted	2,400.		☐☐☐☐☐
k.		Black inscription omitted	2,000.		☐☐☐☐☐
l.		Imperf.	9,000.		☐☐☐☐☐
2217		Sheet of 9	3.50		☐☐☐☐☐
a.-i.	A1599	22c any single	38	20	☐☐☐☐☐
2218		Sheet of 9	3.50		☐☐☐☐☐
a.-i.	A1599	22c any single	38	20	☐☐☐☐☐
j.		Brown omitted	—		☐☐☐☐☐
k.		Black inscription omitted	2,600.		☐☐☐☐☐
2219		Sheet of 9	3.50		☐☐☐☐☐
a.-i.	A1599	22c any single	38	20	☐☐☐☐☐
2220	A1600	22c multicolored	55	15	☐☐☐☐☐
2221	A1601	22c multicolored	55	15	☐☐☐☐☐
2222	A1602	22c multicolored	55	15	☐☐☐☐☐
2223	A1603	22c multicolored	55	15	☐☐☐☐☐
a.		Block of 4, #2220-2223 ...	2.40	1.00	☐☐☐☐☐
b.		As "a," black (engr.) omitted	—		☐☐☐☐☐
2224	A1604	22c scarlet & dark blue	40	15	☐☐☐☐☐

1986-87, Coil stamps, Perf. 10 Vertically

Scott No.	Illus No.	Description	Unused Value	Used Value	//////
2225	A1604a	1c violet	15	15	☐☐☐☐☐
a.		Untagged	15	15	☐☐☐☐☐
b.		Imperf., pair	—		☐☐☐☐☐
2226	A1604b	2c black	15	15	☐☐☐☐☐
2228	A1285	4c reddish brown	15	15	☐☐☐☐☐
b.		Imperf., pair	400.00		☐☐☐☐☐
2231	A1511	8.3c green (Bureau precancel).	16	16	☐☐☐☐☐

1986

Scott No.	Illus No.	Description	Unused Value	Used Value	//////
2235	A1605	22c multicolored	42	15	☐☐☐☐☐
2236	A1606	22c multicolored	42	15	☐☐☐☐☐
2237	A1607	22c multicolored	42	15	☐☐☐☐☐
2238	A1608	22c multicolored	42	15	☐☐☐☐☐
a.		Block of 4, #2235-2238 ...	1.75	1.00	☐☐☐☐☐
b.		As "a," black (engr.) omitted	350.00		☐☐☐☐☐
2239	A1609	22c copper red	40	15	☐☐☐☐☐
2240	A1610	22c multicolored	42	15	☐☐☐☐☐
2241	A1611	22c multicolored	42	15	☐☐☐☐☐
2242	A1612	22c multicolored	42	15	☐☐☐☐☐
2243	A1613	22c multicolored	42	15	☐☐☐☐☐
a.		Block of 4, #2240-2243 ...	1.75	1.00	☐☐☐☐☐
b.		As "a," imperf. vert.	1,500		☐☐☐☐☐

A1581-1584

A1600-1603

A1605-1608

A1604a

A1604

A1604b

A1610-1613

A1609

A1616

A1614

A1615

A1618

A1617

A1637

A1619

A1620

A1638

A1639

A1640

A1621

A1641

A1642

A1645

A1643

A1644

200

Scott No.	Illus No.		Description	Unused Value	Used Value	//////
2244	A1614	22c	multicolored	40	15	☐☐☐☐☐
2245	A1615	22c	multicolored	40	15	☐☐☐☐☐

1987

2246	A1616	22c	multicolored	40	15	☐☐☐☐☐
2247	A1617	22c	multicolored	40	15	☐☐☐☐☐
a.			Silver omitted	1,500.		☐☐☐☐☐
2248	A1618	22c	multicolored	40	15	☐☐☐☐☐
2249	A1619	22c	multicolored	40	15	☐☐☐☐☐
2250	A1620	22c	multicolored	40	15	☐☐☐☐☐
a.			Black (engr.) omitted	—		☐☐☐☐☐
2251	A1621	22c	multicolored	40	15	☐☐☐☐☐

1987-88, Coil stamps, Perf. 10 Vertically

2252	A1622	3c	claret	15	15	☐☐☐☐☐
a.			Untagged	15	15	☐☐☐☐☐
2253	A1623	5c	black	15	15	☐☐☐☐☐
2254	A1624	5.3c	black (Bureau precancel in scarlet)	15	15	☐☐☐☐☐
2255	A1625	7.6c	brown (Bureau precancel in scarlet)	15	15	☐☐☐☐☐
2256	A1626	8.4c	dp claret (Bureau precancel in red)	15	15	☐☐☐☐☐
a.			Imperf., pair	750.00		☐☐☐☐☐
2257	A1627	10c	sky blue	18	15	☐☐☐☐☐
2258	A1628	13c	black (Bureau precancel in red)	22	22	☐☐☐☐☐
2259	A1629	13.2c	slate green (Bureau precancel in red)	22	22	☐☐☐☐☐
a.			Imperf., pair	160.00		☐☐☐☐☐
2260	A1630	15c	violet	24	15	☐☐☐☐☐
2261	A1631	16.7c	rose (Bureau precancel in black)	28	28	☐☐☐☐☐
a.			Imperf., pair	225.00		☐☐☐☐☐
2262	A1632	17.5c	dark violet	30	15	☐☐☐☐☐
a.			Untagged (Bureau precancel)	30	30	☐☐☐☐☐
b.			Imperf., pair	1,500.		☐☐☐☐☐
2263	A1633	20c	blue violet	35	15	☐☐☐☐☐
a.			Imperf., pair	90.00		☐☐☐☐☐
2264	A1634	20.5c	rose (Bureau precancel in black)	38	38	☐☐☐☐☐
2265	A1635	21c	olive green (Bureau precancel in red)	38	38	☐☐☐☐☐
a.			Imperf., pair	75.00		☐☐☐☐☐
2266	A1636	24.1c	deep ultra (Bureau precancel)	42	42	☐☐☐☐☐

A1622	A1623	A1624	A1625

A1626	A1627	A1628	A1629

A1630	A1631	A1632	A1633

A1634	A1635	A1636

HOW TO USE THIS BOOK

The number in the first column is its Scott number or identifying number. The letter and number that come next (A41) indicate the design and refer to the illustration so designated. Following that is the denomination of the stamp and its color. Finally, the value, unused and used is shown.

Scott No.	Illus No.		Description	Unused Value	Used Value	//////
1987, Perf. 10 on 1, 2 or 3 sides						
2267	A1637	22c	multicolored	55	15	☐☐☐☐☐
2268	A1638	22c	multicolored	55	15	☐☐☐☐☐
2269	A1639	22c	multicolored	55	15	☐☐☐☐☐
2270	A1640	22c	multicolored	55	15	☐☐☐☐☐
2271	A1641	22c	multicolored	55	15	☐☐☐☐☐
2272	A1642	22c	multicolored	55	15	☐☐☐☐☐
2273	A1643	22c	multicolored	55	15	☐☐☐☐☐
2274	A1644	22c	multicolored	55	15	☐☐☐☐☐
a.			Bklt. pane of 10, #2268-2271, 2273-2274, 2 each #2267, 2272	6.75	—	☐☐☐☐☐
2275	A1645	22c	multicolored	40	15	☐☐☐☐☐
2276	A1646	22c	multicolored	40	15	☐☐☐☐☐
a.			Booklet pane of 20	8.50	—	☐☐☐☐☐
2277	A1647	(25c)	multicolored	45	15	☐☐☐☐☐
2278	A1648	25c	multicolored	40	15	☐☐☐☐☐
2279	A1647	(25c)	multicolored	45	15	☐☐☐☐☐
a.			Imperf., pair	120.00		☐☐☐☐☐
2280	A1649	25c	Green trees	45	15	☐☐☐☐☐
a.			Imperf., pair	20.00		☐☐☐☐☐
b.			Black trees	—		☐☐☐☐☐
d.			Pair, imperf. between	—		☐☐☐☐☐
2281	A1649d	25c	multicolored	45	15	☐☐☐☐☐
a.			Imperf., pair	45.00		☐☐☐☐☐
b.			Black (engr.) omitted	70.00		☐☐☐☐☐
c.			Black (litho.) omitted	550.00		☐☐☐☐☐
d.			Pair, imperf. between	—		☐☐☐☐☐
2282	A1647	(25c)	multicolored	45	15	☐☐☐☐☐
a.			Booklet pane of 10	4.75	—	☐☐☐☐☐
2283	A1649a	25c	multicolored	50	15	☐☐☐☐☐
a.			Booklet pane of 10	4.75	—	☐☐☐☐☐
b.		25c	multi, red removed from sky	50	15	☐☐☐☐☐
c.			As "b," bklt. pane of 10 ...	50.00	—	☐☐☐☐☐
d.			As "a," horiz. imperf. btwn.	—		☐☐☐☐☐
2284	A1649b	25c	multicolored	45	15	☐☐☐☐☐
2285	A1649c	25c	multicolored	45	15	☐☐☐☐☐
b.			Bklt. pane of 10, 5 each #2284-2285	4.50	—	☐☐☐☐☐
d.			Pair, #2284-2285	1.00	—	☐☐☐☐☐
2285A	A1648	25c	multicolored	45	15	☐☐☐☐☐
c.			Booklet pane of 6	2.75	—	☐☐☐☐☐
2286	A1650	22c	Barn swallow	85	15	☐☐☐☐☐
2287	A1651	22c	Monarch butterfly	85	15	☐☐☐☐☐
2288	A1652	22c	Bighorn sheep	85	15	☐☐☐☐☐
2289	A1653	22c	Broad-tailed hummingbird	85	15	☐☐☐☐☐
2290	A1654	22c	Cottontail	85	15	☐☐☐☐☐
2291	A1655	22c	Osprey	85	15	☐☐☐☐☐

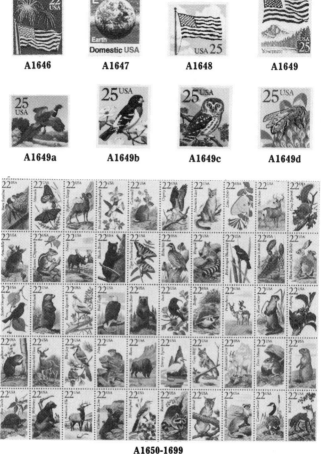

A1646 A1647 A1648 A1649

A1649a A1649b A1649c A1649d

A1650-1699

HOW TO USE THIS BOOK

The number in the first column is its Scott number or identifying number. The letter and number that come next (A41) indicate the design and refer to the illustration so designated. Following that is the denomination of the stamp and its color. Finally, the value, unused and used is shown.

Scott No.	Illus No.		Description	Unused Value	Used Value	//////
2292	A1656	22c	Mountain lion	85	15	☐☐☐☐☐
2293	A1657	22c	Luna moth	85	15	☐☐☐☐☐
2294	A1658	22c	Mule deer	85	15	☐☐☐☐☐
2295	A1659	22c	Gray squirrel..................	85	15	☐☐☐☐☐
2296	A1660	22c	Armadillo	85	15	☐☐☐☐☐
2297	A1661	22c	Eastern chipmunk	85	15	☐☐☐☐☐
2298	A1662	22c	Moose	85	15	☐☐☐☐☐
2299	A1663	22c	Black bear	85	15	☐☐☐☐☐
2300	A1664	22c	Tiger swallowtail	85	15	☐☐☐☐☐
2301	A1665	22c	Bobwhite	85	15	☐☐☐☐☐
2302	A1666	22c	Ringtail	85	15	☐☐☐☐☐
2303	A1667	22c	Red-winged blackbird	85	15	☐☐☐☐☐
2304	A1668	22c	American lobster	85	15	☐☐☐☐☐
2305	A1669	22c	Black-tailed jack rabbit ...	85	15	☐☐☐☐☐
2306	A1670	22c	Scarlet tanager	85	15	☐☐☐☐☐
2307	A1671	22c	Woodchuck	85	15	☐☐☐☐☐
2308	A1672	22c	Roseate spoonbill	85	15	☐☐☐☐☐
2309	A1673	22c	Bald eagle	85	15	☐☐☐☐☐
2310	A1674	22c	Alaskan brown bear.........	85	15	☐☐☐☐☐
2311	A1675	22c	Iiwi	85	15	☐☐☐☐☐
2312	A1676	22c	Badger	85	15	☐☐☐☐☐
2313	A1677	22c	Pronghorn	85	15	☐☐☐☐☐
2314	A1678	22c	River otter	85	15	☐☐☐☐☐
2315	A1679	22c	Ladybug	85	15	☐☐☐☐☐
2316	A1680	22c	Beaver	85	15	☐☐☐☐☐
2317	A1681	22c	White-tailed deer	85	15	☐☐☐☐☐
2318	A1682	22c	Blue jay	85	15	☐☐☐☐☐
2319	A1683	22c	Pika	85	15	☐☐☐☐☐
2320	A1684	22c	Bison	85	15	☐☐☐☐☐
2321	A1685	22c	Snowy egret....................	85	15	☐☐☐☐☐
2322	A1686	22c	Gray wolf	85	15	☐☐☐☐☐
2323	A1687	22c	Mountain goat	85	15	☐☐☐☐☐
2324	A1688	22c	Deer mouse	85	15	☐☐☐☐☐
2325	A1689	22c	Black-tailed prairie dog ...	85	15	☐☐☐☐☐
2326	A1690	22c	Box turtle.......................	85	15	☐☐☐☐☐
2327	A1691	22c	Wolverine	85	15	☐☐☐☐☐
2328	A1692	22c	American elk	85	15	☐☐☐☐☐
2329	A1693	22c	California sea lion	85	15	☐☐☐☐☐
2330	A1694	22c	Mockingbird	85	15	☐☐☐☐☐
2331	A1695	22c	Raccoon	85	15	☐☐☐☐☐
2332	A1696	22c	Bobcat	85	15	☐☐☐☐☐
2333	A1697	22c	Black-footed ferret	85	15	☐☐☐☐☐
2334	A1698	22c	Canada goose	85	15	☐☐☐☐☐
2335	A1699	22c	Red fox	85	15	☐☐☐☐☐
a.			Pane of 50, #2286-2335 ..	46.50		☐☐☐☐☐
			2286b-2335b, any single, red omitted	—		☐☐☐☐☐

Dec 7, 1787   USA
Delaware 22

A1700

Dec 12, 1787
Pennsylvania

A1701

Dec 18, 1787   USA
New Jersey 22

A1702

22
USA
January 2, 1788
Georgia

A1703

22
USA
January 9, 1788
Connecticut

A1704

22
USA
Feb 6, 1788
Massachusetts

A1705

April 28, 1788   USA
Maryland 22

A1706

25
USA
May 23, 1788
South Carolina

A1707

25
USA
June 21, 1788
New Hampshire

A1708

June 25, 1788   USA
Virginia 25

A1709

July 26, 1788   USA
New York 25

A1710

25
USA
November 21, 1789
North Carolina

A1711

25
USA
May 29, 1790
Rhode Island

A1712

Scott No.	Illus No.		Description	Unused Value	Used Value	//////
1987-88						
2336	A1700	22c	multicolored	40	15	☐☐☐☐☐
2337	A1701	22c	multicolored	42	15	☐☐☐☐☐
2338	A1702	22c	multicolored	42	15	☐☐☐☐☐
a.			Black (engr.) omitted	5,000.		☐☐☐☐☐
2339	A1703	22c	multicolored	40	15	☐☐☐☐☐
2340	A1704	22c	multicolored	40	15	☐☐☐☐☐
2341	A1705	22c	dark blue & dark red	40	15	☐☐☐☐☐
2342	A1706	22c	multicolored	40	15	☐☐☐☐☐
2343	A1707	25c	multicolored	45	15	☐☐☐☐☐
a.			Strip of 3, vert. imperf. between	—		☐☐☐☐☐
2344	A1708	25c	multicolored	45	15	☐☐☐☐☐
2345	A1709	25c	multicolored	45	15	☐☐☐☐☐
2346	A1710	25c	multicolored	45	15	☐☐☐☐☐
2347	A1711	25c	multicolored	45	15	☐☐☐☐☐
2348	A1712	25c	multicolored	45	15	☐☐☐☐☐
2349	A1713	22c	scarlet & black	40	15	☐☐☐☐☐
a.			Black (engr.) omitted	300.00		☐☐☐☐☐
2350	A1714	22c	bright green	40	15	☐☐☐☐☐
2351	A1715	22c	ultra & white	42	15	☐☐☐☐☐
2352	A1716	22c	ultra & white	42	15	☐☐☐☐☐
2353	A1717	22c	ultra & white	42	15	☐☐☐☐☐
2354	A1718	22c	ultra & white	42	15	☐☐☐☐☐
a.			Block of 4, #2351-2354 ...	1.75	1.00	☐☐☐☐☐
b.			As "a," white omitted	1,250.		☐☐☐☐☐
2355	A1719	22c	multicolored	50	15	☐☐☐☐☐
a.			Grayish green (background) omitted	—		☐☐☐☐☐
2356	A1720	22c	multicolored	50	15	☐☐☐☐☐
a.			Grayish green (background) omitted	—		☐☐☐☐☐
2357	A1721	22c	multicolored	50	15	☐☐☐☐☐
a.			Grayish green (background) omitted	—		☐☐☐☐☐
2358	A1722	22c	multicolored	50	15	☐☐☐☐☐
a.			Grayish green (background) omitted	—		☐☐☐☐☐
2359	A1723	22c	multicolored	50	15	☐☐☐☐☐
a.			Bklt. pane of 5, #2355-2359	2.75	—	☐☐☐☐☐
b.			Grayish green (background) omitted	—		☐☐☐☐☐
2360	A1724	22c	multicolored	40	15	☐☐☐☐☐
2361	A1725	22c	multicolored	1.90	15	☐☐☐☐☐
a.			Black (engr.) omitted	850.00		☐☐☐☐☐
2362	A1726	22c	multicolored	50	15	☐☐☐☐☐
2363	A1727	22c	multicolored	50	15	☐☐☐☐☐

A1713

A1714

A1724

A1725

A1715-1718

A1731

A1733

A1732

A1719-1723

A1726-1730

A1736-1739

A1735

A1734

A1740

A1741

A1742

A1743

A1744

A1745-1749

A1754-1757

Scott No.	Illus No.		Description	Unused Value	Used Value	/ / / / / /
2364	A1728	22c	multicolored	50	15	☐☐☐☐☐
2365	A1729	22c	multicolored	50	15	☐☐☐☐☐
a.			Red omitted	—		☐☐☐☐☐
2366	A1730	22c	multicolored	50	15	☐☐☐☐☐
a.			Booklet pane of 5,			
			#2362-2366	2.75	—	☐☐☐☐☐
b.			As "a," black omitted on			
			#2366	—		☐☐☐☐☐
2367	A1731	22c	multicolored	40	15	☐☐☐☐☐
2368	A1732	22c	multicolored	40	15	☐☐☐☐☐

1988

Scott No.	Illus No.		Description	Unused Value	Used Value	/ / / / / /
2369	A1733	22c	multicolored	40	15	☐☐☐☐☐
2370	A1734	22c	multicolored	40	15	☐☐☐☐☐
2371	A1735	22c	multicolored	40	15	☐☐☐☐☐
2372	A1736	22c	multicolored	42	15	☐☐☐☐☐
2373	A1737	22c	multicolored	42	15	☐☐☐☐☐
2374	A1738	22c	multicolored	42	15	☐☐☐☐☐
2375	A1739	22c	multicolored	42	15	☐☐☐☐☐
a.			Block of 4, #2372-2375 ...	2.00	1.00	☐☐☐☐☐
2376	A1740	22c	multicolored	40	15	☐☐☐☐☐
2377	A1741	25c	multicolored	45	15	☐☐☐☐☐
2378	A1742	25c	multicolored	45	15	☐☐☐☐☐
2379	A1743	45c	multicolored	65	20	☐☐☐☐☐
2380	A1744	25c	multicolored	45	15	☐☐☐☐☐
2381	A1745	25c	multicolored	45	15	☐☐☐☐☐
2382	A1746	25c	multicolored	45	15	☐☐☐☐☐
2383	A1747	25c	multicolored	45	15	☐☐☐☐☐
2384	A1748	25c	multicolored	45	15	☐☐☐☐☐
2385	A1749	25c	multicolored	45	15	☐☐☐☐☐
a.			Booklet pane of 5,			
			#2381-2385	2.50	—	☐☐☐☐☐
2386	A1750	25c	multicolored	50	15	☐☐☐☐☐
2387	A1751	25c	multicolored	50	15	☐☐☐☐☐
2388	A1752	25c	multicolored	50	15	☐☐☐☐☐
2389	A1753	25c	multicolored	50	15	☐☐☐☐☐
a.			Block of 4, #2386-2389 ...	2.25	1.00	☐☐☐☐☐
b.			Black (engr.) omitted	1,500.		☐☐☐☐☐
c.			As "a," imperf. horiz.	2,500.		☐☐☐☐☐
2390	A1754	25c	multicolored	55	15	☐☐☐☐☐
2391	A1755	25c	multicolored	55	15	☐☐☐☐☐
2392	A1756	25c	multicolored	55	15	☐☐☐☐☐
2393	A1757	25c	multicolored	55	15	☐☐☐☐☐
a.			Block of 4, #2390-2393 ...	2.45	1.00	☐☐☐☐☐
2394	A1758	$8.75	multicolored	13.50	7.75	☐☐☐☐☐
2395	A1759	25c	multicolored	45	15	☐☐☐☐☐

A1750-1753

A1758

A1759

A1760

A1761

A1762

A1764

A1763

A1765

Scott No.	Illus No.		Description	Unused Value	Used Value	//////
2396	A1760	25c	multicolored	45	15	☐☐☐☐☐
a.			Bklt. pane, 3 #2395 & 3 #2396 with gutter btwn.	3.00	—	☐☐☐☐☐
2397	A1761	25c	multicolored	45	15	☐☐☐☐☐
2398	A1762	25c	multicolored	45	15	☐☐☐☐☐
a.			Bklt. pane, 3 #2397 & 3 #2398 with gutter btwn.	3.00	—	☐☐☐☐☐
b.			As "a," imperf. horiz.	—		☐☐☐☐☐
2399	A1763	25c	multicolored	45	15	☐☐☐☐☐
a.			Gold omitted....................	40.00		☐☐☐☐☐
2400	A1764	25c	multicolored	45	15	☐☐☐☐☐

1989

Scott No.	Illus No.		Description	Unused Value	Used Value	//////
2401	A1765	25c	multicolored	45	15	☐☐☐☐☐
2402	A1766	25c	multicolored	45	15	☐☐☐☐☐
2403	A1767	25c	multicolored	45	15	☐☐☐☐☐
2404	A1768	25c	multicolored	45	15	☐☐☐☐☐
2405	A1769	25c	multicolored	45	15	☐☐☐☐☐
2406	A1770	25c	multicolored	45	15	☐☐☐☐☐
2407	A1771	25c	multicolored	45	15	☐☐☐☐☐
2408	A1772	25c	multicolored	45	15	☐☐☐☐☐
2409	A1773	25c	multicolored	45	15	☐☐☐☐☐
a.			Bklt. pane of 5, #2405-2409	2.50	—	☐☐☐☐☐
2410	A1774	25c	grysh brn, blk & car rose	45	15	☐☐☐☐☐
2411	A1775	25c	multicolored	45	15	☐☐☐☐☐

1989-90

Scott No.	Illus No.		Description	Unused Value	Used Value	//////
2412	A1776	25c	multicolored	45	15	☐☐☐☐☐
2413	A1777	25c	multicolored	45	15	☐☐☐☐☐
2414	A1778	25c	multicolored	45	15	☐☐☐☐☐
2415	A1779	25c	multicolored	45	15	☐☐☐☐☐

1989

Scott No.	Illus No.		Description	Unused Value	Used Value	//////
2416	A1780	25c	multicolored	45	15	☐☐☐☐☐
2417	A1781	25c	multicolored	60	15	☐☐☐☐☐
2418	A1782	25c	multicolored	45	15	☐☐☐☐☐
2419	A1783	$2.40	multicolored	4.25	2.00	☐☐☐☐☐
a.			Black (engr.) omitted.......	3,500.		☐☐☐☐☐
b.			Imperf., pair....................	1,500.		☐☐☐☐☐
c.			Black (litho.) omitted	—		☐☐☐☐☐
2420	A1784	25c	multicolored	45	15	☐☐☐☐☐
2421	A1785	25c	multicolored	45	15	☐☐☐☐☐
a.			Black (engr.) omitted.......	275.00		☐☐☐☐☐
2422	A1786	25c	multicolored	45	15	☐☐☐☐☐
2423	A1787	25c	multicolored	45	15	☐☐☐☐☐
2424	A1788	25c	multicolored	45	15	☐☐☐☐☐

A1766

A1767

A1768

A1769-1773

A1774

A1775

A1776

A1777

A1778

A1779

214

A1781

A1782

A1785

A1790

A1780

A1784

A1783

A1786-1789

215

A1792

A1791

A1793

A1794

A1795-1798

A1800

A1799

A1801

A1802

Scott No.	Illus No.		Description	Unused Value	Used Value	/ / / / / /
2425	A1789	25c	multicolored	45	15	
a.			Block of 4, #2422-2425 ...	2.00	1.00	
b.			As "a," black (engr.)			
			omitted	1,100.		
2426	A1790	25c	multicolored	45	15	
2427	A1791	25c	multicolored	45	15	
a.			Booklet pane of 10	4.50	—	
2428	A1792	25c	multicolored	45	15	
a.			Vert. pair, imperf. horiz. ..	—		

Booklet stamp, Perf. 11½ on 2 or 3 sides

2429	A1792	25c	multicolored	45	15	
a.			Booklet pane of 10	4.50	—	
b.			As "a," horiz. imperf. btwn.	—		
c.			As "a," red omitted	—		

Die cut, Self-adhesive

2431	A1793	25c	multicolored	50	20	
a.			Booklet pane of 18	9.00		
b.			Vert. pair, no die cutting			
			between	850.00		
2433	A1794		Sheet of 4	10.00	9.00	
a.		90c	like No. 122	1.85	1.75	
b.		90c	like No. 132TC (blue frame,			
			brown center)	1.85	1.75	
c.		90c	like No. 132TC (green frame,			
			blue center)	1.85	1.75	
d.		90c	like No. 132TC (scarlet			
			frame, blue center)	1.85	1.75	
2434	A1795	25c	multicolored	45	15	
2435	A1796	25c	multicolored	45	15	
2436	A1797	25c	multicolored	45	15	
2437	A1798	25c	multicolored	45	15	
a.			Block of 4, #2434-2437 ...	3.00	2.00	
b.			As "a," dark blue (engr.)			
			omitted	1,100.		
2438			Sheet of 4	4.00	1.75	
a.	A1795	25c	multicolored	60	25	
b.	A1796	25c	multicolored	60	25	
c.	A1797	25c	multicolored	60	25	
d.	A1798	25c	multicolored	60	25	
e.			Dark blue & gray (engr.)			
			omitted	—		

1990

2439	A1799	25c	multicolored	45	15	
2440	A1800	25c	brt bl, dk pink & emer grn	45	15	
a.			Imperf., pair	850.00		

A1803

A1808

A1804-07

A1810

A1811

A1812

A1816

A1823

A1827

A1829-33

Scott No.	Illus No.		Description	Unused Value	Used Value	//////
Booklet stamp, Perf. 11½ on 2 or 3 sides						
2441	A1800	25c	ultra, bright pink & dk grn	45	15	☐☐☐☐☐
a.			Booklet pane of 10	4.50	—	☐☐☐☐☐
b.			As "a," bright pink omitted	*1,800.*		☐☐☐☐☐
2442	A1801	25c	multicolored	45	15	☐☐☐☐☐
2443	A1802	15c	multicolored	28	15	☐☐☐☐☐
a.			Booklet pane of 10	2.80	—	☐☐☐☐☐
b.			As "a," blue omitted	*2,000.*		☐☐☐☐☐
2444	A1803	25c	multicolored	45	15	☐☐☐☐☐
a.			Black (engr.) omitted	—	—	☐☐☐☐☐
2445	A1804	25c	multicolored	70	15	☐☐☐☐☐
2446	A1805	25c	multicolored	70	15	☐☐☐☐☐
2447	A1806	25c	multicolored	70	15	☐☐☐☐☐
2448	A1807	25c	multicolored	70	15	☐☐☐☐☐
a.			Block of 4, #2445-2448 ...	3.25	1.00	☐☐☐☐☐
2449	A1808	25c	multicolored	45	15	☐☐☐☐☐
1909-92, Coil stamps, Perf. 10 Vertically						
2451	A1810	4c	claret	15	15	☐☐☐☐☐
a.			Imperf., pair	*600.00*		☐☐☐☐☐
b.			Untagged	15	15	☐☐☐☐☐
2452	A1811	5c	red	15	15	☐☐☐☐☐
a.			Untagged	15	15	☐☐☐☐☐
2452B	A1811	5c	carmine	15	15	☐☐☐☐☐
2453	A1812	5c	brown (Bureau precancel in gray).................	15	15	☐☐☐☐☐
a.			Imperf., pair	*600.00*		☐☐☐☐☐
2454	A1812	5c	red (Bureau precancel in gray).................	15	15	☐☐☐☐☐
2457	A1816	10c	green (Bureau precancel in gray).................	18	18	☐☐☐☐☐
a.			Imperf., pair	*600.00*		☐☐☐☐☐
2464	A1823	23c	dark blue	42	15	☐☐☐☐☐
a.			Imperf., pair	*400.00*		☐☐☐☐☐
2468	A1827	$1	blue & scarlet	1.75	50	☐☐☐☐☐
1990						
2470	A1829	25c	multicolored	45	15	☐☐☐☐☐
2471	A1830	25c	multicolored	45	15	☐☐☐☐☐
2472	A1831	25c	multicolored	45	15	☐☐☐☐☐
2473	A1832	25c	multicolored	45	15	☐☐☐☐☐
2474	A1833	25c	multicolored	45	15	☐☐☐☐☐
a.			Bklt. pane of 5, #2470-2474	2.50	—	☐☐☐☐☐
b.			As "a," white (USA 25) omitted	*90.00*		☐☐☐☐☐

A1834

A1835

A1837

A1840

A1841

A1855-59

A1860-64

Scott No.	Illus No.		Description	Unused Value	Used Value	/ / / / / /
Die cut, Self-adhesive						
2475	A1834	25c	dark red & dark blue	50	25	☐☐☐☐☐
a.			Pane of 12	6.00		☐☐☐☐☐
1990-93						
2476	A1835	$2	multicolored	3.50	1.25	☐☐☐☐☐
a.			Black (engr.) omitted	—		☐☐☐☐☐
Die cut, Self-adhesive						
2478	A1837	29c	multicolored	58	25	☐☐☐☐☐
a.			Pane of 18	10.50		☐☐☐☐☐
2481	A1840	1c	multicolored	15	15	☐☐☐☐☐
2482	A1841	3c	multicolored	15	15	☐☐☐☐☐
2487	A1846	19c	multicolored	35	15	☐☐☐☐☐
2489	A1848	30c	multicolored	50	15	☐☐☐☐☐
2491	A1850	45c	multicolored	78	15	☐☐☐☐☐
1991, Booklet stamp, Perf. 10 on 2 or 3 sides						
2493	A1852	29c	black & multi	50	15	☐☐☐☐☐
a.			Booklet pane of 10	5.00		☐☐☐☐☐
b.			As "a," horiz. imperf. btwn.	—		☐☐☐☐☐
Booklet stamp, Perf. 11 on 2 or 3 sides						
2494	A1852	29c	red & multi	50	15	☐☐☐☐☐
a.			Booklet pane of 10	5.00		☐☐☐☐☐
1990						
2496	A1855	25c	multicolored	45	15	☐☐☐☐☐
2497	A1856	25c	multicolored	45	15	☐☐☐☐☐
2498	A1857	25c	multicolored	45	15	☐☐☐☐☐
2499	A1858	25c	multicolored	45	15	☐☐☐☐☐
2500	A1859	25c	multicolored	45	15	☐☐☐☐☐
a.			Strip of 5, #2496-2500	2.50	—	☐☐☐☐☐
2501	A1860	25c	multicolored	45	15	☐☐☐☐☐
2502	A1861	25c	multicolored	45	15	☐☐☐☐☐
2503	A1862	25c	multicolored	45	15	☐☐☐☐☐
2504	A1863	25c	multicolored	45	15	☐☐☐☐☐
2505	A1864	25c	multicolored	45	15	☐☐☐☐☐
a.			Bklt. pane, 2 each #2501-2505	5.00	—	☐☐☐☐☐
b.			As "a," black (engr.) omitted	—		☐☐☐☐☐
c.			Strip of 5, #2501-2505	2.25	—	☐☐☐☐☐
d.			As "a," horiz. imperf. btwn.	—		☐☐☐☐☐
2506	A1865	25c	multicolored	45	15	☐☐☐☐☐
a.			Black (engr.) omitted	—		☐☐☐☐☐
2507	A1866	25c	multicolored	45	15	☐☐☐☐☐
a.			Pair, #2506-2507	1.00	16	☐☐☐☐☐

A1846

A1848

A1850

A1852

A1865-66

A1867-70

A1871

A1872

A1873

A1874

A1875

A1876

A1877

222

Scott No.	Illus No.		Description	Unused Value	Used Value	//////
2508	A1867	25c	multicolored	45	15	☐☐☐☐☐
2509	A1868	25c	multicolored	45	15	☐☐☐☐☐
2510	A1869	25c	multicolored	45	15	☐☐☐☐☐
2511	A1870	25c	multicolored	45	15	☐☐☐☐☐
a.			Block of 4, #2508-2511 ...	2.00	—	☐☐☐☐☐
b.			As "a," black (engr.) omitted	1,250.		☐☐☐☐☐
2512	A1871	25c	multicolored	45	15	☐☐☐☐☐
2513	A1872	25c	multicolored	45	15	☐☐☐☐☐
a.			Imperf., pair	1,750.		☐☐☐☐☐
2514	A1873	25c	multicolored	45	15	☐☐☐☐☐
a.			Booklet pane of 10	4.50	—	☐☐☐☐☐
2515	A1874	25c	multicolored	45	15	☐☐☐☐☐

Booklet stamp, Perf. 11½x11 on 2 or 3 sides

Scott No.	Illus No.		Description	Unused Value	Used Value	//////
2516	A1874	25c	multicolored	45	15	☐☐☐☐☐
a.			Booklet pane of 10	4.50	—	☐☐☐☐☐

1991

Scott No.	Illus No.		Description	Unused Value	Used Value	//////
2517	A1875	(29c)	yel, blk, red & yel grn	50	15	☐☐☐☐☐
a.			Imperf., pair	750.00		☐☐☐☐☐
b.			Horiz. pair, imperf. vert. ..	—		☐☐☐☐☐

Coil stamp, Perf. 10 Vertically

Scott No.	Illus No.		Description	Unused Value	Used Value	//////
2518	A1875	(29c)	yel, blk, dull red & dk yel grn	50	15	☐☐☐☐☐
a.			Imperf., pair	50.00		☐☐☐☐☐

Booklet stamps, Perf. 11 on 2 or 3 sides

Scott No.	Illus No.		Description	Unused Value	Used Value	//////
2519	A1875	(29c)	yel, blk, dull red & dk grn	50	15	☐☐☐☐☐
a.			Booklet pane of 10	5.00		☐☐☐☐☐
2520	A1875	(29c)	pale yel, blk, red & brt grn	50	15	☐☐☐☐☐
a.			Booklet pane of 10	5.50		☐☐☐☐☐
2521	A1876	(4c)	gold & carmine	15	15	☐☐☐☐☐
a.			Vert. pair, imperf. horiz. ..	200.00		☐☐☐☐☐
b.			Double impression of gold	—		☐☐☐☐☐

Die cut, Self-adhesive

Scott No.	Illus No.		Description	Unused Value	Used Value	//////
2522	A1877	(29c)	black, dark blue & red	50	25	☐☐☐☐☐
a.			Pane of 12	6.00		☐☐☐☐☐

Coil stamps, Perf. 10 Vertically

Scott No.	Illus No.		Description	Unused Value	Used Value	//////
2523	A1878	29c	blue, red & claret	50	15	☐☐☐☐☐
b.			Imperf., pair	35.00		☐☐☐☐☐
c.			Blue, red & brown	5.00	—	☐☐☐☐☐
2523A	A1878	29c	blue, red & brown	50	15	☐☐☐☐☐

A1878　　　　**A1879**　　　　**A1880**　　　　**A1881**

A1882　　　　**A1883**　　　　**A1884**

A1887　　　　**A1888**　　　　**A1889**

A1890　　　　**A1891**　　　　**A1892**

Scott No.	Illus No.		Description	Unused Value	Used Value	//////
1991-92						
2524	A1879	29c	dull yel, blk, red & pale yel grn	50	15	☐☐☐☐☐
a.			Perf. 13	50	15	☐☐☐☐☐
Coil stamps, Rouletted 10 Vertically						
2525	A1879	29c	pale yel, blk, red & yel grn	50	15	☐☐☐☐☐
Perf. 10 Vertically						
2526	A1879	29c	pale yel, blk, red & yel grn	50	15	☐☐☐☐☐
2527	A1879	29c	pale yel, blk, red & brt grn	50	15	☐☐☐☐☐
a.			Booklet pane of 10	5.00	—	☐☐☐☐☐
b.			As "a," vert. imperf. btwn.	—	—	☐☐☐☐☐
1991						
2528	A1880	29c	multicolored	50	15	☐☐☐☐☐
a.			Booklet pane of 10	5.00	—	☐☐☐☐☐
b.			As "a," horiz. imperf. btwn.	—	—	☐☐☐☐☐
Coil stamp, Perf. 10 Vertically						
2529	A1881	19c	multicolored	35	15	☐☐☐☐☐
Booklet stamp, Perf. 10 on 2 or 3 sides						
2530	A1882	19c	multicolored	35	15	☐☐☐☐☐
a.			Booklet pane of 10	3.50	—	☐☐☐☐☐
2531	A1883	29c	multicolored	50	15	☐☐☐☐☐
Die cut, Self-adhesive						
2531A	A1884	29c	black, gold & green	58	25	☐☐☐☐☐
b.			Pane of 18	10.50		☐☐☐☐☐
2532	A1887	50c	multicolored	1.00	25	☐☐☐☐☐
2533	A1888	29c	multicolored	50	15	☐☐☐☐☐
2534	A1889	29c	multicolored	50	15	☐☐☐☐☐
Perf. 12½x13						
2535	A1890	29c	multicolored	50	15	☐☐☐☐☐
a.			Perf. 11	58	15	☐☐☐☐☐
b.			Imperf., pair.....................	—		☐☐☐☐☐
Booklet stamp, Perf. 11 on 1 or 2 sides						
2536	A1890	29c	multicolored	50	15	☐☐☐☐☐
a.			Booklet pane of 10	5.00		☐☐☐☐☐
2537	A1891	52c	multicolored	90	20	☐☐☐☐☐
2538	A1892	29c	multicolored	50	15	☐☐☐☐☐
2539	A1893	$1	gold & multi	1.75	50	☐☐☐☐☐

A1893

A1897

A1894

A1899-A1903

A1895

A1896

A1904

A1905   **A1912**   **A1914**

A1915   **A1921**

1941: A World at War

A1913

A1907-A1911   A1916-A1920

Scott No.	Illus No.		Description	Unused Value	Used Value	//////
1991-93						
2540	A1894	$2.90	Priority	5.00	—	☐☐☐☐☐
2541	A1895	$9.95	Domestic express	17.50	—	☐☐☐☐☐
2542	A1896	$14	International express	25.00	—	☐☐☐☐☐
2543	A1897	$2.90	Priority	5.80	—	☐☐☐☐☐
1991						
2545	A1899	29c	multicolored	50	15	☐☐☐☐☐
2546	A1900	29c	multicolored	50	15	☐☐☐☐☐
2547	A1901	29c	multicolored	50	15	☐☐☐☐☐
2548	A1902	29c	multicolored	50	15	☐☐☐☐☐
2549	A1903	29c	multicolored	50	15	☐☐☐☐☐
a.			Bklt. pane of 5, #2545-2549	2.90	—	☐☐☐☐☐
2550	A1904	29c	multicolored	50	15	☐☐☐☐☐
a.			Vert. pair, imperf. horiz. ..	*550.00*		☐☐☐☐☐
2551	A1905	29c	multicolored	50	15	☐☐☐☐☐
2552	A1905	29c	multicolored	50	15	☐☐☐☐☐
a.			Booklet pane of 5	2.50	—	☐☐☐☐☐
2553	A1907	29c	multicolored	50	15	☐☐☐☐☐
2554	A1908	29c	multicolored	50	15	☐☐☐☐☐
2555	A1909	29c	multicolored	50	15	☐☐☐☐☐
2556	A1910	29c	multicolored	50	15	☐☐☐☐☐
2557	A1911	29c	multicolored	50	15	☐☐☐☐☐
a.			Strip of #2553-2557	2.90	—	☐☐☐☐☐
2558	A1912	29c	multicolored	50	15	☐☐☐☐☐
2559	A1913		Block of 10	5.80	—	☐☐☐☐☐
a.-j.		29c	any single	58	29	☐☐☐☐☐
k.			Black (engr.) omitted.......	—		☐☐☐☐☐
2560	A1914	29c	multicolored	50	15	☐☐☐☐☐
2561	A1915	29c	multicolored	50	15	☐☐☐☐☐
a.			Black (engr.) omitted.......	*350.00*		☐☐☐☐☐
2562	A1916	29c	multicolored	58	15	☐☐☐☐☐
2563	A1917	29c	multicolored	58	15	☐☐☐☐☐
2564	A1918	29c	multicolored	58	15	☐☐☐☐☐
2565	A1919	29c	multicolored	58	15	☐☐☐☐☐
2566	A1920	29c	multicolored	58	15	☐☐☐☐☐
a.			Bklt. pane, 2 each #2562-2566	6.00	—	☐☐☐☐☐
b.			As "a," scarlet & brt vio (engr.) omitted	*650.00*		☐☐☐☐☐
c.			Strip of 5, #2562-2566	2.90	—	☐☐☐☐☐
2567	A1921	29c	multicolored	50	15	☐☐☐☐☐
a.			Horiz. pair, imperf. vert. ..	—		☐☐☐☐☐
b.			Vert. pair, imperf. horiz. ..	—		☐☐☐☐☐
2568	A1922	29c	multicolored	50	15	☐☐☐☐☐
2569	A1923	29c	multicolored	50	15	☐☐☐☐☐
2570	A1924	29c	multicolored	50	15	☐☐☐☐☐

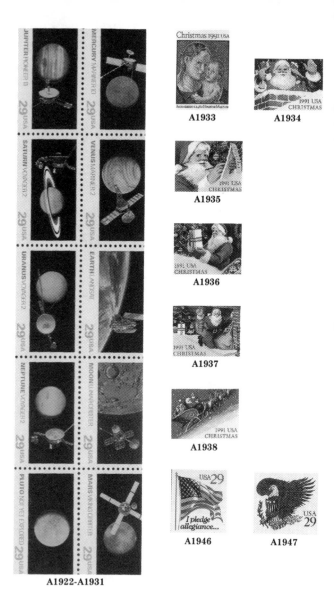

A1922-A1931

A1933

A1934

A1935

A1936

A1937

A1938

A1946

A1947

Scott No.	Illus No.		Description	Unused Value	Used Value	//////
2571	A1925	29c	multicolored	50	15	☐☐☐☐☐
2572	A1926	29c	multicolored	50	15	☐☐☐☐☐
2573	A1927	29c	multicolored	50	15	☐☐☐☐☐
2574	A1928	29c	multicolored	50	15	☐☐☐☐☐
2575	A1929	29c	multicolored	50	15	☐☐☐☐☐
2576	A1930	29c	multicolored	50	15	☐☐☐☐☐
2577	A1931	29c	multicolored	50	15	☐☐☐☐☐
a.			Bklt. pane of 10, #2568-2577	6.00	—	☐☐☐☐☐
2578	A1933	(29c)	multicolored	58	15	☐☐☐☐☐
a.			Booklet pane of 10	5.80	—	☐☐☐☐☐
b.			As "a," single, red & black (engr.) omitted	3,000.		☐☐☐☐☐
2579	A1934	(29c)	multicolored	58	15	☐☐☐☐☐
a.			Horiz. pair, imperf. vert. ..	550.00		☐☐☐☐☐
b.			Vert. pair, imperf. horiz. ..	—		☐☐☐☐☐
2580	A1934	(29c)	Type I	58	15	☐☐☐☐☐
2581	A1934	(29c)	Type II	58	15	☐☐☐☐☐
a.			Pair, #2580, 2581	1.16	25	☐☐☐☐☐
b.			Bklt. pane, 2 each #2580, 2581	2.40	—	☐☐☐☐☐
2582	A1935	(29c)	multicolored	58	15	☐☐☐☐☐
a.			Booklet pane of 4	2.40	—	☐☐☐☐☐
2583	A1936	(29c)	multicolored	58	15	☐☐☐☐☐
a.			Booklet pane of 4	2.40	—	☐☐☐☐☐
2584	A1937	(29c)	multicolored	58	15	☐☐☐☐☐
a.			Booklet pane of 4	2.40	—	☐☐☐☐☐
2585	A1938	(29c)	multicolored	58	15	☐☐☐☐☐
a.			Booklet pane of 4	2.40	—	☐☐☐☐☐

1992-93, Booklet stamps
Perf. 10 on 2 or 3 sides

2594	A1946	29c	black denomination	50	15	☐☐☐☐☐
a.			Booklet pane of 10	5.00	—	☐☐☐☐☐

Perf. 11x10 on 2 or 3 sides

2594B	A1946	29c	red denomination	50	15	☐☐☐☐☐
c.			Booklet pane of 10	5.00	—	☐☐☐☐☐

Die cut, Self-adhesive

2595	A1947	29c	brown & multi	50	25	☐☐☐☐☐
a.			Pane of 17 + label	8.50		☐☐☐☐☐
2596	A1947	29c	green & multi	50	25	☐☐☐☐☐
a.			Pane of 17 + label	8.50		☐☐☐☐☐
2597	A1947	29c	red & multi	50	25	☐☐☐☐☐
a.			Pane of 17 + label	8.50		☐☐☐☐☐

A1956

A1957

A1959

A1960

A1961

A1968

A1969

A1970

A1971

A1963-A1967

Scott No.	Illus No.		Description	Unused Value	Used Value	//////

1991-93, Coil stamps, Perf. 10 Vertically

Scott No.	Illus No.		Description	Unused Value	Used Value	//////
2604	A1956	(10c)	multicolored	20	15	☐☐☐☐☐
a.			Imperf. pair	—		☐☐☐☐☐
2605	A1957	(10c)	orange yellow & multi	20	20	☐☐☐☐☐
2606	A1957	(10c)	gold & multi	20	20	☐☐☐☐☐
2607	A1959	23c	multi (Bureau precancel in blue)	46	46	☐☐☐☐☐
2608	A1960	23c	multi (Bureau precanceled)	40	40	☐☐☐☐☐
2608A	A1960	23c	multi (Bureau precanceled)	40	40	☐☐☐☐☐
2608B	A1960	23c	First Class ⅝ x½mm long	40	40	☐☐☐☐☐
2609	A1961	29c	blue & red	50	15	☐☐☐☐☐

1992

Scott No.	Illus No.		Description	Unused Value	Used Value	//////
2611	A1963	29c	multicolored	50	15	☐☐☐☐☐
2612	A1964	29c	multicolored	50	15	☐☐☐☐☐
2613	A1965	29c	multicolored	50	15	☐☐☐☐☐
2614	A1966	29c	multicolored	50	15	☐☐☐☐☐
2615	A1967	29c	multicolored	50	15	☐☐☐☐☐
a.			Strip of 5, #2611-2615	2.90	—	☐☐☐☐☐
2616	A1968	29c	multicolored	50	15	☐☐☐☐☐
2617	A1969	29c	multicolored	50	15	☐☐☐☐☐
2618	A1970	29c	multicolored	50	15	☐☐☐☐☐
2619	A1971	29c	multicolored	50	15	☐☐☐☐☐
2620	A1972	29c	multicolored	50	15	☐☐☐☐☐
2621	A1973	29c	multicolored	50	15	☐☐☐☐☐
2622	A1974	29c	multicolored	50	15	☐☐☐☐☐
2623	A1975	29c	multicolored	50	15	☐☐☐☐☐
a.			Block of 4, #2620-2623	2.00	1.00	☐☐☐☐☐

Perf. 10½

Scott No.	Illus No.		Description	Unused Value	Used Value	//////
2624	A1976		Sheet of 3	2.10	—	☐☐☐☐☐
a.	A71	1c	deep blue	15	15	☐☐☐☐☐
b.	A74	4c	ultramarine	15	15	☐☐☐☐☐
c.	A82	$1	salmon	2.00	1.00	☐☐☐☐☐
2625	A1977		Sheet of 3	8.10	—	☐☐☐☐☐
a.	A72	2c	brown violet	15	15	☐☐☐☐☐
b.	A73	3c	green	15	15	☐☐☐☐☐
c.	A85	$4	crimson lake	8.00	4.00	☐☐☐☐☐
2626	A1978		Sheet of 3	1.70	—	☐☐☐☐☐
a.	A75	5c	chocolate	15	15	☐☐☐☐☐
b.	A80	30c	orange brown	60	30	☐☐☐☐☐
c.	A81	50c	slate blue	1.00	50	☐☐☐☐☐
2627	A1979		Sheet of 3	6.28	—	☐☐☐☐☐
a.	A76	6c	purple	15	15	☐☐☐☐☐
b.	A77	8c	magenta	16	15	☐☐☐☐☐
c.	A84	$3	yellow green	6.00	3.00	☐☐☐☐☐

A1972-A1975

A1976-A1981

A1982

A1983-A1986

A1987

A1988

A1989-A1993

235

A1994-A1998

A2050   **A2051**

A2052-A2055

Scott No.	Illus No.		Description	Unused Value	Used Value	//////
2628	A1980		Sheet of 3	4.50	—	
a.	A78	10c	black brown	20	15	
b.	A79	15c	dark green	30	15	
c.	A83	$2	brown red	4.00	2.00	
2629	A1981	$5	Sheet of 1, type A86	10.00	—	
2630	A1982	29c	green, red & black	50	15	
2631	A1983	29c	multicolored	50	15	
2632	A1984	29c	multicolored	50	15	
2633	A1985	29c	multicolored	50	15	
2634	A1986	29c	multicolored	50	15	
a.			Block of 4, #2631-2634 ...	2.00	—	
2635	A1987	29c	multicolored	50	15	
a.			Black (engr.) omitted	—		
2636	A1988	29c	multicolored	50	15	
2637	A1989	29c	multicolored	50	15	
2638	A1990	29c	multicolored	50	15	
2639	A1991	29c	multicolored	50	15	
2640	A1992	29c	multicolored	50	15	
2641	A1993	29c	multicolored	50	15	
a.			Strip of 5, #2637-2641	2.90	—	
2642	A1994	29c	multicolored	50	15	
2643	A1995	29c	multicolored	50	15	
2644	A1996	29c	multicolored	50	15	
2645	A1997	29c	multicolored	50	15	
2646	A1998	29c	multicolored	50	15	
a.			Bklt. pane of 5, #2642-2646	2.50	—	
2647	A1999	29c	Indian paintbrush	50	15	
2648	A2000	29c	Fragrant water lily	50	15	
2649	A2001	29c	Meadow beauty	50	15	
2650	A2002	29c	Jack-in-the-pulpit	50	15	
2651	A2003	29c	California poppy	50	15	
2652	A2004	29c	Large-flowered trillium ...	50	15	
2653	A2005	29c	Tickseed	50	15	
2654	A2006	29c	Shooting star..................	50	15	
2655	A2007	29c	Stream violet	50	15	
2656	A2008	29c	Bluets	50	15	
2657	A2009	29c	Herb Robert	50	15	
2658	A2010	29c	Marsh marigold	50	15	
2659	A2011	29c	Sweet white violet	50	15	
2660	A2012	29c	Claret cup cactus	50	15	
2661	A2013	29c	White mountain avens	50	15	
2662	A2014	29c	Sessile bellwort	50	15	
2663	A2015	29c	Blue flag	50	15	
2664	A2016	29c	Harlequin lupine	50	15	
2665	A2017	29c	Twinflower.....................	50	15	
2666	A2018	29c	Common sunflower	50	15	
2667	A2019	29c	Sego lily	50	15	

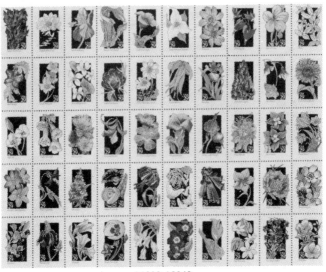

A1999-A2048

A2049

238

Scott No.	Illus No.		Description	Unused Value	Used Value	//////
2668	A2020	29c	Virginia bluebells	50	15	☐☐☐☐☐
2669	A2021	29c	Ohia lehua	50	15	☐☐☐☐☐
2670	A2022	29c	Rosebud orchid	50	15	☐☐☐☐☐
2671	A2023	29c	Showy evening primrose .	5⸍	15	☐☐☐☐☐
2672	A2024	29c	Fringed gentian	50	15	☐☐☐☐☐
2673	A2025	29c	Yellow ladys slipper	50	15	☐☐☐☐☐
2674	A2026	29c	Passionflower	50	15	☐☐☐☐☐
2675	A2027	29c	Bunchberry	50	15	☐☐☐☐☐
2676	A2028	29c	Pasqueflower	50	15	☐☐☐☐☐
2677	A2029	29c	Round-lobed hepatica	50	15	☐☐☐☐☐
2678	A2030	29c	Wild columbine	50	15	☐☐☐☐☐
2679	A2031	29c	Fireweed	50	15	☐☐☐☐☐
2680	A2032	29c	Indian pond lily	50	15	☐☐☐☐☐
2681	A2033	29c	Turks cap lily	50	15	☐☐☐☐☐
2682	A2034	29c	Dutchmans breeches	50	15	☐☐☐☐☐
2683	A2035	29c	Trumpet honeysuckle	50	15	☐☐☐☐☐
2684	A2036	29c	Jacobs ladder	50	15	☐☐☐☐☐
2685	A2037	29c	Plains prickly pear	50	15	☐☐☐☐☐
2686	A2038	29c	Moss campion	50	15	☐☐☐☐☐
2687	A2039	29c	Bearberry	50	15	☐☐☐☐☐
2688	A2040	29c	Mexican hat	50	15	☐☐☐☐☐
2689	A2041	29c	Harebell	50	15	☐☐☐☐☐
2690	A2042	29c	Desert five spot	50	15	☐☐☐☐☐
2691	A2043	29c	Smooth Solomons seal	50	15	☐☐☐☐☐
2692	A2044	29c	Red maids	50	15	☐☐☐☐☐
2693	A2045	29c	Yellow skunk cabbage	50	15	☐☐☐☐☐
2694	A2046	29c	Rue anemone	50	15	☐☐☐☐☐
2695	A2047	29c	Standing cypress	50	15	☐☐☐☐☐
2696	A2048	29c	Wild flax	50	15	☐☐☐☐☐
a.			Pane of 50, #2647-2696 ..	25.00	—	☐☐☐☐☐
2697	A2049		Block of 10	5.80	2.90	☐☐☐☐☐
a.-j.		29c	any single	58	29	☐☐☐☐☐
2698	A2050	29c	multicolored	50	15	☐☐☐☐☐
2699	A2051	29c	multicolored	50	15	☐☐☐☐☐
2700	A2052	29c	multicolored	50	15	☐☐☐☐☐
2701	A2053	29c	multicolored	50	15	☐☐☐☐☐
2702	A2054	29c	multicolored	50	15	☐☐☐☐☐
2703	A2055	29c	multicolored	50	15	☐☐☐☐☐
a.			Block or strip of 4, #2700-2703	2.00	1.10	☐☐☐☐☐
2704	A2056	29c	multicolored	50	15	☐☐☐☐☐
2705	A2057	29c	multicolored	50	15	☐☐☐☐☐
2706	A2058	29c	multicolored	50	15	☐☐☐☐☐
2707	A2059	29c	multicolored	50	15	☐☐☐☐☐
2708	A2060	29c	multicolored	50	15	☐☐☐☐☐
2709	A2061	29c	multicolored	50	15	☐☐☐☐☐
a.			Booklet pane of 5, #2705-2709	2.50	—	☐☐☐☐☐

A2056

A2062

A2067

King Penguins

White Bengal Tiger

A2057-A2061

A2068

A2063-A2066

Scott No.	Illus No.		Description	Unused Value	Used Value	//////
2710	A2062	29c	multicolored	50	15	
a.			Booklet pane of 10	5.00	—	
2711	A2063	29c	multicolored	50	15	
2712	A2064	29c	multicolored	50	15	
2713	A2065	29c	multicolored	50	15	
2714	A2066	29c	multicolored	50	15	
a.			Block of 4, #2711-2714 ...	2.00	1.10	
2715	A2063	29c	multicolored	50	15	
2716	A2064	29c	multicolored	50	15	
2717	A2065	29c	multicolored	50	15	
2718	A2066	29c	multicolored	50	15	
a.			Booklet pane of 4, #2715-2718	2.00	—	

Die cut, Self-adhesive

Scott No.	Illus No.		Description	Unused Value	Used Value	//////
2719	A2064	29c	multicolored	58	15	
a.			Booklet pane of 18	10.50		
2720	A2067	29c	multicolored	50	15	

1993

Scott No.	Illus No.		Description	Unused Value	Used Value	//////
2721	A2068	29c	multicolored	50	15	
2722	A2068	29c	Oklahoma	50	15	

Perf. 10

Scott No.	Illus No.		Description	Unused Value	Used Value	//////
2723	A2068	29c	Hank Williams	50	15	
2724	A2068	29c	Elvis Presley	50	15	
2725	A2068	29c	Bill Haley	50	15	
2726	A2068	29c	Clyde McPhatter	50	15	
2727	A2068	29c	Ritchie Valens	50	15	
2728	A2068	29c	Otis Redding	50	15	
2729	A2068	29c	Buddy Holly	50	15	
2730	A2068	29c	Dinah Washington	50	15	
a.			Vert. strip of 7, #2724-2730	3.50	—	

Booklet stamps, Perf. 11 Horiz.

Scott No.	Illus No.		Description	Unused Value	Used Value	//////
2731	A2068	29c	Presley	50	15	
2732	A2068	29c	Haley	50	15	
2733	A2068	29c	McPhatter	50	15	
2734	A2068	29c	Valens	50	15	
2735	A2068	29c	Redding	50	15	
2736	A2068	29c	Holly	50	15	
2737	A2068	29c	Washington	50	15	
a.			Booklet pane, 2 #2731, 1 each #2732-2737	4.00	—	
b.			Booklet pane, #2731, 2735-2737	2.00	—	
2741	A2086	29c	multicolored	50	15	
2742	A2087	29c	multicolored	50	15	

A2086-A2090

A2092

A2091

A2093

A2094

A2095-A2098

A2099

A2100

A2111

A2101-A2104

A2105-A2109

A2110

243

Scott No.	Illus No.		Description	Unused Value	Used Value	//////
2743	A2088	29c	multicolored	50	15	☐☐☐☐☐
2744	A2089	29c	multicolored	50	15	☐☐☐☐☐
2745	A2090	29c	multicolored	50	15	☐☐☐☐☐
a.			Booklet pane of 5, #2741-2745	2.50	—	☐☐☐☐☐
2746	A2091	29c	multicolored	50	15	☐☐☐☐☐
2747	A2092	29c	multicolored	50	15	☐☐☐☐☐
2748	A2093	29c	multicolored	50	15	☐☐☐☐☐
2749	A2094	29c	blue	50	15	☐☐☐☐☐
2750	A2095	29c	multicolored	50	15	☐☐☐☐☐
2751	A2096	29c	multicolored	50	15	☐☐☐☐☐
2752	A2097	29c	multicolored	50	15	☐☐☐☐☐
2753	A2098	29c	multicolored	50	15	☐☐☐☐☐
a.			Block of 4, #2750-2753 ...	2.00	1.10	☐☐☐☐☐
2754	A2099	29c	multicolored	50	15	☐☐☐☐☐
2755	A2100	29c	greenish gray	50	15	☐☐☐☐☐
2756	A2101	29c	multicolored	50	15	☐☐☐☐☐
2757	A2102	29c	multicolored	50	15	☐☐☐☐☐
2758	A2103	29c	multicolored	50	15	☐☐☐☐☐
2759	A2104	29c	multicolored	50	15	☐☐☐☐☐
2760	A2105	29c	multicolored	50	15	☐☐☐☐☐
2761	A2106	29c	multicolored	50	15	☐☐☐☐☐
2762	A2107	29c	multicolored	50	15	☐☐☐☐☐
2763	A2108	29c	multicolored	50	15	☐☐☐☐☐
2764	A2109	29c	multicolored	50	15	☐☐☐☐☐
2765	A2110		Block of 10	5.80	3.00	☐☐☐☐☐
a.-j.		29c	any single	58	30	☐☐☐☐☐
2766	A2111	29c	multicolored	50	15	☐☐☐☐☐
2767	A2068	29c	Show Boat	50	15	☐☐☐☐☐
2768	A2068	29c	Porgy & Bess	50	15	☐☐☐☐☐
2769	A2068	29c	Oklahoma	50	15	☐☐☐☐☐
2770	A2068	29c	My Fair Lady	50	15	☐☐☐☐☐
a.			Booklet pane of 4, #2767-2770	2.00	—	☐☐☐☐☐
			_____			☐☐☐☐☐
			_____			☐☐☐☐☐
			_____			☐☐☐☐☐
			_____			☐☐☐☐☐
			_____			☐☐☐☐☐
			_____			☐☐☐☐☐
			_____			☐☐☐☐☐
			_____			☐☐☐☐☐
			_____			☐☐☐☐☐
			_____			☐☐☐☐☐
			_____			☐☐☐☐☐
			_____			☐☐☐☐☐
			_____			☐☐☐☐☐
			_____			☐☐☐☐☐

AP1 AP2 AP3 AP4

AP5 AP6

AP7

AP8

AP9 AP10

AP11 AP12

AP13

AP14 AP15

246

Scott No.	Illus No.		Description	Unused Value	Used Value	//////
AIR POST STAMPS						
1918						
C1	AP1	6c	orange	55.00	25.00	☐☐☐☐☐
C2	AP1	16c	green	80.00	27.50	☐☐☐☐☐
C3	AP1	24c	carmine rose & blue	80.00	32.50	☐☐☐☐☐
a.			Center inverted	*135,000.*		☐☐☐☐☐
1923						
C4	AP2	8c	dark green	22.50	12.00	☐☐☐☐☐
C5	AP3	16c	dark blue	80.00	27.50	☐☐☐☐☐
C6	AP4	24c	carmine	80.00	22.50	☐☐☐☐☐
1926-28, Perf. 11						
C7	AP5	10c	dark blue	2.50	25	☐☐☐☐☐
C8	AP5	15c	olive brown	3.00	1.90	☐☐☐☐☐
C9	AP5	20c	yellow green	8.50	1.65	☐☐☐☐☐
C10	AP6	10c	dark blue	6.75	1.65	☐☐☐☐☐
a.			Booklet pane of 3	82.50	*50.00*	☐☐☐☐☐
C11	AP7	5c	carmine & blue	3.75	40	☐☐☐☐☐
a.			Vert. pair, imperf. btwn. ..	*5,500.*		☐☐☐☐☐
C12	AP8	5c	violet	8.00	25	☐☐☐☐☐
a.			Horiz. pair, imperf. btwn.	*4,500.*		☐☐☐☐☐
1930						
C13	AP9	65c	green	250.00	150.00	☐☐☐☐☐
C14	AP10	$1.30	brown	575.00	350.00	☐☐☐☐☐
C15	AP11	$2.60	blue	900.00	500.00	☐☐☐☐☐
1931-32, Perf. 10½x11						
C16	AP8	5c	violet	5.00	35	☐☐☐☐☐
C17	AP8	8c	olive bister	1.90	20	☐☐☐☐☐
1933						
C18	AP12	50c	green	75.00	65.00	☐☐☐☐☐
1934						
C19	AP8	6c	dull orange	2.25	15	☐☐☐☐☐
1935						
C20	AP13	25c	blue	1.10	75	☐☐☐☐☐
1937						
C21	AP14	20c	green	8.50	1.25	☐☐☐☐☐
C22	AP14	50c	carmine	8.00	4.00	☐☐☐☐☐

AP16

AP17

AP19

AP18

AP20

AP21

AP22

AP24

AP23

AP25

AP26

AP27

AP28

AP29

AP30

Scott No.	Illus No.		Description	Unused Value	Used Value	/ / / / / /
1938						
C23	AP15	6c	dark blue & carmine	40	15	☐☐☐☐☐
a.			Vert. pair, imperf. horiz. ..	300.00		☐☐☐☐☐
b.			Horiz. pair, imperf. vert ...	*10,000.*		☐☐☐☐☐
c.		6c	ultramarine & carmine	150.00		☐☐☐☐☐
1939						
C24	AP16	30c	dull blue	7.50	1.00	☐☐☐☐☐
1941-44						
C25	AP17	6c	carmine	15	15	☐☐☐☐☐
a.			Booklet pane of 3	3.50	*1.00*	☐☐☐☐☐
b.			Horiz. pair, imperf. btwn.	*1,500.*		☐☐☐☐☐
C26	AP17	8c	olive green	16	15	☐☐☐☐☐
C27	AP17	10c	violet	1.10	20	☐☐☐☐☐
C28	AP17	15c	brown carmine	2.25	35	☐☐☐☐☐
C29	AP17	20c	bright green	1.75	30	☐☐☐☐☐
C30	AP17	30c	blue	2.00	30	☐☐☐☐☐
C31	AP17	50c	orange	10.00	3.75	☐☐☐☐☐
1946						
C32	AP18	5c	carmine	15	15	☐☐☐☐☐
1947, Perf. 10½x11						
C33	AP19	5c	carmine	15	15	☐☐☐☐☐
C34	AP20	10c	black	25	15	☐☐☐☐☐
C35	AP21	15c	bright blue green	35	15	☐☐☐☐☐
a.			Horiz. pair, imperf. btwn.	*1,500.*		☐☐☐☐☐
C36	AP22	25c	blue	85	15	☐☐☐☐☐
1948, Coil stamp, Perf. 10 Horizontally						
C37	AP19	5c	carmine	80	75	☐☐☐☐☐
1948						
C38	AP23	5c	bright carmine	15	15	☐☐☐☐☐
1949, Perf. 10½x11						
C39	AP19	6c	carmine	15	15	☐☐☐☐☐
a.			Booklet pane of 6	9.50	*4.00*	☐☐☐☐☐
1949						
C40	AP24	6c	carmine	15	15	☐☐☐☐☐
Coil stamp, Perf. 10 Horizontally						
C41	AP19	6c	carmine	2.75	15	☐☐☐☐☐
1949						
C42	AP25	10c	violet	20	18	☐☐☐☐☐

AP31

AP32

AP33

AP34

AP35

AP36

AP38

AP37

AP39

AP40

AP42

AP41-Redrawn

AP43

AP44

AP45

AP47

AP46

250

Scott No.	Illus No.	Description	Unused Value	Used Value	//////
C43	AP26	15c ultramarine	30	25	☐☐☐☐☐
C44	AP27	25c rose carmine	50	40	☐☐☐☐☐
C45	AP28	6c magenta	15	15	☐☐☐☐☐

1952-58

C46	AP29	80c bright red violet	6.00	1.00	☐☐☐☐☐
C47	AP30	6c carmine	15	15	☐☐☐☐☐
C48	AP31	4c bright blue	15	15	☐☐☐☐☐
C49	AP32	6c blue	15	15	☐☐☐☐☐
C50	AP31	5c rose red	15	15	☐☐☐☐☐

Perf. 10½x11

C51	AP33	7c blue	15	15	☐☐☐☐☐
a.		Booklet pane of 6	11.00	*6.00*	☐☐☐☐☐

Coil stamp, Perf. 10 Horizontally

C52	AP33	7c blue	2.25	15	☐☐☐☐☐

1959

C53	AP34	7c dark blue	15	15	☐☐☐☐☐
C54	AP35	7c dark blue & red	15	15	☐☐☐☐☐
C55	AP36	7c rose red	15	15	☐☐☐☐☐
C56	AP37	10c violet blue & bright red ..	24	24	☐☐☐☐☐

1959-66

C57	AP38	10c black & green	1.40	70	☐☐☐☐☐
C58	AP39	15c black & orange	35	15	☐☐☐☐☐
C59	AP40	25c black & maroon	48	15	☐☐☐☐☐
a.		Tagged	60	25	☐☐☐☐☐

Perf. 10½x11

C60	AP33	7c carmine	15	15	☐☐☐☐☐
a.		Booklet pane of 6	15.00	*7.00*	☐☐☐☐☐

Coil stamp, Perf. 10 Horizontally

C61	AP33	7c carmine	4.00	25	☐☐☐☐☐

1961-67

C62	AP38	13c black & red	40	15	☐☐☐☐☐
a.		Tagged	75	50	☐☐☐☐☐
C63	AP41	15c black & orange	30	15	☐☐☐☐☐
a.		Tagged	40	15	☐☐☐☐☐
b.		As "a," horiz. pair, imperf. vert.	*15,000.*		☐☐☐☐☐

AP50

AP48

AP51

AP49

AP52

AP53

AP54

AP55

AP56

AP57

AP58

AP59

AP60

AP61

AP62

AP63

AP70

252

Scott No.	Illus No.		Description	Unused Value	Used Value	//////
Perf. 10½x11						
C64	AP42	8c	carmine	15	15	☐☐☐☐☐
a.			Tagged	20	15	☐☐☐☐☐
b.			Booklet pane 5 + label	6.75	*2.50*	☐☐☐☐☐
c.			As "b," tagged	1.75	*50*	☐☐☐☐☐
Coil stamp, Perf. 10 horizontally						
C65	AP42	8c	carmine	40	15	☐☐☐☐☐
a.			Tagged	35	15	☐☐☐☐☐
1963-67						
C66	AP43	15c	carmine, deep claret & blue	60	55	☐☐☐☐☐
C67	AP44	6c	red	15	15	☐☐☐☐☐
a.			Tagged	2.75	80	☐☐☐☐☐
C68	AP45	8c	carmine & maroon	20	15	☐☐☐☐☐
C69	AP46	8c	blue, red & bister	45	15	☐☐☐☐☐
C70	AP47	8c	brown	24	15	☐☐☐☐☐
C71	AP48	20c	multicolored	80	15	☐☐☐☐☐
1968, Perf. 11x10½						
C72	AP49	10c	carmine	20	15	☐☐☐☐☐
b.			Booklet pane of 8	2.00	75	☐☐☐☐☐
c.			Booklet pane of 5 + label	3.75	75	☐☐☐☐☐
Coil stamp, Perf. 10 Vertically						
C73	AP49	10c	carmine	30	15	☐☐☐☐☐
a.			Imperf., pair	*600.00*		☐☐☐☐☐
1968						
C74	AP50	10c	blue, black & red	25	15	☐☐☐☐☐
a.			Red (tail stripe) omitted ...	—		☐☐☐☐☐
C75	AP51	20c	red, blue & black	48	15	☐☐☐☐☐
1969						
C76	AP52	10c	multicolored	20	15	☐☐☐☐☐
a.			Rose red (litho.) omitted ..	*425.00*	—	☐☐☐☐☐
1971-73						
C77	AP53	9c	red	18	15	☐☐☐☐☐
C78	AP54	11c	carmine	20	15	☐☐☐☐☐
a.			Booklet pane of 4 + 2 labels	1.25	75	☐☐☐☐☐
b.			Untagged (Bureau precanceled)		30	☐☐☐☐☐
C79	AP55	13c	carmine	22	15	☐☐☐☐☐
a.			Booklet pane of 5 + label	1.25	75	☐☐☐☐☐
b.			Untagged (Bureau precanceled)		28	☐☐☐☐☐

AP64

AP66

AP68

AP65

AP67

AP69

Philip Mazzei
Patriot Remembered

AP72

AP71

AP73

AP81

AP86

AP87

AP88

AP89

AP90

Scott No.	Illus No.		Description	Unused Value	Used Value	//////
C80	AP56	17c	bluish black, red & dark green	35	15	☐☐☐☐☐
C81	AP51	21c	red, blue & black	40	15	☐☐☐☐☐

Coil stamps, Perf. 10 vertically

C82	AP54	11c	carmine	25	15	☐☐☐☐☐
a.			Imperf., pair	*175.00*		☐☐☐☐☐
C83	AP55	13c	carmine	26	15	☐☐☐☐☐
a.			Imperf., pair	80.00		☐☐☐☐☐

1972-74

C84	AP57	11c	orange & multi	20	15	☐☐☐☐☐
a.			Blue & green (litho) omitted	*1,400.*		☐☐☐☐☐
C85	AP58	11c	multicolored	22	15	☐☐☐☐☐
C86	AP59	11c	rose lilac & multi	22	15	☐☐☐☐☐
a.			Vermilion & olive (litho.) omitted	*1,500.*		☐☐☐☐☐
C87	AP60	18c	carmine, black & ultra	40	25	☐☐☐☐☐
C88	AP61	26c	ultra, black & carmine	48	15	☐☐☐☐☐

1976

C89	AP62	25c	ultra, red & black	45	15	☐☐☐☐☐
C90	AP63	31c	ultra, red & black	55	15	☐☐☐☐☐

1978

C91	AP64	31c	ultra & multi	65	30	☐☐☐☐☐
C92	AP65	31c	ultra & multi	65	30	☐☐☐☐☐
a.			Vert. pair, #C91-C92	1.30	85	☐☐☐☐☐
b.			As "a," ultramarine & black (engr.) omitted	*900.00*		☐☐☐☐☐
c.			As "a," black (engr.) omitted	—		☐☐☐☐☐
d.			As "a," black, yellow, magenta, blue & brown (litho.) omitted	*2,250.*		☐☐☐☐☐

1979

C93	AP66	21c	ultra & multi	70	32	☐☐☐☐☐
C94	AP67	21c	ultra & multi	70	32	☐☐☐☐☐
a.			Vert. pair, #C93-C94	1.40	95	☐☐☐☐☐
b.			As "a," ultramarine & black (engr.) omitted	*4,000.*		☐☐☐☐☐
C95	AP68	25c	ultra & multi	1.10	35	☐☐☐☐☐
C96	AP69	25c	ultra & multi	1.10	35	☐☐☐☐☐
a.			Vert. pair, #C95-C96	2.25	95	☐☐☐☐☐
C97	AP70	31c	multicolored	65	30	☐☐☐☐☐

AP91

AP92

AP93

AP94

AP95-98

AP99

AP100

AP101

AP102

AP103

Scott No.	Illus No.		Description	Unused Value	Used Value	//////
1980						
C98	AP71	40c	multicolored	70	15	☐☐☐☐☐
a.			Perf. 10½x11	3.00	—	☐☐☐☐☐
b.			Imperf., pair	*3,250.*		☐☐☐☐☐
c.			Horiz. pair, imperf. vert. ..	—		☐☐☐☐☐
C99	AP72	28c	multicolored	55	15	☐☐☐☐☐
C100	AP73	35c	multicolored	60	15	☐☐☐☐☐
1983						
C101	AP81	28c	Gymnast	60	28	☐☐☐☐☐
C102	AP81	28c	Hurdler	60	28	☐☐☐☐☐
C103	AP81	28c	Basketball	60	28	☐☐☐☐☐
C104	AP81	28c	Soccer	60	28	☐☐☐☐☐
a.			Block of 4, #C101-C104 .	2.50	1.75	☐☐☐☐☐
b.			As "a," imperf. vert.	—		☐☐☐☐☐
C105	AP81	40c	Shot put	90	40	☐☐☐☐☐
a.			Perf. 11x10½	1.00	45	☐☐☐☐☐
C106	AP81	40c	Gymnast	90	40	☐☐☐☐☐
a.			Perf. 11x10½	1.00	45	☐☐☐☐☐
C107	AP81	40c	Swimmer	90	40	☐☐☐☐☐
a.			Perf. 11x10½	1.00	45	☐☐☐☐☐
C108	AP81	40c	Weightlifting	90	40	☐☐☐☐☐
a.			Block of 4, #C105-C108 .	3.60	2.00	☐☐☐☐☐
b.			As "a," imperf.	*1,350.*		☐☐☐☐☐
c.			Perf. 11x10½	1.00	45	☐☐☐☐☐
d.			As "a," perf. 11x10½	4.25	—	☐☐☐☐☐
C109	AP81	35c	Womens fencing..............	90	35	☐☐☐☐☐
C110	AP81	35c	Cycling	90	35	☐☐☐☐☐
C111	AP81	35c	Womens volleyball	90	35	☐☐☐☐☐
C112	AP81	35c	Pole vaulting...................	90	35	☐☐☐☐☐
a.			Block of 4, #C109-C112 .	3.60	1.85	☐☐☐☐☐
1985						
C113	AP86	33c	multicolored	60	20	☐☐☐☐☐
a.			Imperf., pair....................	850.00		☐☐☐☐☐
C114	AP87	39c	multicolored	70	20	☐☐☐☐☐
a.			Imperf., pair....................	*1,250.*		☐☐☐☐☐
C115	AP88	44c	multicolored	80	20	☐☐☐☐☐
a.			Imperf., pair....................	800.00		☐☐☐☐☐
C116	AP89	44c	multicolored	80	20	☐☐☐☐☐
a.			Imperf., pair....................	—		☐☐☐☐☐
1988						
C117	AP90	44c	multicolored	1.00	20	☐☐☐☐☐
C118	AP91	45c	multicolored	80	20	☐☐☐☐☐
C119	AP92	36c	multicolored	65	20	☐☐☐☐☐

Scott No.	Illus No.		Description	Unused Value	Used Value	//////
1989						
C120	AP93	45c	multicolored	80	22	☐☐☐☐☐
C121	AP94	45c	multicolored	80	22	☐☐☐☐☐
C122	AP95	45c	multicolored	90	30	☐☐☐☐☐
C123	AP96	45c	multicolored	90	30	☐☐☐☐☐
C124	AP97	45c	multicolored	90	30	☐☐☐☐☐
C125	AP98	45c	multicolored	90	30	☐☐☐☐☐
a.			Block of 4, #C122-C125 .	3.60	2.25	☐☐☐☐☐
b.			As "a," light blue (engr.) omitted	1,500.		☐☐☐☐☐
C126			Sheet of 4	3.60	2.25	☐☐☐☐☐
a.	AP95	45c	multicolored	90	50	☐☐☐☐☐
b.	AP96	45c	multicolored	90	50	☐☐☐☐☐
c.	AP97	45c	multicolored	90	50	☐☐☐☐☐
d.	AP98	45c	multicolored	90	50	☐☐☐☐☐
1990						
C127	AP99	45c	multicolored	90	20	☐☐☐☐☐
1991						
C128	AP100	50c	multicolored	1.00	24	☐☐☐☐☐
a.			Vert. pair, imperf. horiz. ..	—		☐☐☐☐☐
C129	AP101	40c	multicolored	80	22	☐☐☐☐☐
C130	AP102	50c	multicolored	1.00	24	☐☐☐☐☐
C131	AP103	50c	multicolored	1.10	24	☐☐☐☐☐

259

ASPD1

SD1

SD2

SD3

SD4

SD5

SD6

SD7

SD8

SD9

Scott No.	Illus No.	Description	Unused Value	Used Value	//////

AIR POST SPECIAL DELIVERY STAMPS

1934

Scott No.	Illus No.	Description	Unused Value	Used Value	
CE1	APSD1	16c dark blue	55	65	☐☐☐☐☐

1936

Scott No.	Illus No.	Description	Unused Value	Used Value	
CE2	APSD1	16c red & blue	30	20	☐☐☐☐☐
a.		Horiz. pair, imperf. vert. ..	*3,750.*		☐☐☐☐☐

SPECIAL DELIVERY STAMPS

1885-93

Scott No.	Illus No.	Description	Unused Value	Used Value	
E1	SD1	10c blue	185.00	27.50	☐☐☐☐☐
E2	SD2	10c blue	175.00	7.50	☐☐☐☐☐
E3	SD2	10c orange	110.00	15.00	☐☐☐☐☐

1894, Line under "TEN CENTS"

Scott No.	Illus No.	Description	Unused Value	Used Value	
E4	SD3	10c blue	450.00	14.00	☐☐☐☐☐

1895, Watermark 191

Scott No.	Illus No.	Description	Unused Value	Used Value	
E5	SD3	10c blue	90.00	1.90	☐☐☐☐☐
b.		Printed on both sides	*1,250.*		☐☐☐☐☐

1902

Scott No.	Illus No.	Description	Unused Value	Used Value	
E6	SD4	10c ultramarine	55.00	1.90	☐☐☐☐☐

1908

Scott No.	Illus No.	Description	Unused Value	Used Value	
E7	SD5	10c green	40.00	24.00	☐☐☐☐☐

1911, Watermark 190, Perf. 12

Scott No.	Illus No.	Description	Unused Value	Used Value	
E8	SD4	10c ultramarine	55.00	2.50	☐☐☐☐☐
b.		10c violet blue	55.00	2.50	☐☐☐☐☐

1914, Perf. 10

Scott No.	Illus No.	Description	Unused Value	Used Value	
E9	SD4	10c ultramarine	110.00	3.00	☐☐☐☐☐

1916, Perf. 10, Unwatermarked

Scott No.	Illus No.	Description	Unused Value	Used Value	
E10	SD4	10c pale ultramarine	200.00	15.00	☐☐☐☐☐

1917-25, Perf. 11

Scott No.	Illus No.	Description	Unused Value	Used Value	
E11	SD4	10c ultramarine	10.00	25	☐☐☐☐☐
b.		10c gray violet	10.00	25	☐☐☐☐☐
c.		10c blue	20.00	60	☐☐☐☐☐
E12	SD6	10c gray violet	18.00	15	☐☐☐☐☐
a.		10c deep ultramarine	25.00	20	☐☐☐☐☐
E13	SD6	15c deep orange	15.00	50	☐☐☐☐☐
E14	SD7	20c black	1.65	85	☐☐☐☐☐

Scott No.	Illus No.	Description	Unused Value	Used Value	/////
1927-51, Perf. 11x10½					
E15	SD6	10c gray violet	60	15	☐☐☐☐☐
a.		10c red lilac	60	15	☐☐☐☐☐
b.		10c gray lilac	60	15	☐☐☐☐☐
c.		Horiz. pair, imperf. btwn.	275.00		☐☐☐☐☐
E16	SD6	15c orange	70	15	☐☐☐☐☐
E17	SD6	13c blue	60	15	☐☐☐☐☐
E18	SD6	17c orange yellow	2.75	1.75	☐☐☐☐☐
E19	SD7	20c black	1.25	15	☐☐☐☐☐
1954-57					
E20	SD8	20c deep blue	40	15	☐☐☐☐☐
E21	SD8	30c lake	50	15	☐☐☐☐☐
1969-71					
E22	SD9	45c carmine & violet blue	1.25	15	☐☐☐☐☐
E23	SD9	60c violet blue & carmine	1.10	15	☐☐☐☐☐
					☐☐☐☐☐
					☐☐☐☐☐
					☐☐☐☐☐
					☐☐☐☐☐
					☐☐☐☐☐
					☐☐☐☐☐
					☐☐☐☐☐
					☐☐☐☐☐
					☐☐☐☐☐
					☐☐☐☐☐
					☐☐☐☐☐
					☐☐☐☐☐
					☐☐☐☐☐
					☐☐☐☐☐
					☐☐☐☐☐
					☐☐☐☐☐
					☐☐☐☐☐
					☐☐☐☐☐
					☐☐☐☐☐
					☐☐☐☐☐
					☐☐☐☐☐
					☐☐☐☐☐
					☐☐☐☐☐
					☐☐☐☐☐
					☐☐☐☐☐
					☐☐☐☐☐

RS1

CM1

Scott No.	Illus No.	Description	Unused Value	Used Value	//////
REGISTRATION STAMP					
1911					
F1	RS1	10c ultramarine	55.00	3.00	☐☐☐☐☐
CERTIFIED MAIL STAMP					
1955					
FA1	CM1	15c red	30	20	☐☐☐☐☐

D1

D2

D3   D4   D5

HOW TO USE THIS BOOK

The number in the first column is its Scott number or identifying number. The letter and number that come next (A41) indicate the design and refer to the illustration so designated. Following that is the denomination of the stamp and its color. Finally, the value, unused and used is shown.

POSTAGE DUE STAMPS
1879, Perf. 12

J1	D1	1c	brown	30.00	5.00	☐☐☐☐☐
J2	D1	2c	brown	200.00	4.00	☐☐☐☐☐
J3	D1	3c	brown	25.00	2.50	☐☐☐☐☐
J4	D1	5c	brown	300.00	30.00	☐☐☐☐☐
J5	D1	10c	brown	350.00	15.00	☐☐☐☐☐
a.			Imperf., pair	1,600.		☐☐☐☐☐
J6	D1	30c	brown	175.00	35.00	☐☐☐☐☐
J7	D1	50c	brown	225.00	40.00	☐☐☐☐☐

1879, Special Printing

J8	D1	1c	deep brown	6,250.	☐☐☐☐☐
J9	D1	2c	deep brown	4,250.	☐☐☐☐☐
J10	D1	3c	deep brown	3,900.	☐☐☐☐☐
J11	D1	5c	deep brown	3,250.	☐☐☐☐☐
J12	D1	10c	deep brown	2,250.	☐☐☐☐☐
J13	D1	30c	deep brown	2,250.	☐☐☐☐☐
J14	D1	50c	deep brown	2,400.	☐☐☐☐☐

1884-89

J15	D1	1c	red brown	30.00	2.50	☐☐☐☐☐
J16	D1	2c	red brown	40.00	2.50	☐☐☐☐☐
J17	D1	3c	red brown	500.00	100.00	☐☐☐☐☐
J18	D1	5c	red brown	250.00	15.00	☐☐☐☐☐
J19	D1	10c	red brown	225.00	10.00	☐☐☐☐☐
J20	D1	30c	red brown	110.00	30.00	☐☐☐☐☐
J21	D1	50c	red brown	1,000.	125.00	☐☐☐☐☐

1891-93

J22	D1	1c	bright claret	14.00	50	☐☐☐☐☐
J23	D1	2c	bright claret	15.00	45	☐☐☐☐☐
J24	D1	3c	bright claret	32.50	5.00	☐☐☐☐☐
J25	D1	5c	bright claret	35.00	5.00	☐☐☐☐☐
J26	D1	10c	bright claret	70.00	11.00	☐☐☐☐☐
J27	D1	30c	bright claret	250.00	90.00	☐☐☐☐☐
J28	D1	50c	bright claret	275.00	90.00	☐☐☐☐☐

1894

J29	D2	1c	vermilion	650.00	200.00	☐☐☐☐☐
J30	D2	2c	vermilion	300.00	60.00	☐☐☐☐☐
J31	D2	1c	deep claret	22.50	3.00	☐☐☐☐☐
b.			Vert. pair, imperf. horiz.	—		☐☐☐☐☐
J32	D2	2c	deep claret	17.50	1.75	☐☐☐☐☐
J33	D2	3c	deep claret	75.00	20.00	☐☐☐☐☐
J34	D2	5c	deep claret	100.00	22.50	☐☐☐☐☐
J35	D2	10c	deep claret	100.00	17.50	☐☐☐☐☐

Scott No.	Illus No.		Description	Unused Value	Used Value	//////
J36	D2	30c	deep claret	225.00	60.00	
a.		30c	carmine	225.00	60.00	
b.		30c	pale rose	210.00	55.00	
J37	D2	50c	deep claret	500.00	150.00	
a.		50c	pale rose	450.00	135.00	

1895, Watermark 191
Scott No.	Illus No.		Description	Unused Value	Used Value	//////
J38	D2	1c	deep claret	5.00	30	
J39	D2	2c	deep claret	5.00	20	
J40	D2	3c	deep claret	35.00	1.00	
J41	D2	5c	deep claret	37.50	1.00	
J42	D2	10c	deep claret	40.00	2.00	
J43	D2	30c	deep claret	300.00	25.00	
J44	D2	50c	deep claret	190.00	20.00	

1910-12, Watermark 190
Scott No.	Illus No.		Description	Unused Value	Used Value	//////
J45	D2	1c	deep claret	20.00	2.00	
a.		1c	rose carmine	17.50	1.75	
J46	D2	2c	deep claret	20.00	30	
a.		2c	rose carmine	17.50	30	
J47	D2	3c	deep claret	350.00	17.50	
J48	D2	5c	deep claret	60.00	3.50	
a.		5c	rose carmine	—	—	
J49	D2	10c	deep claret	75.00	7.50	
a.		10c	rose carmine	—	—	
J50	D2	50c	deep claret	600.00	75.00	

1914-15, Perf. 10
Scott No.	Illus No.		Description	Unused Value	Used Value	//////
J52	D2	1c	carmine lake	40.00	7.50	
a.		1c	dull rose	40.00	7.50	
J53	D2	2c	carmine lake	32.50	20	
a.		2c	dull rose	32.50	20	
b.		2c	vermilion	32.50	20	
J54	D2	3c	carmine lake	425.00	20.00	
a.		3c	dull rose	425.00	20.00	
J55	D2	5c	carmine lake	25.00	1.50	
a.		5c	dull rose	25.00	1.50	
J56	D2	10c	carmine lake	40.00	1.00	
a.		10c	dull rose	40.00	1.00	
J57	D2	30c	carmine lake	145.00	12.00	
J58	D2	50c	carmine lake	6,500.	375.00	

1916, Perf. 10, Unwatermarked
Scott No.	Illus No.		Description	Unused Value	Used Value	//////
J59	D2	1c	rose	1,100.	175.00	
J60	D2	2c	rose	85.00	10.00	

Scott No.	Illus No.		Description	Unused Value	Used Value	//////
1917, Perf. 11						
J61	D2	1c	carmine rose	1.75	15	
a.		1c	rose red	1.75	15	
b.		1c	deep claret	1.75	15	
J62	D2	2c	carmine rose	1.50	15	
a.		2c	rose red	1.50	15	
b.		2c	deep claret	1.50	15	
J63	D2	3c	carmine rose	8.50	15	
a.		3c	rose red	8.50	15	
b.		3c	deep claret	8.50	25	
J64	D2	5c	carmine	8.50	15	
a.		5c	rose red	8.50	15	
b.		5c	deep claret	8.50	15	
J65	D2	10c	carmine rose	12.50	20	
a.		10c	rose red	12.50	15	
b.		10c	deep claret	12.50	15	
J66	D2	30c	carmine rose	60.00	40	
a.		30c	deep claret	60.00	40	
J67	D2	50c	carmine rose	75.00	15	
a.		50c	rose red	75.00	15	
b.		50c	deep claret	75.00	15	
1925						
J68	D2	½c	dull red	70	15	
1930-31, Perf. 11						
J69	D3	½c	carmine	3.50	1.00	
J70	D3	1c	carmine	2.50	15	
J71	D3	2c	carmine	3.00	15	
J72	D3	3c	carmine	15.00	1.00	
J73	D3	5c	carmine	14.00	1.50	
J74	D3	10c	carmine	30.00	50	
J75	D3	30c	carmine	85.00	1.00	
J76	D3	50c	carmine	100.00	30	
J77	D4	$1	carmine	25.00	15	
a.		$1	scarlet	20.00	15	
J78	D4	$5	carmine	30.00	15	
a.		$5	scarlet	25.00	15	
1931-56, Perf. 11x10½, 10½x11						
J79	D3	½c	dull carmine	75	15	
J80	D3	1c	dull carmine	15	15	
J81	D3	2c	dull carmine	15	15	
J82	D3	3c	dull carmine	25	15	
J83	D3	5c	dull carmine	35	15	
J84	D3	10c	dull carmine	1.10	15	
J85	D3	30c	dull carmine	8.00	15	
J86	D3	50c	dull carmine	9.50	15	

Scott No.	Illus No.		Description	Unused Value	Used Value	//////
J79a	D3	½c	scarlet	75	15	☐☐☐☐☐
J80a	D3	1c	scarlet	15	15	☐☐☐☐☐
J81a	D3	2c	scarlet	15	15	☐☐☐☐☐
J82a	D3	3c	scarlet	25	15	☐☐☐☐☐
J83a	D3	5c	scarlet	35	15	☐☐☐☐☐
J84a	D3	10c	scarlet	1.10	15	☐☐☐☐☐
J85a	D3	30c	scarlet	8.00	15	☐☐☐☐☐
J86a	D3	50c	scarlet	9.50	15	☐☐☐☐☐
J87	D4	$1	scarlet	35.00	20	☐☐☐☐☐

1959

Scott No.	Illus No.		Description	Unused Value	Used Value	//////
J88	D5	½c	carmine rose	1.25	85	☐☐☐☐☐
J89	D5	1c	carmine rose	15	15	☐☐☐☐☐
a.			1 CENT omitted	375.00		☐☐☐☐☐
b.			Pair, one without 1 CENT	—		☐☐☐☐☐
J90	D5	2c	carmine rose	15	15	☐☐☐☐☐
J91	D5	3c	carmine rose	15	15	☐☐☐☐☐
a.			Pair, one without 3 CENTS	800.00		☐☐☐☐☐
J92	D5	4c	carmine rose	15	15	☐☐☐☐☐
J93	D5	5c	carmine rose	15	15	☐☐☐☐☐
a.			Pair, one without 5 CENTS	—		☐☐☐☐☐
J94	D5	6c	carmine rose	15	15	☐☐☐☐☐
a.			Pair, one without 6 CENTS	800.00		☐☐☐☐☐
J95	D5	7c	carmine rose	15	15	☐☐☐☐☐
J96	D5	8c	carmine rose	16	15	☐☐☐☐☐
a.			Pair, one without 8 CENTS	800.00		☐☐☐☐☐
J97	D5	10c	carmine rose	20	15	☐☐☐☐☐
J98	D5	30c	carmine rose	55	15	☐☐☐☐☐
J99	D5	50c	carmine rose	90	15	☐☐☐☐☐
J100	D5	$1	carmine rose	1.50	15	☐☐☐☐☐
J101	D5	$5	carmine rose	8.00	15	☐☐☐☐☐

1978

Scott No.	Illus No.		Description	Unused Value	Used Value	//////
J102	D5	11c	carmine rose	25	15	☐☐☐☐☐
J103	D5	13c	carmine rose	25	15	☐☐☐☐☐

1985

Scott No.	Illus No.		Description	Unused Value	Used Value	//////
J104	D5	17c	carmine rose	40	15	☐☐☐☐☐

SHANGHAI

2¢

CHINA

Scott No.	Illus No.	Description	Unused Value	Used Value	/ / / / / /
U.S. OFFICES IN CHINA					
1919					
K1	A140	2c on 1c green	17.50	20.00	
K2	A140	4c on 2c rose, type I	17.50	20.00	
K3	A140	6c on 3c violet, type II	32.50	45.00	
K4	A140	8c on 4c brown	40.00	45.00	
K5	A140	10c on 5c blue	45.00	52.50	
K6	A140	12c on 6c red orange	55.00	67.50	
K7	A140	14c on 7c black	60.00	72.50	
K8	A148	16c on 8c olive bister	45.00	50.00	
a.		16c on 8c olive green	40.00	42.50	
K9	A148	18c on 9c salmon red	45.00	55.00	
K10	A148	20c on 10c orange yellow	40.00	47.50	
K11	A148	24c on 12c brown carmine	47.50	60.00	
a.		24c on 12c claret brown	67.50	90.00	
K12	A148	30c on 15c gray	57.50	80.00	
K13	A148	40c on 20c deep ultra	85.00	125.00	
K14	A148	60c on 30c orange red	80.00	100.00	
K15	A148	$1 on 50c light violet............	300.00	400.00	
K16	A148	$2 on $1 violet brown	275.00	325.00	
a.		Double surcharge	2,500.	2,500	

SHANGHAI

2 Cts.

CHINA

1922, Surcharged locally

K17	A140	2c on 1c green	80.00	80.00	
K18	A140	4c on 2c carmine, type VII ...	70.00	70.00	

01

08

06

011

012

013

014

Scott No.	Illus No.	Description	Unused Value	Used Value	//////
OFFICIAL STAMPS					
1873, Agriculture Dept.					
O1	O1	1c yellow	90.00	60.00	☐☐☐☐☐
O2	O1	2c yellow	70.00	25.00	☐☐☐☐☐
O3	O1	3c yellow	65.00	3.50	☐☐☐☐☐
O4	O1	6c yellow	75.00	15.00	☐☐☐☐☐
O5	O1	10c yellow	150.00	70.00	☐☐☐☐☐
O6	O1	12c yellow	200.00	95.00	☐☐☐☐☐
O7	O1	15c yellow	150.00	70.00	☐☐☐☐☐
O8	O1	24c yellow	175.00	70.00	☐☐☐☐☐
O9	O1	30c yellow	225.00	110.00	☐☐☐☐☐
Executive Dept.					
O10	O1	1c carmine	350.00	150.00	☐☐☐☐☐
O11	O1	2c carmine	225.00	80.00	☐☐☐☐☐
O12	O1	3c carmine	275.00	75.00	☐☐☐☐☐
a.		3c violet rose	275.00	75.00	☐☐☐☐☐
O13	O1	6c carmine	400.00	250.00	☐☐☐☐☐
O14	O1	10c carmine	375.00	200.00	☐☐☐☐☐
Interior Dept.					
O15	O1	1c vermilion	20.00	3.50	☐☐☐☐☐
O16	O1	2c vermilion	17.50	2.00	☐☐☐☐☐
O17	O1	3c vermilion	27.50	2.00	☐☐☐☐☐
O18	O1	6c vermilion	20.00	2.00	☐☐☐☐☐
O19	O1	10c vermilion	19.00	4.00	☐☐☐☐☐
O20	O1	12c vermilion	30.00	3.00	☐☐☐☐☐

Scott No.	Illus No.		Description	Unused Value	Used Value	//////
Justice Dept.						
O21	O1	15c	vermilion	50.00	6.00	□□□□□
O22	O1	24c	vermilion	37.50	5.00	□□□□□
O23	O1	30c	vermilion	50.00	6.00	□□□□□
O24	O1	90c	vermilion	110.00	15.00	□□□□□
O25	O1	1c	purple	60.00	30.00	□□□□□
O26	O1	2c	purple	95.00	30.00	□□□□□
O27	O1	3c	purple	95.00	6.00	□□□□□
O28	O1	6c	purple	90.00	10.00	□□□□□
O29	O1	10c	purple	100.00	27.50	□□□□□
O30	O1	12c	purple	75.00	15.00	□□□□□
O31	O1	15c	purple	165.00	50.00	□□□□□
O32	O1	24c	purple	450.00	135.00	□□□□□
O33	O1	30c	purple	400.00	75.00	□□□□□
O34	O1	90c	purple	600.00	200.00	□□□□□
Navy Dept.						
O35	O1	1c	ultramarine	45.00	10.00	□□□□□
a.		1c	dull blue	52.50	8.50	□□□□□
O36	O1	2c	ultramarine	32.50	9.00	□□□□□
a.		2c	dull blue	42.50	7.50	□□□□□
O37	O1	3c	ultramarine	37.50	4.00	□□□□□
a.		3c	dull blue	42.50	5.50	□□□□□
O38	O1	6c	ultramarine	32.50	5.00	□□□□□
a.		6c	dull blue	42.50	5.00	□□□□□
O39	O1	7c	ultramarine	225.00	70.00	□□□□□
a.		7c	dull blue	250.00	70.00	□□□□□
O40	O1	10c	ultramarine	45.00	12.50	□□□□□
a.		10c	dull blue	50.00	13.00	□□□□□
O41	O1	12c	ultramarine	57.50	7.00	□□□□□
O42	O1	15c	ultramarine	95.00	20.00	□□□□□
O43	O1	24c	ultramarine	95.00	25.00	□□□□□
a.		24c	dull blue	110.00	—	□□□□□
O44	O1	30c	ultramarine	85.00	10.00	□□□□□
O45	O1	90c	ultramarine	400.00	70.00	□□□□□
a.			Double impression		3,250.	□□□□□
Post Office Dept.						
O47	O6	1c	black	7.25	3.00	□□□□□
O48	O6	2c	black	7.00	2.50	□□□□□
a.			Double impression	300.00		□□□□□
O49	O6	3c	black	2.50	55	□□□□□
a.			Printed on both sides		2,750.	□□□□□
O50	O6	6c	black	8.00	1.40	□□□□□
a.			Diagonal half used as 3c on cover		2,750.	□□□□□
O51	O6	10c	black	40.00	15.00	□□□□□
O52	O6	12c	black	22.50	3.50	□□□□□

271

Scott No.	Illus No.		Description	Unused Value	Used Value	//////
State Dept.						
O53	O6	15c	black	25.00	5.00	
a.			Imperf., pair	600.00		
O54	O6	24c	black	32.50	6.00	
O55	O6	30c	black	32.50	5.50	
O56	O6	90c	black	47.50	7.50	
O57	O1	1c	dark green	60.00	15.00	
O58	O1	2c	dark green	125.00	25.00	
O59	O1	3c	bright green	50.00	9.00	
O60	O1	6c	bright green	47.50	10.00	
O61	O1	7c	dark green	90.00	17.50	
O62	O1	10c	dark green	75.00	13.50	
O63	O1	12c	dark green	110.00	35.00	
O64	O1	15c	dark green	125.00	25.00	
O65	O1	24c	dark green	250.00	75.00	
O66	O1	30c	dark green	250.00	45.00	
O67	O1	90c	dark green	400.00	125.00	
O68	O8	$2	green & black	550.00	400.00	
O69	O8	$5	green & black	4,250.	2,000.	
O70	O8	$10	green & black	3,000.	1,500.	
O71	O8	$20	green & black	2,250.	800.00	
Treasury Dept.						
O72	O1	1c	brown	22.50	1.75	
O73	O1	2c	brown	25.00	1.75	
O74	O1	3c	brown	16.00	75	
O75	O1	6c	brown	22.50	1.50	
O76	O1	7c	brown	57.50	10.00	
O77	O1	10c	brown	57.50	3.00	
O78	O1	12c	brown	57.50	1.75	
O79	O1	15c	brown	50.00	2.50	
O80	O1	24c	brown	250.00	30.00	
O81	O1	30c	brown	82.50	3.00	
O82	O1	90c	brown	87.50	3.00	
War Dept.						
O83	O1	1c	rose	82.50	3.25	
O84	O1	2c	rose	75.00	4.50	
O85	O1	3c	rose	72.50	1.00	
O86	O1	6c	rose	250.00	2.00	
O87	O1	7c	rose	75.00	30.00	
O88	O1	10c	rose	22.50	4.00	
O89	O1	12c	rose	75.00	2.00	
O90	O1	15c	rose	20.00	2.50	
O91	O1	24c	rose	20.00	3.00	
O92	O1	30c	rose	22.50	2.50	
O93	O1	90c	rose	50.00	10.00	

Scott No.	Illus No.		Description	Unused Value	Used Value	//////
1879, Agriculture Dept.						
O94	O1	1c	yellow, no gum	1,500.		☐☐☐☐☐
O95	O1	3c	yellow	175.00	35.00	☐☐☐☐☐
Interior Dept.						
O96	O1	1c	vermilion	110.00	85.00	☐☐☐☐☐
O97	O1	2c	vermilion	2.50	1.00	☐☐☐☐☐
O98	O1	3c	vermilion	2.00	60	☐☐☐☐☐
O99	O1	6c	vermilion	3.00	2.50	☐☐☐☐☐
O100	O1	10c	vermilion	32.50	27.50	☐☐☐☐☐
O101	O1	12c	vermilion	65.00	40.00	☐☐☐☐☐
O102	O1	15c	vermilion	150.00	65.00	☐☐☐☐☐
O103	O1	24c	vermilion	1,500.	—	☐☐☐☐☐
Justice Dept.						
O106	O1	3c	bluish purple	50.00	22.50	☐☐☐☐☐
O107	O1	6c	bluish purple	110.00	80.00	☐☐☐☐☐
Post Office Dept.						
O108	O6	3c	black	7.50	1.75	☐☐☐☐☐
Treasury Dept.						
O109	O1	3c	brown	27.50	2.50	☐☐☐☐☐
O110	O1	6c	brown	50.00	16.00	☐☐☐☐☐
O111	O1	10c	brown	70.00	17.50	☐☐☐☐☐
O112	O1	30c	brown	800.00	125.00	☐☐☐☐☐
O113	O1	90c	brown	825.00	125.00	☐☐☐☐☐
War Dept.						
O114	O1	1c	rose red	2.00	1.50	☐☐☐☐☐
O115	O1	2c	rose red	3.00	1.50	☐☐☐☐☐
O116	O1	3c	rose red	3.00	75	☐☐☐☐☐
a.			Imperf., pair	*800.00*		☐☐☐☐☐
b.			Double impression	500.00		☐☐☐☐☐
O117	O1	6c	rose red	2.50	80	☐☐☐☐☐
O118	O1	10c	rose red	20.00	15.00	☐☐☐☐☐
O119	O1	12c	rose red	15.00	3.00	☐☐☐☐☐
O120	O1	30c	rose red	47.50	30.00	☐☐☐☐☐
1911, Official Postal Savings Mail						
Watermark 191						
O121	O11	2c	black	9.00	1.10	☐☐☐☐☐
O122	O11	50c	dark green	110.00	25.00	☐☐☐☐☐
O123	O11	$1	ultramarine	100.00	7.00	☐☐☐☐☐
Watermark 190						
O124	O11	1c	dark violet	5.50	1.00	☐☐☐☐☐
O125	O11	2c	black	30.00	3.50	☐☐☐☐☐
O126	O11	10c	carmine	10.00	1.00	☐☐☐☐☐

Scott No.	Illus No.		Description	Unused Value	Used Value	//////
1983-85						
O127	O12	1c	red, blue & black	15	15	☐☐☐☐☐
O128	O12	4c	red, blue & black	15	20	☐☐☐☐☐
O129	O12	13c	red, blue & black	26	75	☐☐☐☐☐
O129A	O12	14c	red, blue & black	28	50	☐☐☐☐☐
O130	O12	17c	red, blue & black	34	40	☐☐☐☐☐
O132	O12	$1	red, blue & black	1.75	1.00	☐☐☐☐☐
O133	O12	$5	red, blue & black	9.00	5.00	☐☐☐☐☐

Coil stamps, Perf 10 Vertically

O135	O12	20c	red, blue & black	2.00	*2.00*	☐☐☐☐☐
a.			Imperf., pair	*1,500.*		☐☐☐☐☐
O136	O12	22c	red, blue & black	60	*2.00*	☐☐☐☐☐

1985

O138	O12	(14c)	red, blue & black	3.50	*5.00*	☐☐☐☐☐

1985-88, Coil stamps, Perf. 10 Vertically

O138A	O13	15c	red, blue & black	30	15	☐☐☐☐☐
O138B	O13	20c	red, blue & black	40	15	☐☐☐☐☐
O139	O12	(22c)	red, blue & black	4.50	*3.00*	☐☐☐☐☐
O140	O13	(25c)	red, blue & black	50	*2.00*	☐☐☐☐☐
O141	O13	25c	red, blue & black	50	20	☐☐☐☐☐
a.			Imperf., pair	—	—	☐☐☐☐☐

1989

O143	O13	1c	red, blue & black	15	—	☐☐☐☐☐

1991, Coil stamps, Perf. 10 Vertically

O144	O14	(29c)	red, blue & black	58	50	☐☐☐☐☐
O145	O13	29c	red, blue & black	58	25	☐☐☐☐☐

1991

O146	O13	4c	red, blue & black	15	15	☐☐☐☐☐
O147	O13	19c	red, blue & black	38	50	☐☐☐☐☐
O148	O13	23c	red, blue & black	46	25	☐☐☐☐☐

N1

N2

N3

N4

N5

N6

N7

N8

N9

N10

N11

N12

N13

N14

Scott No.	Illus No.		Description	Unused Value	Used Value	//////

NEWSPAPER STAMPS

1865, Thin hard paper, no gum

Scott No.	Illus No.		Description	Unused Value	Used Value	//////
PR1	N1	5c	dark blue	185.00	—	
a.		5c	light blue	185.00	—	
PR2	N2	10c	blue green	85.00	—	
a.		10c	green	85.00	—	
b.			Pelure paper	125.00	—	
PR3	N3	25c	orange red	125.00	—	
a.		25c	carmine red	150.00	—	
b.			Pelure paper	125.00		

White border, Yellowish paper

Scott No.	Illus No.		Description	Unused Value	Used Value	//////
PR4	N1	5c	light blue	50.00	30.00	
a.		5c	dark blue	50.00	30.00	
b.			Pelure paper	50.00	—	

1875, Reprints, Hard White Paper, Without Gum

Scott No.	Illus No.		Description	Unused Value	Used Value	//////
PR5	N1	5c	dull blue	70.00		
a.			Printed on both sides	—		
PR6	N2	10c	dark bluish green	50.00		
a.			Printed on both sides	1,750.		
PR7	N3	25c	dark carmine	80.00		

1880, Soft Porous Paper, White Border

Scott No.	Illus No.		Description	Unused Value	Used Value	//////
PR8	N1	5c	dark blue	125.00		

1875, Thin hard paper

Scott No.	Illus No.		Description	Unused Value	Used Value	//////
PR9	N4	2c	black	14.00	11.00	
PR10	N4	3c	black	17.50	14.50	
PR11	N4	4c	black	15.00	12.50	
PR12	N4	6c	black	20.00	17.00	
PR13	N4	8c	black	27.50	22.50	
PR14	N4	9c	black	60.00	50.00	
PR15	N4	10c	black	27.50	20.00	
PR16	N5	12c	rose	65.00	40.00	
PR17	N5	24c	rose	82.50	45.00	
PR18	N5	36c	rose	92.50	50.00	
PR19	N5	48c	rose	165.00	85.00	
PR20	N5	60c	rose	82.50	45.00	
PR21	N5	72c	rose	200.00	110.00	
PR22	N5	84c	rose	300.00	135.00	
PR23	N5	96c	rose	165.00	100.00	
PR24	N6	$1.92	dark brown	225.00	125.00	
PR25	N7	$3	vermilion	300.00	135.00	
PR26	N8	$6	ultramarine	500.00	185.00	
PR27	N9	$9	yellow	650.00	250.00	
PR28	N10	$12	blue green	750.00	350.00	
PR29	N11	$24	dark gray violet	750.00	325.00	

Scott No.	Illus No.		Description	Unused Value	Used Value	//////
PR30	N12	$36	brown rose	800.00	450.00	□□□□□
PR31	N13	$48	red brown	1,050.	500.00	□□□□□
PR32	N14	$60	violet	1,050.	500.00	□□□□□

Special Printing, Hard White Paper, Without Gum

Scott No.	Illus No.		Description	Unused Value	Used Value	//////
PR33	N4	2c	gray black	100.00		□□□□□
PR34	N4	3c	gray black	105.00		□□□□□
PR35	N4	4c	gray black	110.00		□□□□□
PR36	N4	6c	gray black	150.00		□□□□□
PR37	N4	8c	gray black	175.00		□□□□□
PR38	N4	9c	gray black	200.00		□□□□□
PR39	N4	10c	gray black	250.00		□□□□□
PR40	N5	12c	pale rose	300.00		□□□□□
PR41	N5	24c	pale rose	425.00		□□□□□
PR42	N5	36c	pale rose	500.00		□□□□□
PR43	N5	48c	pale rose	600.00		□□□□□
PR44	N5	60c	pale rose	675.00		□□□□□
PR45	N5	72c	pale rose	825.00		□□□□□
PR46	N5	84c	pale rose	850.00		□□□□□
PR47	N5	96c	pale rose	1,500.		□□□□□
PR48	N6	$1.92	dark brown	*3,500.*		□□□□□
PR49	N7	$3	vermilion	*7,000.*		□□□□□
PR50	N8	$6	ultra	*8,500.*		□□□□□
PR51	N9	$9	yellow	*20,000.*		□□□□□
PR52	N10	$12	blue green	*18,500.*		□□□□□
PR53	N11	$24	dark gray violet	—		□□□□□
PR54	N12	$36	brown rose	—		□□□□□
PR55	N13	$48	red brown	—		□□□□□
PR56	N14	$60	violet	—		□□□□□

1879, Soft porous paper

Scott No.	Illus No.		Description	Unused Value	Used Value	//////
PR57	N4	2c	black	6.00	4.50	□□□□□
PR58	N4	3c	black	7.50	5.00	□□□□□
PR59	N4	4c	black	7.50	5.00	□□□□□
PR60	N4	6c	black	15.00	11.00	□□□□□
PR61	N4	8c	black	15.00	11.00	□□□□□
PR62	N4	10c	black	15.00	11.00	□□□□□
PR63	N5	12c	red	55.00	25.00	□□□□□
PR64	N5	24c	red	55.00	22.50	□□□□□
PR65	N5	36c	red	170.00	95.00	□□□□□
PR66	N5	48c	red	135.00	60.00	□□□□□
PR67	N5	60c	red	100.00	60.00	□□□□□
a.			Imperf., pair	*600.00*		□□□□□
PR68	N5	72c	red	210.00	115.00	□□□□□
PR69	N5	84c	red	165.00	85.00	□□□□□
PR70	N5	96c	red	110.00	60.00	□□□□□
PR71	N6	$1.92	pale brown	90.00	55.00	□□□□□
PR72	N7	$3	red vermilion	90.00	55.00	□□□□□

Scott No.	Illus No.		Description	Unused Value	Used Value	//////
PR73	N8	$6	blue	150.00	90.00	
PR74	N9	$9	orange	110.00	60.00	
PR75	N10	$12	yellow green	160.00	85.00	
PR76	N11	$24	dark violet	200.00	110.00	
PR77	N12	$36	indian red	250.00	135.00	
PR78	N13	$48	yellow brown	325.00	165.00	
PR79	N14	$60	purple	325.00	165.00	

1883, Special Printing

PR80	N4	2c	intense black	275.00		

1885

PR81	N4	1c	black	8.50	5.00	
PR82	N5	12c	carmine	27.50	12.50	
PR83	N5	24c	carmine	30.00	15.00	
PR84	N5	36c	carmine	42.50	17.50	
PR85	N5	48c	carmine	60.00	30.00	
PR86	N5	60c	carmine	85.00	40.00	
PR87	N5	72c	carmine	95.00	45.00	
PR88	N5	84c	carmine	200.00	110.00	
PR89	N5	96c	carmine	140.00	85.00	

1894

PR90	N4	1c	intense black	55.00		
PR91	N4	2c	intense black	55.00		
PR92	N4	4c	intense black	75.00		
PR93	N4	6c	intense black	950.00		
PR94	N4	10c	intense black	125.00		
PR95	N5	12c	pink	550.00		
PR96	N5	24c	pink	575.00		
PR97	N5	36c	pink	3,500.		
PR98	N5	60c	pink	3,500.	—	
PR99	N5	96c	pink	4,000.		
PR100	N7	$3	scarlet	5,500.		
PR101	N8	$6	pale blue			
PR102	N15	1c	black	25.00	7.50	
PR103	N15	2c	black	25.00	7.50	
PR104	N15	5c	black	35.00	12.50	
PR105	N15	10c	black	75.00	32.50	
PR106	N16	25c	carmine	100.00	35.00	
PR107	N16	50c	carmine	235.00	95.00	
PR108	N17	$2	scarlet	275.00	65.00	
PR109	N18	$5	ultramarine	375.00	150.00	
PR110	N19	$10	green	350.00	165.00	
PR111	N20	$20	slate	675.00	300.00	
PR112	N21	$50	dull rose	700.00	300.00	
PR113	N22	$100	purple	775.00	350.00	

N15

N16

N17

N18

N19

N20

N21

N22

Scott No.	Illus No.		Description	Unused Value	Used Value	//////
1895-97, Watermark 191						
PR114	N15	1c	black	3.50	3.00	☐☐☐☐☐
PR115	N15	2c	black	4.00	3.50	☐☐☐☐☐
PR116	N15	5c	black	6.00	5.00	☐☐☐☐☐
PR117	N15	10c	black	4.00	3.50	☐☐☐☐☐
PR118	N16	25c	carmine	8.00	8.00	☐☐☐☐☐
PR119	N16	50c	carmine	10.00	12.50	☐☐☐☐☐
PR120	N17	$2	scarlet	12.00	15.00	☐☐☐☐☐
PR121	N18	$5	dark blue	20.00	25.00	☐☐☐☐☐
a.		$5	light blue	100.00	45.00	☐☐☐☐☐
PR122	N19	$10	green	18.00	25.00	☐☐☐☐☐
PR123	N20	$20	slate	20.00	27.50	☐☐☐☐☐
PR124	N21	$50	dull rose	25.00	30.00	☐☐☐☐☐
PR125	N22	$100	purple	30.00	37.50	☐☐☐☐☐

PP1

PP2   PP3

PP4

PP5   PP6

PP7   PP8

PP9   PP10

PP11   PP12   PP13

282

PPD1

Scott No.	Illus No.	Description	Unused Value	Used Value	//////
PARCEL POST STAMPS					
1913					
Q1	PP1	1c carmine rose	2.50	85	
Q2	PP2	2c carmine rose	3.00	60	
Q3	PP3	3c carmine	5.75	4.50	
Q4	PP4	4c carmine rose	16.00	1.90	
Q5	PP5	5c carmine rose	15.00	1.25	
Q6	PP6	10c carmine rose	25.00	1.75	
Q7	PP7	15c carmine rose	35.00	7.75	
Q8	PP8	20c carmine rose	77.50	15.00	
Q9	PP9	25c carmine rose	35.00	4.00	
Q10	PP10	50c carmine rose	160.00	27.50	
Q11	PP11	75c carmine rose	45.00	22.50	
Q12	PP12	$1 carmine rose	260.00	17.00	
SPECIAL HANDLING STAMPS					
1925-29					
QE1	PP13	10c yellow green	1.00	80	
QE2	PP13	15c yellow green	1.00	70	
QE3	PP13	20c yellow green	1.75	1.00	
QE4	PP13	25c yellow green	13.00	5.50	
a.		25c deep green	22.50	4.50	
PARCEL POST POSTAGE DUE STAMPS					
1912					
JQ1	PPD1	1c dark green	5.00	2.75	
JQ2	PPD1	2c dark green	45.00	13.00	
JQ3	PPD1	5c dark green	7.00	3.50	
JQ4	PPD1	10c dark green	110.00	30.00	
JQ5	PPD1	25c dark green	50.00	3.25	

CVP1

CVP2

CVP3

Scott No.	Illus No.	Description	Unused Value	Used Value	/ / / / /
COMPUTER VENDED POSTAGE					
1989, Aug. 23, Washington, D.C., Machine 82					
1	CVP1 25c	1st Class	—	—	☐☐☐☐☐
a.		1st day dated, serial #12501-15500	4.50	—	☐☐☐☐☐
b.		1st day dated, serial #00001-12500	4.50	—	☐☐☐☐☐
c.		1st day dated, serial over #27500	—	—	☐☐☐☐☐
2	CVP1 $1	3rd Class	—	—	☐☐☐☐☐
a.		1st day dated, serial #24501-27500	—	—	☐☐☐☐☐
b.		1st day dated, serial over #27500	—	—	☐☐☐☐☐
3	CVP2 $1.69	Parcel Post	—	—	☐☐☐☐☐
a.		1st day dated, serial #21501-24500	—	—	☐☐☐☐☐
b.		1st day dated, serial over #27500	—	—	☐☐☐☐☐
4	CVP1 $2.40	Priority Mail	—	—	☐☐☐☐☐
a.		1st day dated, serial #18501-21500	—	—	☐☐☐☐☐
b.		Priority Mail ($2.74), with bar code (CVP2)	—	—	☐☐☐☐☐
c.		1st day dated, serial over #27500	—	—	☐☐☐☐☐

Scott No.	Illus No.	Description	Unused Value	Used Value	//////
5	CVP1	$8.75 Express Mail	—	—	☐☐☐☐☐
a.		1st day dated, serial #15501-18500	—	—	☐☐☐☐☐
b.		1st day dated, serial over #27500	—	—	☐☐☐☐☐

Washington, D.C., Machine 83

6	CVP1	25c 1st Class	—	—	☐☐☐☐☐
a.		1st day dated, serial #12501-15500	4.50	—	☐☐☐☐☐
b.		1st day dated, serial #00001-12500	—	—	☐☐☐☐☐
c.		1st day dated, serial over #27500	—	—	☐☐☐☐☐
7	CVP1	$1 3rd Class	—	—	☐☐☐☐☐
a.		1st day dated, serial #24501-27500	—	—	☐☐☐☐☐
b.		1st day dated, serial over #27500	—	—	☐☐☐☐☐
8	CVP2	$1.69 Parcel Post	—	—	☐☐☐☐☐
a.		1st day dated, serial #21501-24500	—	—	☐☐☐☐☐
b.		1st day dated, serial over #27500	—	—	☐☐☐☐☐
9	CVP1	$2.40 Priority Mail	—	—	☐☐☐☐☐
a.		1st day dated, serial #18501-21500	—	—	☐☐☐☐☐
b.		1st day dated, serial over #27500	—	—	☐☐☐☐☐
c.		Priority Mail ($2.74), with bar code (CVP2)	*100.00*		☐☐☐☐☐
10	CVP1	$8.75 Express Mail	—	—	☐☐☐☐☐
a.		1st day dated, serial #15501-18500	—	—	☐☐☐☐☐
b.		1st day dated, serial over #27500	—	—	☐☐☐☐☐

1989, Sept. 1, Kensington, MD, Machine 82

11	CVP1	25c 1st Class	—	—	☐☐☐☐☐
a.		1st day dated, serial #12501-15500	4.50	—	☐☐☐☐☐
b.		1st day dated, serial #00001-12500	—	—	☐☐☐☐☐
c.		1st day dated, serial over #27500	—	—	☐☐☐☐☐

Scott No.	Illus No.		Description	Unused Value	Used Value	/ / / / / /
12	CVP1	$1	3rd Class	—	—	☐☐☐☐☐
a.			1st day dated, serial #24501-27500	—	—	☐☐☐☐☐
b.			1st day dated, serial over #27500	—	—	☐☐☐☐☐
13	CVP2	$1.69	Parcel Post	—	—	☐☐☐☐☐
a.			1st day dated, serial #21501-24500	—	—	☐☐☐☐☐
b.			1st day dated, serial over #27500	—	—	☐☐☐☐☐
14	CVP1	$2.40	Priority Mail	—	—	☐☐☐☐☐
a.			1st day dated, serial #18501-21500	—	—	☐☐☐☐☐
b.			1st day dated, serial over #27500	—	—	☐☐☐☐☐
c.			Priority Mail ($2.74), with bar code (CVP2)	*100.00*		☐☐☐☐☐
15	CVP1	$8.75	Express Mail....................	—	—	☐☐☐☐☐
a.			1st day dated, serial #15501-18500	—	—	☐☐☐☐☐
b.			1st day dated, serial over #27500	—	—	☐☐☐☐☐

Kensington, MD, Machine 83

Scott No.	Illus No.		Description	Unused Value	Used Value	/ / / / / /
16	CVP1	25c	1st Class	6.00	—	☐☐☐☐☐
a.			1st day dated, serial #12501-15500	4.50	—	☐☐☐☐☐
b.			1st day dated, serial #00001-12500	4.50	—	☐☐☐☐☐
c.			1st day dated, serial over #27500	—	—	☐☐☐☐☐
17	CVP1	$1	3rd Class	—	—	☐☐☐☐☐
a.			1st day dated, serial #24501-27500	—	—	☐☐☐☐☐
b.			1st day dated, serial over #27500	—	—	☐☐☐☐☐
18	CVP2	$1.69	Parcel Post	—	—	☐☐☐☐☐
a.			1st day dated, serial #21501-24500	—	—	☐☐☐☐☐
b.			1st day dated, serial over #27500	—	—	☐☐☐☐☐
19	CVP1	$2.40	Priority Mail	—	—	☐☐☐☐☐
a.			1st day dated, serial #18501-21500	—	—	☐☐☐☐☐
b.			1st day dated, serial over #27500	—	—	☐☐☐☐☐
c.			Priority Mail ($2.74), with bar code (CVP2)	100.00		☐☐☐☐☐

Scott No.	Illus No.	Description	Unused Value	Used Value	/ / / / /
20	CVP1 $8.75	Express Mail	—	—	☐☐☐☐☐
a.		1st day dated, serial #15501-18500	—	—	☐☐☐☐☐
b.		1st day dated, serial over #27500	—	—	☐☐☐☐☐

1989, Nov., Washington, D.C., Machine 11

21	CVP1 25c	1st Class	*150.00*		☐☐☐☐☐
a.		1st Class, with bar code (CVP2)	—		☐☐☐☐☐
22	CVP1 $1	3rd Class	*500.00*		☐☐☐☐☐
23	CVP2 $1.69	Parcel Post	*500.00*		☐☐☐☐☐
24	CVP1 $2.40	Priority Mail	*500.00*		☐☐☐☐☐
a.		Priority Mail ($2.74), with bar code (CVP2)	—		☐☐☐☐☐
25	CVP1 $8.75	Express Mail	*500.00*		☐☐☐☐☐

Washington, D.C., Machine 12

26	CVP1 25c	1st Class	*150.00*		☐☐☐☐☐
27	CVP1 $1	3rd Class	—		☐☐☐☐☐
28	CVP2 $1.69	Parcel Post	—		☐☐☐☐☐
29	CVP1 $2.40	Priority Mail	—		☐☐☐☐☐
a.		Priority Mail ($2.74), with bar code (CVP2)	—		☐☐☐☐☐
30	CVP1 $8.75	Express Mail	—		☐☐☐☐☐
31	CVP3 29c	red & blue	60	—	☐☐☐☐☐

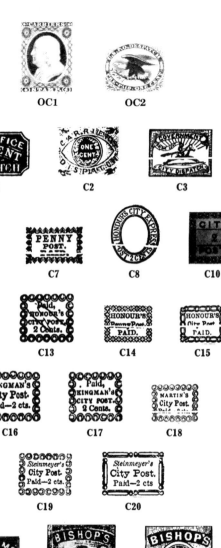

OC1

OC2

C1

C2

C3

C6

C7

C8

C10

C11

C13

C14

C15

C16

C17

C18

C19

C20

C20a

C20b

C20c

Scott No.	Illus No.		Description	Unused Value	Used Value	//////
CARRIER'S STAMPS						
OFFICIAL ISSUES						
1851						
LO1	OC1	(1c)	dull blue, *rose*	2,750.	2,500.	☐☐☐☐☐
LO2	OC2	1c	blue	15.00	30.00	☐☐☐☐☐
1875						
LO3	OC1	(1c)	blue, *rose*	40.00		☐☐☐☐☐
LO4	OC1	(1c)	blue, perf. 12	2,500.		☐☐☐☐☐
LO5	OC2	1c	blue, *rose*, imperf.	20.00		☐☐☐☐☐
LO6	OC2	1c	blue, perf. 12	175.00		☐☐☐☐☐
SEMI-OFFICIAL ISSUES						
1850-55						
1LB1	C1	1c	red, *bluish*	100.00	60.00	☐☐☐☐☐
1LB2	C1	1c	blue, *bluish*	125.00	90.00	☐☐☐☐☐
a.			Bluish laid paper	—	—	☐☐☐☐☐
1LB3	C1	1c	blue	75.00	50.00	☐☐☐☐☐
a.			Laid paper	150.00	100.00	☐☐☐☐☐
1LB4	C1	1c	green	—	600.00	☐☐☐☐☐
1LB5	C1	1c	red	350.00	275.00	☐☐☐☐☐
1856						
1LB6	C2	1c	blue	90.00	60.00	☐☐☐☐☐
1LB7	C2	1c	red	90.00	60.00	☐☐☐☐☐
1857						
1LB8	C3	1c	black	40.00	30.00	☐☐☐☐☐
a.			SENT	45.00	35.00	☐☐☐☐☐
b.			Short rays	45.00	35.00	☐☐☐☐☐
1LB9	C3	1c	red	60.00	45.00	☐☐☐☐☐
a.			SENT	75.00	50.00	☐☐☐☐☐
b.			Short rays	75.00	50.00	☐☐☐☐☐
1849-50						
3LB1	C6	1c	blue	150.00	75.00	☐☐☐☐☐
1851						
3LB2	C7	1c	blue (shades), *slate*	125.00	65.00	☐☐☐☐☐
1849						
4LB1	C8	2c	black, *brown rose*	2,500.	2,500.	☐☐☐☐☐
4LB2	C8	2c	black, *yellow*		2,500.	☐☐☐☐☐
1854						
4LB3	C10	2c	black		1,000.	☐☐☐☐☐

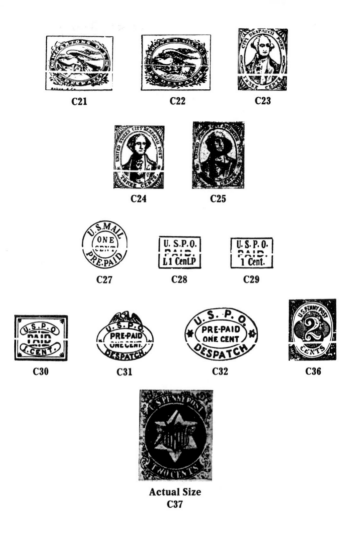

C21   C22   C23

C24   C25

C27   C28   C29

C30   C31   C32   C36

Actual Size
C37

HOW TO USE THIS BOOK

The number in the first column is its Scott number or identifying number. The letter and number that come next (A41) indicate the design and refer to the illustration so designated. Following that is the denomination of the stamp and its color. Finally, the value, unused and used is shown.

Scott No.	Illus No.		Description	Unused Value	Used Value	//////
1849-50						
4LB5	C11	2c	black, *bluish*, pelure	*400.00*	*300.00*	☐☐☐☐☐
4LB7	C11	2c	black, *yellow*	*400.00*	*400.00*	☐☐☐☐☐
1851-58						
4LB8	C13	2c	black, *bluish*	175.00	100.00	☐☐☐☐☐
a.			Period after Paid	350.00	150.00	☐☐☐☐☐
b.			Cens		700.00	☐☐☐☐☐
c.			Conours and Bents		—	☐☐☐☐☐
4LB9	C13	2c	black, *bluish*, pelure	*375.00*	*425.00*	☐☐☐☐☐
4LB11	C14	(2c)	black, *bluish*	—	250.00	☐☐☐☐☐
4LB12	C14	(2c)	black, *bluish*, pelure	—	250.00	☐☐☐☐☐
4LB13	C15	(2c)	black, *bluish*	250.00	125.00	☐☐☐☐☐
a.			Comma after PAID	300.00		☐☐☐☐☐
b.			No period after Post	400.00		☐☐☐☐☐
1851-58						
4LB14	C16	2c	black, *bluish*	*400.00*	*450.00*	☐☐☐☐☐
4LB15	C17	2c	black, *bluish*	*500.00*	*500.00*	☐☐☐☐☐
1858						
4LB16	C18	2c	black, *bluish*	*2,000.*		☐☐☐☐☐
1860						
4LB17	C19	2c	black		—	☐☐☐☐☐
1859						
4LB18	C19	2c	black, *bluish*	*2,500.*		☐☐☐☐☐
4LB19	C20	2c	black, *bluish*	*2,500.*	—	☐☐☐☐☐
4LB20	C20	2c	black, *pink*	*150.00*	—	☐☐☐☐☐
4LB21	C20	2c	black, *yellow*	125.00		☐☐☐☐☐
1854						
9LB1	C20a	2c	brown	*1,500.*	1,500.	☐☐☐☐☐
1854						
10LB1	C20b		blue	*1,000.*	1,000.	☐☐☐☐☐
10LB2	C20c	2c	black, *bluish*	750.00	750.00	☐☐☐☐☐
1857						
5LB1	C21	(2c)	bluish green	*75.00*		☐☐☐☐☐
1858						
5LB2	C22	(2c)	blue	150.00	150.00	☐☐☐☐☐
5LB3	C22	(2c)	black	*600.00*	*1,750.*	☐☐☐☐☐

Scott No.	Illus No.		Description	Unused Value	Used Value	/ / / / / /
1842						
6LB1	C23	3c	black, *grayish*		1,250.	☐☐☐☐☐
1842-45						
6LB2	C24	3c	black, *rosy buff*	600.00		☐☐☐☐☐
6LB3	C24	3c	black, *light blue*	400.00	300.00	☐☐☐☐☐
6LB4	C24	3c	black, *green*	2,000.		☐☐☐☐☐
6LB5	C24	3c	black, *blue green (shades)*	125.00	100.00	☐☐☐☐☐
a.			Double impression		500.00	☐☐☐☐☐
b.		3c	black, *blue*	400.00	125.00	☐☐☐☐☐
c.			As "b," double impression		750.00	☐☐☐☐☐
d.		3c	black, *green*	650.00	500.00	☐☐☐☐☐
e.			As "d," double impression	—		☐☐☐☐☐
1846						
6LB7	C25	2c	on 3c, on cover		—	☐☐☐☐☐
1849						
6LB9	C27	1c	black, *rose*	60.00	50.00	☐☐☐☐☐
1849-50						
6LB10	C27	1c	black, *yellow*	60.00	60.00	☐☐☐☐☐
6LB11	C27	1c	black, *buff*	60.00	50.00	☐☐☐☐☐
a.			Pair, one stamp sideways.	1,000.		☐☐☐☐☐
1849-50						
7LB1	C28	1c	black, *rose* (with letters L.P.)	175.00		☐☐☐☐☐
7LB2	C28	1c	black, *rose* (with letter S)	500.00		☐☐☐☐☐
7LB3	C28	1c	black, *rose* (with letter H)	175.00		☐☐☐☐☐
7LB4	C28	1c	black, *rose* (with letters L.S.)	175.00		☐☐☐☐☐
7LB5	C28	1c	black, *rose* (with letters J.J.)	2,000.		☐☐☐☐☐
7LB6	C29	1c	black, *rose*	150.00	125.00	☐☐☐☐☐
7LB7	C29	1c	black, *blue,* glazed	600.00		☐☐☐☐☐
7LB8	C29	1c	black, *vermilion,* glazed ..	500.00		☐☐☐☐☐
7LB9	C29	1c	black, *yellow,* glazed	2,500.		☐☐☐☐☐
1850-52						
7LB11	C30	1c	gold, *black,* glazed	100.00	75.00	☐☐☐☐☐
7LB12	C30	1c	blue	200.00	150.00	☐☐☐☐☐
7LB13	C30	1c	black	650.00	500.00	☐☐☐☐☐
7LB14	C31	1c	blue, *buff*	1,000.		☐☐☐☐☐
1855						
7LB16	C31	1c	black		1,650.	☐☐☐☐☐

Scott No.	Illus No.	Description	Unused Value	Used Value	//////
1856					
7LB18	C32	1c black	900.00	1,400.	☐☐☐☐☐
1849					
8LB1	C36	2c black	4,000.	5,000.	☐☐☐☐☐
1857					
8LB2	C37	2c blue		5,000.	☐☐☐☐☐

HP1

HP2

HP3

HP4

HP5

HP6

HP7

HP8

HP9

HUNTING PERMIT STAMPS

Scott No.	Illus No.	Description	Unused Value	Used Value	//////
1934					
RW1	HP1	$1 blue	425.00	85.00	☐☐☐☐☐
a.		Imperf., pair	—		☐☐☐☐☐
b.		Vert. pair, imperf. horiz. ..	—		☐☐☐☐☐
1935					
RW2		$1 *Canvasback Ducks Taking to Flight*	400.00	100.00	☐☐☐☐☐
1936					
RW3		$1 *Canada Geese in Flight* ...	210.00	50.00	☐☐☐☐☐
1937					
RW4		$1 *Scaup Ducks Taking to Flight*	170.00	35.00	☐☐☐☐☐
1938					
RW5		$1 *Pintail Drake and Duck Alighting*	170.00	35.00	☐☐☐☐☐
1939					
RW6	HP2	$1 chocolate	120.00	15.00	☐☐☐☐☐
1940					
RW7		$1 *Black Mallards*	115.00	15.00	☐☐☐☐☐
1941					
RW8		$1 *Family of Ruddy Ducks* ...	115.00	15.00	☐☐☐☐☐
1942					
RW9		$1 *Baldpates*	115.00	15.00	☐☐☐☐☐
1943					
RW10		$1 *Wood Ducks*	50.00	15.00	☐☐☐☐☐
1944					
RW11		$1 *White-fronted Geese*	40.00	14.00	☐☐☐☐☐
1945					
RW12		$1 *Shoveller Ducks in Flight*	40.00	10.00	☐☐☐☐☐
1946					
RW13		$1 *Redhead Ducks*	35.00	9.00	☐☐☐☐☐
a.		$1 bright rose pink	—		☐☐☐☐☐
1947					
RW14		$1 *Snow Geese*	35.00	9.00	☐☐☐☐☐

Scott No.	Illus No.		Description	Unused Value	Used Value	//////
1948 RW15		$1	*Bufflehead Ducks in Flight*	30.00	9.00	☐☐☐☐☐
1949 RW16	HP3	$2	bright green	40.00	7.00	☐☐☐☐☐
1950 RW17		$2	*Trumpeter Swans in Flight*	45.00	7.00	☐☐☐☐☐
1951 RW18		$2	*Gadwall Ducks*	45.00	5.00	☐☐☐☐☐
1952 RW19		$2	*Harlequin Ducks*	45.00	5.00	☐☐☐☐☐
1953 RW20		$2	*Blue-winged Teal*	45.00	5.00	☐☐☐☐☐
1954 RW21		$2	*Ring-necked Ducks*	45.00	5.00	☐☐☐☐☐
1955 RW22		$2	*Blue Geese*	50.00	5.00	☐☐☐☐☐
1956 RW23		$2	*American Merganser*	45.00	5.00	☐☐☐☐☐
1957 RW24		$2	*American Eider*	42.50	5.00	☐☐☐☐☐
1958 RW25		$2	*Canada Geese*	45.00	5.00	☐☐☐☐☐
1959 RW26	HP4	$3	blue, ocher & black	60.00	5.00	☐☐☐☐☐
1960 RW27	HP5	$3	red brown, dark blue & bister	60.00	5.00	☐☐☐☐☐
1961 RW28		$3	*Mallard Hen and Ducklings*	65.00	5.00	☐☐☐☐☐
1962 RW29	HP6	$3	dk bl, dk red brn & black .	70.00	6.00	☐☐☐☐☐

Scott No.	Illus No.	Description	Unused Value	Used Value	//////
1963 RW30		\$3 *Pair of Brant landing*	70.00	6.00	☐☐☐☐☐
1964 RW31		\$3 *Hawaiian Nene Geese*	70.00	6.00	☐☐☐☐☐
1965 RW32		\$3 *3 Canvasback Drakes*	65.00	6.00	☐☐☐☐☐
1966 RW33	HP7	\$3 ultra, slate grn & blk	65.00	5.00	☐☐☐☐☐
1967 RW34		\$3 *Old Squaw Ducks*	65.00	5.00	☐☐☐☐☐
1968 RW35		\$3 *Hooded Mergansers*	50.00	5.00	☐☐☐☐☐
1969 RW36	HP8	\$3 gray, brown, indigo & brown red	50.00	5.00	☐☐☐☐☐
1970 RW37		\$3 *Ross Geese*	47.50	4.00	☐☐☐☐☐
1971 RW38		\$3 *3 Cinnamon Teal*	27.50	4.00	☐☐☐☐☐
1972 RW39		\$5 *Emperor Geese*	20.00	4.00	☐☐☐☐☐
1973 RW40		\$5 *Stellers Eiders*	17.00	4.00	☐☐☐☐☐
1974 RW41		\$5 *Wood Ducks*	14.00	4.00	☐☐☐☐☐
1975 RW42		\$5 *Canvasback duck decoy and flying ducks*	10.00	4.00	☐☐☐☐☐
1976 RW43		\$5 *Family of Canada Geese* .	10.00	4.00	☐☐☐☐☐
1977 RW44		\$5 *Ross Geese, pair*	11.00	4.00	☐☐☐☐☐
1978 RW45	HP9	\$5 multicolored	9.50	3.75	☐☐☐☐☐

297

Scott No.	Illus No.		Description	Unused Value	Used Value	//////
1979 RW46		$7.50	*Green-winged teal*	12.00	4.00	☐☐☐☐☐
1980 RW47		$7.50	*Mallards*	12.00	4.00	☐☐☐☐☐
1981 RW48		$7.50	*Ruddy Ducks*	12.00	4.00	☐☐☐☐☐
1982 RW49		$7.50	*Canvasbacks*	11.00	4.00	☐☐☐☐☐
1983 RW50		$7.50	*Pintails*	11.00	4.00	☐☐☐☐☐
1984 RW51		$7.50	*Widgeon*	11.00	4.00	☐☐☐☐☐
1985 RW52		$7.50	*Cinnamon Teal*	11.00	4.00	☐☐☐☐☐
1986 RW53 a.		$7.50	*Fulvous Whistling Duck* .. Black omitted	11.00 *3,250.*	4.00	☐☐☐☐☐ ☐☐☐☐☐
1987 RW54		$10	*Redheads*	12.50	5.00	☐☐☐☐☐
1988 RW55		$10	*Snow Goose*	14.00	5.00	☐☐☐☐☐
1989 RW56		$12.50	*Lesser Scaups*	17.50	5.00	☐☐☐☐☐
1990 RW57 a.		$12.50	*Black Bellied* *Whistling Duck*............ Back printing omitted	17.50 *850.00*	5.00	☐☐☐☐☐ ☐☐☐☐☐
1991 RW58 a.	HP10	$15	multicolored .... Black (engr.) omitted	20.00 —	5.00	☐☐☐☐☐ ☐☐☐☐☐
1992 RW59		$15	*Spectacled Eider*.............	20.00	5.00	☐☐☐☐☐
1993 RW60		$15	*Canvasbacks*...................	20.00	5.00	☐☐☐☐☐

Scott No.	Illus No.	Description	Unused Value	Used Value	//////

A5

A6

A7

A8

A9

A10

A11

A12

A13

A14

Scott No.	Illus No.		Description	Unused Value	Used Value	//////
MARSHALL ISLANDS						
1984						
31	A5	20c	Outrigger canoe	50	50	☐☐☐☐☐
32	A5	20c	Fishnet	50	50	☐☐☐☐☐
33	A5	20c	Navigational stick chart ...	50	50	☐☐☐☐☐
34	A5	20c	Islet	50	50	☐☐☐☐☐
a.			Block of 4, #31-34	2.00	2.00	☐☐☐☐☐
1984-85						
35	A6	1c	shown	15	15	☐☐☐☐☐
36	A6	3c	Likiep, Azimuth compass	15	15	☐☐☐☐☐
37	A6	5c	Ebon, 16th cent. compass	15	15	☐☐☐☐☐
38	A6	10c	Jaluit, anchor buoys	20	20	☐☐☐☐☐
39	A6	13c	Ailinginae, Nocturnal	26	26	☐☐☐☐☐
a.			Booklet pane of 10	7.00	—	☐☐☐☐☐
40	A6	14c	Wotho Atoll, navigational stick chart....................	28	28	☐☐☐☐☐
a.			Booklet pane of 10	7.00	—	☐☐☐☐☐
41	A6	20c	Kwajalein and Ebeye, stick chart	40	40	☐☐☐☐☐
a.			Booklet pane of 10	9.00	—	☐☐☐☐☐
b.			Booklet pane, 5 each 13c, 20c	8.00	—	☐☐☐☐☐
42	A6	22c	Enewetak, 18th cent. lodestone storage case	44	44	☐☐☐☐☐
a.			Booklet pane of 10	9.00	—	☐☐☐☐☐
b.			Booklet pane, 5 each 14c, 22c	8.00	—	☐☐☐☐☐
43	A6	28c	Ailinglaplap, printed compass	56	56	☐☐☐☐☐
44	A6	30c	Majuro, navigational stick-chart	60	60	☐☐☐☐☐
45	A6	33c	Namu, stick chart	66	66	☐☐☐☐☐
46	A6	37c	Rongelap, quadrant	74	74	☐☐☐☐☐
47	A6	39c	Taka, map compass, 16th cent. sea chart	78	78	☐☐☐☐☐
48	A6	44c	Ujelang, chronograph	88	88	☐☐☐☐☐
49	A6	50c	Maloelap and Aur, nocturlabe	1.00	1.00	☐☐☐☐☐
49A	A6	$1	Arno, 16th cent. sector compass	2.00	2.00	☐☐☐☐☐
1984						
50	A7	40c	shown	75	75	☐☐☐☐☐
51	A7	40c	No. 13	75	75	☐☐☐☐☐
52	A7	40c	No. 4	75	75	☐☐☐☐☐

Scott No.	Illus No.		Description	Unused Value	Used Value	//////
53	A7	40c	No. 25	75	75	
a.			Block of 4, #50-53	3.00	3.00	
54	A8	20c	Common	45	45	
55	A8	20c	Rissos	45	45	
56	A8	20c	Spotter	45	45	
57	A8	20c	Bottlenose	45	45	
a.			Block of 4, #54-57	1.80	1.80	
58			Strip of 4	2.00	2.00	
a.-d.	A9	20c	any single	45	45	
e.			Sheet of 16	9.00		
59	A10	20c	Traditional chief	45	45	
60	A10	20c	Amata Kabua	45	45	
61	A10	20c	Chester Nimitz	45	45	
62	A10	20c	Trygve Lie	45	45	
a.			Block of 4, #59-62	1.80	1.80	

1985

Scott No.	Illus No.		Description	Unused Value	Used Value	//////
63	A11	22c	Forked-tailed Petrel	60	60	
64	A11	22c	Pectoral Sandpiper	60	60	
a.			Pair, #63-64	1.20	1.20	
65	A12	22c	Cymatium lotorium	50	50	
66	A12	22c	Chicoreus cornucervi	50	50	
67	A12	22c	Strombus aurisdanae	50	50	
68	A12	22c	Turbo marmoratus	50	50	
69	A12	22c	Chicoreus palmarosae	50	50	
a.			Strip of 5, #65-69	2.50	2.50	
70	A13	22c	Native drum	50	50	
71	A13	22c	Palm branches	50	50	
72	A13	22c	Pounding stone	50	50	
73	A13	22c	Ak bird	50	50	
a.			Block of 4, #70-73	2.00	2.00	
74	A14	22c	Acanthurus dussumieri	50	50	
75	A14	22c	Adioryx caudimaculatus	50	50	
76	A14	22c	Ostracion meleacaris	50	50	
77	A14	22c	Chaetodon ephippium	50	50	
a.			Block of 4, #74-77	2.00	2.00	
78	A15	22c	multicolored	50	50	
79	A15	22c	multicolored	50	50	
80	A15	22c	multicolored	50	50	
81	A15	22c	multicolored	50	50	
a.			Block of 4, #78-81	2.00	2.00	
82	A16	14c	multicolored	25	25	
83	A16	22c	multicolored	45	45	
84	A16	33c	multicolored	65	65	
85	A16	44c	multicolored	90	90	
86	A17	22c	multicolored	1.10	1.10	
87	A17	22c	multicolored	1.10	1.10	
88	A17	22c	multicolored	1.10	1.10	

A15

A16

A17

A18

A19

A20

A21

A22

Scott No.	Illus No.		Description	Unused Value	Used Value	//////
89	A17	22c	multicolored	1.10	1.10	☐☐☐☐☐
90	A17	22c	multicolored	1.10	1.10	☐☐☐☐☐
a.			Strip of 5, #86-90	5.50	5.50	☐☐☐☐☐
91	A18	22c	Sida fallax	50	50	☐☐☐☐☐
92	A18	22c	Scaevola frutescens	50	50	☐☐☐☐☐
93	A18	22c	Guettarda speciosa	50	50	☐☐☐☐☐
94	A18	22c	Cassytha filiformis	50	50	☐☐☐☐☐
a.			Block of 4, #91-94	2.00	2.00	☐☐☐☐☐

1986-87

107	A6	$2	Wotje and Erikub, terrestrial globe, 1571 .	4.00	4.00	☐☐☐☐☐
108	A6	$5	Bikini, Stick chart............	10.00	10.00	☐☐☐☐☐
109	A6	$10	Stick chart of the atolls	16.00	16.00	☐☐☐☐☐

1986

110	A19	14c	Tritons trumpet	35	35	☐☐☐☐☐
111	A19	14c	Giant clam	35	35	☐☐☐☐☐
112	A19	14c	Small giant clam	35	35	☐☐☐☐☐
113	A19	14c	Coconut crab	35	35	☐☐☐☐☐
a.			Block of 4, #110-113	1.40	1.40	☐☐☐☐☐
114	A20	$1	Douglas C-54 Globester ..	3.25	3.25	☐☐☐☐☐
115	A21	22c	multicolored	50	50	☐☐☐☐☐
116	A21	22c	multicolored	50	50	☐☐☐☐☐
117	A21	22c	multicolored	50	50	☐☐☐☐☐
118	A21	22c	multicolored	50	50	☐☐☐☐☐
a.			Block of 4, #115-118	2.00	2.00	☐☐☐☐☐
119	A12	22c	Ramose murex	50	50	☐☐☐☐☐
120	A12	22c	Orange spider	50	50	☐☐☐☐☐
121	A12	22c	Red-mouth frog shell	50	50	☐☐☐☐☐
122	A12	22c	Laciniate conch	50	50	☐☐☐☐☐
123	A12	22c	Giant frog shell	50	50	☐☐☐☐☐
a.			Strip of 5, #119-123	2.50	2.50	☐☐☐☐☐
124	A22	22c	Blue marlin	50	50	☐☐☐☐☐
125	A22	22c	Wahoo	50	50	☐☐☐☐☐
126	A22	22c	Dolphin fish	50	50	☐☐☐☐☐
127	A22	22c	Yellowfin tuna	50	50	☐☐☐☐☐
a.			Block of 4, #124-127	2.00	2.00	☐☐☐☐☐
128	A23	22c	United Nations UR	70	70	☐☐☐☐☐
129	A23	22c	United Nations UL	70	70	☐☐☐☐☐
130	A23	22c	United Nations LR	70	70	☐☐☐☐☐
131	A23	22c	United Nations LL...........	70	70	☐☐☐☐☐
a.			Block of 4, #128-131	2.80	2.80	☐☐☐☐☐

1987

132	A24	22c	James Arnold, 1854	50	50	☐☐☐☐☐
133	A24	22c	General Scott, 1859	50	50	☐☐☐☐☐
134	A24	22c	Charles W. Morgan, 1865	50	50	☐☐☐☐☐

A24

A23

A25

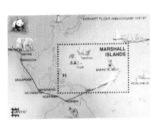
A26

A27

A28

A29

A30

A31

Scott No.	Illus No.		Description	Unused Value	Used Value	//////
135	A24	22c	Lucretia, 1884	50	50	
a.			Block of 4, #132-135	2.00	2.00	
136	A25	33c	multicolored	70	70	
137	A25	33c	multicolored	70	70	
a.			Pair, #136-137	1.40	1.40	
138	A25	39c	multicolored	75	75	
139	A25	39c	multicolored	75	75	
a.			Pair, #138-139	1.50	1.50	
140	A25	44c	multicolored	80	80	
141	A25	44c	multicolored	80	80	
a.			Pair, #140-141	1.60	1.60	
142	A26	$1	Map of flight	2.75	2.75	
143	A27	14c	We,... Marshall	35	35	
144	A27	14c	National seals	35	35	
145	A27	14c	We,... United States	35	35	
a.			Strip of 3, #143-145	1.05	1.05	
146	A27	22c	All we have...	45	45	
147	A27	22c	Flags	45	45	
148	A27	22c	to establish...	45	45	
a.			Strip of 3, #146-148	1.35	1.35	
149	A27	44c	With this Constitution... ..	90	90	
150	A27	44c	Stick chart, Liberty Bell ..	90	90	
151	A27	44c	to promote...	90	90	
a.			Strip of 3, #149-151	2.70	2.70	
152	A12	22c	Magnificent cone	50	50	
153	A12	22c	Partridge tun	50	50	
154	A12	22c	Scorpion spider conch	50	50	
155	A12	22c	Hairy triton	50	50	
156	A12	22c	Chiragra spider conch	50	50	
a.			Strip of 5, #152-156	2.50	2.50	
157	A28	44c	Planting coconut	75	75	
158	A28	44c	Making copra	75	75	
159	A28	44c	Bottling coconut oil	75	75	
a.			Strip of 3, #157-159	2.25	2.25	
160	A29	14c	Matthew 2:1	30	30	
161	A29	22c	Luke 2:14	45	45	
162	A29	33c	Psalms 33:3	70	70	
163	A29	44c	Pslams 150:5	90	90	

1988

164	A30	44c	Pacific reef herons	85	85	
165	A30	44c	Bar-tailed godwit	85	85	
166	A30	44c	Masked booby	85	85	
167	A30	44c	Northern shoveler	85	85	

1988-89

168	A31	1c	Damselfish	15	15	
169	A31	3c	Blackface butterflyfish	15	15	

A32

A33

A34

A35

A36

A37

A38

A39

A42

Scott No.	Illus No.		Description	Unused Value	Used Value	//////
170	A31	14c	Hawkfish	25	25	
a.			Booklet pane of 10	3.00	—	
171	A31	15c	Balloonfish	25	25	
a.			Booklet pane of 10	2.50	—	
172	A31	17c	Trunk fish	30	30	
173	A31	22c	Lyretail wrasse	35	35	
a.			Booklet pane of 10	4.00	—	
b.			Bklt. pane, 5 each 14c, 22c	3.60	—	
174	A31	25c	Parrotfish	40	40	
a.			Booklet pane of 10	4.00	—	
b.			Bklt. pane, 5 each 15c, 25c	3.25	—	
175	A31	33c	White-spotted boxfish	60	60	
176	A31	36c	Spotted boxfish	65	65	
177	A31	39c	Surgeonfish	70	70	
178	A31	44c	Long-snouted butterflyfish	75	75	
179	A31	45c	Trumpetfish	70	70	
180	A31	56c	Sharp-nosed puffer	1.00	1.00	
181	A31	$1	Seahorse	1.75	1.75	
182	A31	$2	Ghost pipefish	3.50	3.50	
183	A31	$5	Big-spotted triggerfish	8.75	8.75	
184	A31	$10	Blue jack	15.00	15.00	
1988						
188			Strip of 5	1.75	1.75	
a.-e.	A32	15c	any single	30	30	
189			Strip of 5	2.25	2.25	
a.-e.	A33	25c	any single	45	45	
190			Sheet of 9	5.75	5.75	
a.-i.	A34	25c	any single	50	50	
191	A35	25c	multicolored	55	55	
192	A35	25c	multicolored	55	55	
193	A35	25c	multicolored	55	55	
194	A35	25c	multicolored	55	55	
a.			Block of 4, #191-194	2.20	2.20	
195	A36	25c	multicolored	50	50	
196	A36	25c	multicolored	50	50	
197	A36	25c	multicolored	50	50	
198	A36	25c	multicolored	50	50	
199	A36	25c	multicolored	50	50	
a.			Strip of 5, #195-199	2.50	2.50	
200	A37	25c	Nuclear threat diminished	60	60	
201	A37	25c	Signing the Test Ban Treaty	60	60	
202	A37	25c	Portrait	60	60	

A40

A41

A43

A44

A45

A46

A47

A57

A58

Scott No.	Illus No.		Description	Unused Value	Used Value	/ / / / / /
203	A37	25c	US-USSR Hotline	60	60	
204	A37	25c	Peace Corps enactment	60	60	
a.			Strip of 5, #200-204	3.00	3.00	
205	A38	25c	multicolored	55	55	
206	A38	25c	multicolored	55	55	
207	A38	25c	multicolored	55	55	
208	A38	25c	multicolored	55	55	
a.			Strip of 4, #205-208	2.20	2.20	

1989

Scott No.	Illus No.		Description	Unused Value	Used Value	/ / / / / /
209	A39	45c	multicolored	85	85	
210	A39	45c	multicolored	85	85	
211	A39	45c	multicolored	85	85	
212	A39	45c	multicolored	85	85	
a.			Block of 4, #209-212	3.40	3.40	
213	A40	45c	Island Woman	85	85	
214	A40	45c	Kotzebue, Alaska	85	85	
215	A40	45c	Marshallese Madonna	85	85	
a.			Strip of 3, #213-215	2.55	2.55	
216	A12	25c	Pontifical miter	55	55	
217	A12	25c	Tapestry turban	55	55	
218	A12	25c	Flame-mouthed helmet	55	55	
219	A12	25c	Prickly Pacific drupe	55	55	
220	A12	25c	Blood-mouthed conch	55	55	
a.			Strip of 5, #216-220	2.75	2.75	
221	A41	$1	multicolored	2.00	2.00	
222	A42	45c	Wandering tattler	85	85	
223	A42	45c	Ruddy turnstone	85	85	
224	A42	45c	Pacific golden plover	85	85	
225	A42	45c	Sanderling	85	85	
a.			Block of 4, #222-225	3.40	3.40	
226	A43	45c	multicolored	85	85	
227	A43	45c	multicolored	85	85	
228	A43	45c	multicolored	85	85	
229	A43	45c	multicolored	85	85	
a.			Block of 4, #226-229	3.40	3.40	
230			Sheet of 6	10.00	3.00	
a.-f.	A44	25c	any single	1.25	1.25	
231	A43	$1	multicolored	10.00	3.00	
232	A45	25c	multicolored	1.25	1.25	
233	A45	25c	multicolored	1.25	1.25	
234	A45	25c	multicolored	1.25	1.25	
235	A45	25c	multicolored	1.25	1.25	
236	A45	25c	multicolored	1.25	1.25	
237	A45	25c	multicolored	1.25	1.25	
238	A45	$1	multicolored	5.00	5.00	
a.			Bklt. pane of 7, #232-238	13.00	—	
239	A46	25c	W1 (1-1)	50	50	

Scott No.	Illus No.		Description	Unused Value	Used Value	/ / / / / /
240	A46	45c	W2 (1-1)	90	90	
241	A46	45c	W3 (1-1)	90	90	
242	A46	45c	W4 (4-1)	90	90	
243	A46	45c	W4 (4-2)	90	90	
244	A46	45c	W4 (4-3)	90	90	
245	A46	45c	W4 (4-4)	90	90	
a.			Block of 4, #242-245	3.60	3.60	

1990

Scott No.	Illus No.		Description	Unused Value	Used Value	/ / / / / /
246	A46	25c	W5 (2-1)	50	50	
247	A46	25c	W5 (2-2)	50	50	
a.			Pair, #246-247	1.00	1.00	
248	A47	25c	W6 (1-1)	50	50	
249	A46	25c	W8 (2-1)	50	50	
250	A46	25c	W8 (2-2)	50	50	
a.			Pair, #249-250	1.00	1.00	
251	A46	45c	W7 (1-1)	90	90	
252	A46	45c	W9 (2-1)	90	90	
253	A46	45c	W9 (2-2)	90	90	
254	A47	45c	W10 (1-1)	90	90	
255	A46	25c	W11 (1-1)	50	50	
256	A47	25c	W12 (1-1)	50	50	
257	A46	45c	W13 (4-1)	90	90	
258	A46	45c	W13 (4-2)	90	90	
259	A46	45c	W13 (4-3)	90	90	
260	A46	45c	W13 (4-4)	90	90	
a.			Block of 4, #257-260	3.60	3.60	
261	A46	45c	W14 (4-1)	90	90	
262	A46	45c	W14 (4-2)	90	90	
263	A46	45c	W14 (4-3)	90	90	
264	A46	45c	W14 (4-4)	90	90	
a.			Block of 4, #261-264	3.60	3.60	
265	A46	45c	W15	90	90	

1990-91

Scott No.	Illus No.		Description	Unused Value	Used Value	/ / / / / /
266	A47	25c	W16	50	50	
267	A46	25c	W17 (4-1)	50	50	
268	A46	25c	W17 (4-2)	50	50	
269	A46	25c	W17 (4-3)	50	50	
270	A46	25c	W17 (4-4)	50	50	
a.			Block of 4, #266-270	2.00	2.00	
271	A46	30c	W18 (4-1)	60	60	
272	A46	30c	W18 (4-2)	60	60	
273	A46	30c	W18 (4-3)	60	60	
274	A46	30c	W18 (4-4)	60	60	
a.			Block of 4, #271-274	2.40	2.40	
275	A46	30c	Tanks, W19	60	60	

Scott No.	Illus No.		Description	Unused Value	Used Value	//////
276	A47	29c	W20 (2-1)	58	58	☐☐☐☐☐
277	A47	29c	W20 (2-2)	58	58	☐☐☐☐☐
a.			Pair, #276-277	1.16	1.16	☐☐☐☐☐
278	A46	50c	W21 (4-1)	1.00	1.00	☐☐☐☐☐
279	A46	50c	W21 (4-2)	1.00	1.00	☐☐☐☐☐
280	A46	50c	W21 (4-3)	1.00	1.00	☐☐☐☐☐
281	A46	50c	W21 (4-4)	1.00	1.00	☐☐☐☐☐
a.			Block of 4, #278-281	4.00	4.00	☐☐☐☐☐
282	A46	30c	Tanks, W22	60	60	☐☐☐☐☐

1991

283	A47	29c	W23 (2-1)	58	58	☐☐☐☐☐
284	A47	29c	W23 (2-2)	58	58	☐☐☐☐☐
a.			Pair, #283-284	1.16	1.16	☐☐☐☐☐
285	A46	29c	W24	58	58	☐☐☐☐☐
286	A46	30c	W25 (2-1)	60	60	☐☐☐☐☐
287	A46	30c	W25 (2-1)	60	60	☐☐☐☐☐
a.			Pair, #286-287	1.20	1.20	☐☐☐☐☐
288	A47	50c	W26 (4-1)	1.00	1.00	☐☐☐☐☐
289	A47	50c	W26 (4-2)	1.00	1.00	☐☐☐☐☐
290	A47	50c	W26 (4-3)	1.00	1.00	☐☐☐☐☐
291	A47	50c	W26 (4-4)	1.00	1.00	☐☐☐☐☐
a.			Block of 4, #288-291	4.00	4.00	☐☐☐☐☐

1991-92

292	A47	29c	W27	58	58	☐☐☐☐☐
293	A46	29c	W28	58	58	☐☐☐☐☐
294	A46	50c	W29 (2-1)	1.00	1.00	☐☐☐☐☐
295	A46	50c	W29 (2-2)	1.00	1.00	☐☐☐☐☐
a.			Pair, #294-295	2.00	2.00	☐☐☐☐☐
296	A46	29c	W30	58	58	☐☐☐☐☐
297	A46	29c	W31	58	58	☐☐☐☐☐
298	A46	50c	W32	1.00	1.00	☐☐☐☐☐
299	A46	29c	W33	58	58	☐☐☐☐☐
300	A46	29c	W34	58	58	☐☐☐☐☐
301	A47	50c	W35	1.00	1.00	☐☐☐☐☐
302	A46	29c	W36	58	58	☐☐☐☐☐
303	A46	29c	W37	58	58	☐☐☐☐☐
304	A46	29c	W38	58	58	☐☐☐☐☐
305	A47	29c	W39	58	58	☐☐☐☐☐
306	A47	50c	W40	1.00	1.00	☐☐☐☐☐
307	A46	29c	W41	58	58	☐☐☐☐☐

1992

308	A46	50c	W42 (4-1)	1.00	1.00	☐☐☐☐☐
309	A46	50c	W42 (4-2)	1.00	1.00	☐☐☐☐☐
310	A46	50c	W42 (4-3)	1.00	1.00	☐☐☐☐☐

A59a

A59

A60

A61

A62

A63

A64

A65

A66

A67

A77

314

Scott No.	Illus No.		Description	Unused Value	Used Value	//////
311	A46	50c	W42 (4-4)	1.00	1.00	☐☐☐☐☐
a.			Block of 4, #308-311	4.00	4.00	☐☐☐☐☐
312	A46	50c	W43 (4-1)	1.00	1.00	☐☐☐☐☐
313	A46	50c	W43 (4-3)	1.00	1.00	☐☐☐☐☐
314	A46	50c	W43 (4-2)	1.00	1.00	☐☐☐☐☐
315	A46	50c	W43 (4-4)	1.00	1.00	☐☐☐☐☐
a.			Block of 4, #312-315	4.00	4.00	☐☐☐☐☐
316	A46	29c	W44	58	58	☐☐☐☐☐
317	A47	29c	W45	58	58	☐☐☐☐☐
318	A46	29c	W46 (2-1)	58	58	☐☐☐☐☐
319	A46	29c	W46 (2-2)	58	58	☐☐☐☐☐
a.			Pair, #318-319	1.16	1.16	☐☐☐☐☐
320	A46	29c	W47	58	58	☐☐☐☐☐
321	A47	29c	W48	58	58	☐☐☐☐☐
322	A46	29c	W49	58	58	☐☐☐☐☐
323	A47	50c	W50	1.00	1.00	☐☐☐☐☐
324	A46	29c	W51	58	58	☐☐☐☐☐
325	A46	50c	W52	1.00	1.00	☐☐☐☐☐
326	A46	29c	W53	58	58	☐☐☐☐☐

1989

Scott No.	Illus No.		Description	Unused Value	Used Value	//////
341	A57	25c	Horn	75	75	☐☐☐☐☐
342	A57	25c	Singing carol	75	75	☐☐☐☐☐
343	A57	25c	Lute	75	75	☐☐☐☐☐
344	A57	25c	Lyre	75	75	☐☐☐☐☐
a.			Block of 4, #341-344	3.00	3.00	☐☐☐☐☐
345			Sheet of 25	30.00	30.00	☐☐☐☐☐
a.-y.	A58	45c	any single	1.00	1.00	☐☐☐☐☐

1990-92

Scott No.	Illus No.		Description	Unused Value	Used Value	//////
346	A59	1c	Black noddy	15	15	☐☐☐☐☐
347	A59	5c	Red-tailed tropic bird	15	15	☐☐☐☐☐
348	A59	10c	Sanderling	20	20	☐☐☐☐☐
349	A59	12c	Black-naped tern	24	24	☐☐☐☐☐
350	A59	15c	Wandering tattler	30	30	☐☐☐☐☐
351	A59	20c	Bristle-thighed curlew	40	40	☐☐☐☐☐
352	A59	23c	Northern shoveler	46	46	☐☐☐☐☐
353	A59	25c	Brown noddy	50	50	☐☐☐☐☐
354	A59	27c	Sooty tern	54	54	☐☐☐☐☐
355	A59	29c	Wedge-tailed shearwater .	58	58	☐☐☐☐☐
356	A59a	29c	Northern pintail	58	58	☐☐☐☐☐
357	A59	30c	Pacific golden plover	60	60	☐☐☐☐☐
358	A59	35c	Brown booby	70	70	☐☐☐☐☐
359	A59	36c	Red footed booby	72	72	☐☐☐☐☐
360	A59	40c	White tern	80	80	☐☐☐☐☐
361	A59	50c	Great frigate bird	1.00	1.00	☐☐☐☐☐
a.			Min. sheet of 4, #347, 350, 353, 361	1.90	1.90	☐☐☐☐☐

A68

A69

A70

A71

A72

A73

A74

A75

A76

A78

316

Scott No.	Illus No.	Description		Unused Value	Used Value	//////
362	A59	52c	Great crested tern	1.04	1.04	□□□□□
363	A59	65c	Lesser sand plover	1.30	1.30	□□□□□
364	A59	75c	Little tern	1.50	1.50	□□□□□
365	A59	$1	Pacific reef heron	2.00	2.00	□□□□□
365A	A59	$2	Masked booby	4.00	4.00	□□□□□

1990

Scott No.	Illus No.	Description		Unused Value	Used Value	//////
366	A60	25c	Lodidean	75	75	□□□□□
367	A60	25c	Lejonjon	75	75	□□□□□
368	A60	25c	Etobobo	75	75	□□□□□
369	A60	25c	Didmakol	75	75	□□□□□
a.			Block of 4, #366-369	3.00	3.00	□□□□□
370	A61	25c	multicolored	75	75	□□□□□
371	A61	25c	multicolored	75	75	□□□□□
372	A61	25c	multicolored	75	75	□□□□□
373	A61	25c	multicolored	75	75	□□□□□
374	A61	25c	multicolored	75	75	□□□□□
375	A61	25c	multicolored	75	75	□□□□□
376	A61	$1	multicolored	3.50	3.50	□□□□□
a.			Bklt. pane of 7, #370-376	8.50	8.50	□□□□□
377	A62	25c	multicolored	75	75	□□□□□
378	A62	25c	multicolored	75	75	□□□□□
379	A62	25c	multicolored	75	75	□□□□□
380	A62	25c	multicolored	75	75	□□□□□
a.			Block of 4, #377-380	3.00	3.00	□□□□□
381	A63	25c	multicolored	60	60	□□□□□
382	A64	45c	multicolored	1.25	1.25	□□□□□
383	A65	25c	Canoe, stick chart	75	75	□□□□□
384	A65	25c	Missionary preaching	75	75	□□□□□
385	A65	25c	Sailors dancing	75	75	□□□□□
386	A65	25c	Youths dancing	75	75	□□□□□
a.			Block of 4, #383-386	3.00	3.00	□□□□□
387	A66	25c	Harvesting	75	75	□□□□□
388	A66	25c	Peeling, slicing	75	75	□□□□□
389	A66	25c	Preserving	75	75	□□□□□
390	A66	25c	Kneading dough	75	75	□□□□□
a.			Block of 4, #387-390	3.00	3.00	□□□□□

1991

Scott No.	Illus No.	Description		Unused Value	Used Value	//////
391	A67	50c	747 ferry	1.00	1.00	□□□□□
392	A67	50c	Orbital release of LDEF ..	1.00	1.00	□□□□□
393	A67	50c	Lift-off	1.00	1.00	□□□□□
394	A67	50c	Landing	1.00	1.00	□□□□□
a.			Block of 4, #391-394	4.00	4.00	□□□□□
395	A68	52c	Ixora carolinensis	1.05	1.05	□□□□□
396	A68	52c	Clerodendrum inerme	1.05	1.05	□□□□□

Scott No.	Illus No.		Description	Unused Value	Used Value	/ / / / / /
397	A68	52c	Messerchmidia argentea ..	1.05	1.05	☐☐☐☐☐
398	A68	52c	Vigna marina	1.05	1.05	☐☐☐☐☐
a.			Min. sheet of 4, #395-398	4.20	4.20	☐☐☐☐☐
399	A69	29c	multicolored	58	58	☐☐☐☐☐
400	A70	29c	Red-footed booby	58	58	☐☐☐☐☐
401	A70	29c	Great frigate bird (7-2)	58	58	☐☐☐☐☐
402	A70	29c	Brown booby	58	58	☐☐☐☐☐
403	A70	29c	White tern	58	58	☐☐☐☐☐
404	A70	29c	Great frigate bird (7-5)	58	58	☐☐☐☐☐
405	A70	29c	Black noddy	58	58	☐☐☐☐☐
406	A70	$1	White-tailed tropic bird ...	2.00	2.00	☐☐☐☐☐
a.			Bklt. pane of 7, #400-406	5.50	5.50	☐☐☐☐☐
407	A71	12c	Dornier 228	24	24	☐☐☐☐☐
408	A71	29c	Douglas DC-8	58	58	☐☐☐☐☐
409	A71	50c	Hawker Siddeley 748	1.00	1.00	☐☐☐☐☐
410	A71	50c	Saab 2000	1.00	1.00	☐☐☐☐☐
411	A72	29c	multicolored	65	65	☐☐☐☐☐
412	A73	30c	multicolored	75	75	☐☐☐☐☐
413	A74	29c	multicolored	58	58	☐☐☐☐☐
1992						
414	A75	29c	multicolored	58	58	☐☐☐☐☐
415	A75	29c	multicolored	58	58	☐☐☐☐☐
416	A75	29c	multicolored	58	58	☐☐☐☐☐
417	A75	29c	multicolored	58	58	☐☐☐☐☐
a.			Strip of 4, #414-417	2.35	2.35	☐☐☐☐☐
418	A76	50c	multicolored	1.00	1.00	☐☐☐☐☐
419	A76	50c	multicolored	1.00	1.00	☐☐☐☐☐
420	A76	50c	multicolored	1.00	1.00	☐☐☐☐☐
421	A76	50c	multicolored	1.00	1.00	☐☐☐☐☐
422	A76	50c	multicolored	1.00	1.00	☐☐☐☐☐
423	A76	50c	multicolored	1.00	1.00	☐☐☐☐☐
424	A76	$1	multicolored	2.00	2.00	☐☐☐☐☐
a.			Bklt. pane of 7, #418-424	8.00	8.00	☐☐☐☐☐
425	A77	29c	Basket weaving	58	58	☐☐☐☐☐
426	A77	29c	Canoe models	58	58	☐☐☐☐☐
427	A77	29c	Wood carving	58	58	☐☐☐☐☐
428	A77	29c	Fan making	58	58	☐☐☐☐☐
a.			Strip of 4, #425-428	2.32	2.32	☐☐☐☐☐
429	A78	29c	multicolored	58	58	☐☐☐☐☐
						☐☐☐☐☐
						☐☐☐☐☐
						☐☐☐☐☐
						☐☐☐☐☐
						☐☐☐☐☐
						☐☐☐☐☐
						☐☐☐☐☐

Scott No.	Illus No.	Description	Unused Value	Used Value	//////

AP1

AP2

AP3

AP4

AP5

HOW TO USE THIS BOOK

The number in the first column is its Scott number or identifying number. The letter and number that come next (A41) indicate the design and refer to the illustration so designated. Following that is the denomination of the stamp and its color. Finally, the value, unused and used is shown.

Scott No.	Illus No.		Description	Unused Value	Used Value	//////

MARSHALL ISLANDS, AIR POST STAMPS

1985

Scott No.	Illus No.		Description	Unused Value	Used Value	
C1	A11	44c	Booby Gannet, vert.	88	88	☐☐☐☐☐
C2	A11	44c	Esquimaux Curlew, vert. .	88	88	☐☐☐☐☐
a.			Pair, #C1-C2	1.80	1.80	☐☐☐☐☐

1986

C3	A20	44c	multicolored	95	95	☐☐☐☐☐
C4	A20	44c	multicolored	95	95	☐☐☐☐☐
C5	A20	44c	multicolored	95	95	☐☐☐☐☐
C6	A20	44c	multicolored	95	95	☐☐☐☐☐
a.			Block of 4, #C3-C6	3.80	3.80	☐☐☐☐☐
C7	A21	44c	USS Saratoga	*4.50*	*4.50*	☐☐☐☐☐
C8	AP1	44c	multicolored	95	95	☐☐☐☐☐
C9	AP2	44c	Community service	85	85	☐☐☐☐☐
C10	AP2	44c	Salute	85	85	☐☐☐☐☐
C11	AP2	44c	Health care	85	85	☐☐☐☐☐
C12	AP2	44c	Learning skills	85	85	☐☐☐☐☐
a.			Block of 4, #C9-C12	3.40	3.40	☐☐☐☐☐

1987

C13	AP3	44c	Wedge-tailed shearwater .	85	85	☐☐☐☐☐
C14	AP3	44c	Red-footed booby	85	85	☐☐☐☐☐
C15	AP3	44c	Red-tailed tropic-bird	85	85	☐☐☐☐☐
C16	AP3	44c	Great frigatebird	85	85	☐☐☐☐☐
a.			Block of 4, #C13-C16	3.40	3.40	☐☐☐☐☐
C17	AP4	44c	multicolored	85	85	☐☐☐☐☐
C18	AP4	44c	multicolored	85	85	☐☐☐☐☐
C19	AP4	44c	multicolored	85	85	☐☐☐☐☐
C20	AP4	44c	multicolored	85	85	☐☐☐☐☐
a.			Block of 4, #C17-C20	3.40	3.40	☐☐☐☐☐

1988

C21	A38	45c	Astronaut, shuttle over Rongelap	90	90	☐☐☐☐☐

1989

C22	AP5	12c	Dornier Do228	25	25	☐☐☐☐☐
a.			Booklet pane of 10	3.00	—	☐☐☐☐☐
C23	AP5	36c	Boeing 737	75	75	☐☐☐☐☐
a.			Booklet pane of 10	8.00	—	☐☐☐☐☐
C24	AP5	39c	Hawker Siddeley 748	90	90	☐☐☐☐☐
a.			Booklet pane of 10	9.00	—	☐☐☐☐☐
C25	AP5	45c	Boeing 727	1.00	1.00	☐☐☐☐☐
a.			Booklet pane of 10	10.00	—	☐☐☐☐☐
b.			Booklet pane, 5 each 36c, 45c	8.75	—	☐☐☐☐☐

A2

A1

A3

A4

A5

A6

A7

A8

Federated States of
Micronesia

LONG-BILLED
WHITE-EYE

Rukia longirostra

3c

A10

A9

A11

322

Scott No.	Illus No.		Description	Unused Value	Used Value	//////
MICRONESIA						
1984						
1	A1	20c	Yap	50	50	
2	A1	20c	Truk	50	50	
3	A1	20c	Pohnpei	50	50	
4	A1	20c	Kosrae	50	50	
a.			Block of 4, #1-4	2.00	2.00	
5	A2	1c	Prussian blue	15	15	
6	A2	2c	deep claret	15	15	
7	A2	3c	dark blue	15	15	
8	A2	4c	green	15	15	
9	A3	5c	yellow brown	15	15	
10	A3	10c	dark violet	16	16	
11	A3	13c	dark blue	20	20	
12	A3	17c	brown lake	25	25	
13	A2	19c	dark violet	28	28	
14	A2	20c	olive green	30	30	
15	A2	30c	rose lake	45	45	
16	A2	37c	deep violet	55	55	
17	A3	50c	brown	75	75	
18	A3	$1	olive	1.50	1.50	
19	A3	$2	Prussian blue	3.00	3.00	
20	A3	$5	brown lake	7.00	7.00	
21	A4	20c	Truk Post Office	48	48	
22	A5	20c	Child in manger	55	55	
1985						
23	A6	22c	U.S.S. Jamestown	60	60	
24	A7	22c	Lelu Protestant Church, Kosrae	60	60	
25	A8	22c	Noddy tern	75	75	
26	A8	22c	Turnstone	75	75	
27	A8	22c	Golden plover	75	75	
28	A8	22c	Black-bellied plover	75	75	
a.			Block of 4, #25-28	3.00	3.00	
1985-88						
31	A9	3c	Long-billed white-eye	15	15	
32	A9	14c	Truk monarch	28	28	
33	A3	15c	Liduduhriap Waterfall, Pohnpei	30	30	
a.			Booklet pane of 10	3.00	—	
34	A10	22c	bright blue green	35	35	
35	A9	22c	Pohnpei mountain starling	44	44	
36	A3	25c	Tonachau Peak, Truk	50	50	
a.			Booklet pane of 10	5.00	—	
b.			Booklet pane, 5 each 15c, 25c	4.00	—	

A16

A17

A18

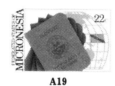

A19

A20

A21

A22

A23

A24

A25

A27

A29

324

A26

A28

HOW TO USE THIS BOOK

The number in the first column is its Scott number or identifying number. The letter and number that come next (A41) indicate the design and refer to the illustration so designated. Following that is the denomination of the stamp and its color. Finally, the value, unused and used is shown.

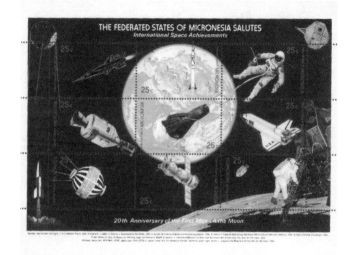

THE FEDERATED STATES OF MICRONESIA SALUTES
International Space Achievements

20th. Anniversary of the First Man on the Moon

A30

A32

A31

A33

A34

A35

Scott No.	Illus No.	Description	Unused Value	Used Value	//////
37	A10	36c ultramarine	72	72	☐☐☐☐☐
38	A3	45c Sleeping Lady, Kosrae	90	90	☐☐☐☐☐
39	A11	$10 bright ultra	15.00	15.00	☐☐☐☐☐

1985

45	A16	22c Land of the Sacred Masonry	60	60	☐☐☐☐☐

1986

46	A17	22c multicolored	60	60	☐☐☐☐☐
48	A1	22c on 20c No. 1	45	45	☐☐☐☐☐
49	A1	22c on 20c No. 2	45	45	☐☐☐☐☐
50	A1	22c on 20c No. 3	45	45	☐☐☐☐☐
51	A1	22c on 20c No. 4	45	45	☐☐☐☐☐
a.		Block of 4, #48-51	1.90	1.90	☐☐☐☐☐
52	A18	22c At ships helm	60	60	☐☐☐☐☐
53	A19	22c multicolored	75	75	☐☐☐☐☐
54	A20	5c multicolored	25	25	☐☐☐☐☐
55	A20	22c multicolored	75	75	☐☐☐☐☐

1987

56	A21	22c Intl. Year of Shelter for the Homeless	65	65	☐☐☐☐☐
57	A21	$1 CAPEX 87	3.00	3.00	☐☐☐☐☐
58	A22	22c multicolored	60	60	☐☐☐☐☐

1988

59	A23	22c German	60	60	☐☐☐☐☐
60	A23	22c Spanish	60	60	☐☐☐☐☐
61	A23	22c Japanese	60	60	☐☐☐☐☐
62	A23	22c US Trust Territory	60	60	☐☐☐☐☐
a.		Block of 4, #59-62	2.40	2.40	☐☐☐☐☐
63	A24	25c Running	55	55	☐☐☐☐☐
64	A24	25c Womens hurdles	55	55	☐☐☐☐☐
a.		Pair, #63-64	1.10	1.10	☐☐☐☐☐
65	A24	45c Basketball	90	90	☐☐☐☐☐
66	A24	45c Womens volleyball	90	90	☐☐☐☐☐
a.		Pair, #65-66	1.80	1.80	☐☐☐☐☐
67	A25	25c multicolored	50	50	☐☐☐☐☐
68	A25	25c multicolored	50	50	☐☐☐☐☐
69	A25	25c multicolored	50	50	☐☐☐☐☐
70	A25	25c multicolored	50	50	☐☐☐☐☐
a.		Block of 4, #67-70	2.00	2.00	☐☐☐☐☐
71		Sheet of 18	7.50	7.50	☐☐☐☐☐
a.-r.	A26	25c any single	40	40	☐☐☐☐☐

A36

A37

A38

A39

A40

A41

A42

A43

A44

Scott No.	Illus No.		Description	Unused Value	Used Value	//////
1989						
72	A27	45c	Plumeria	75	75	
73	A27	45c	Hibiscus	75	75	
74	A27	45c	Jasmine	75	75	
75	A27	45c	Bougainvillea	75	75	
a.			Block of 4, #72-75	3.00	3.00	
76	A28	$1	multicolored	1.65	1.65	
77	A29	25c	Whale	40	40	
78	A29	25c	Hammerhead	40	40	
a.			Pair, #77-78	80	80	
79	A29	45c	Tiger, vert.	75	75	
80	A29	45c	Great white, vert.	75	75	
a.			Pair, #79-80	1.50	1.50	
81	A30		Sheet of 9	3.50	3.50	
a.-i.		25c	any single	38	38	
82	A31	$2.40	multicolored	3.50	3.50	
83	A32	1c	Horses hoof	15	15	
84	A32	3c	Rare spotted cowrie	15	15	
85	A32	15c	Commercial trochus	22	22	
a.			Booklet pane of 10	2.75	—	
87	A32	20c	General cone	30	30	
88	A32	25c	Tritons trumpet	38	38	
a.			Booklet pane of 10	4.75	—	
b.			Booklet pane, 5 each 15c, 25c	3.75	—	
90	A32	30c	Laciniated conch	45	45	
91	A32	36c	Red-mouthed olive	55	55	
93	A32	45c	Map cowrie	70	70	
95	A32	50c	Textile cone	75	75	
100	A32	$1	Orange spider conch	1.50	1.50	
101	A32	$2	Golden cowrie	3.00	3.00	
102	A32	$5	Episcopal miter	7.50	7.50	
103			Sheet of 18	9.50	9.50	
a.-r.	A33	25c	any single	50	50	
104	A34	25c	Heralding angel	40	40	
105	A34	45c	Three wise men	80	80	
1990						
106	A35	10c	Kingfisher (juvenile)	20	20	
107	A35	15c	Kingfisher (adult)	30	30	
108	A35	20c	Pigeon	40	40	
109	A35	25c	Pigeon, diff.	50	50	
110	A36	45c	multicolored	70	70	
111	A36	45c	multicolored	70	70	
112	A36	45c	multicolored	70	70	
113	A36	45c	multicolored	70	70	
a.			Block of 4, #110-113	2.80	2.80	
114	A36	$1	multicolored	1.65	1.65	

329

A45

A46

A47

A48

A49

A50

A51

Scott No.	Illus No.		Description	Unused Value	Used Value	//////
115	A37	$1	Great Britain No. 1	1.65	1.65	☐☐☐☐☐
116	A38	25c	multicolored	40	40	☐☐☐☐☐
117	A38	25c	multicolored	40	40	☐☐☐☐☐
118	A39	25c	multicolored	40	40	☐☐☐☐☐
119	A38	25c	multicolored	40	40	☐☐☐☐☐
120	A38	25c	multicolored	40	40	☐☐☐☐☐
a.			Strip of 5, #116-120	2.00	2.00	☐☐☐☐☐
121	A40	$1	multicolored	1.80	1.80	☐☐☐☐☐
122	A41	25c	multicolored	55	55	☐☐☐☐☐
123	A41	45c	multicolored	1.00	1.00	☐☐☐☐☐
124	A42	25c	multicolored	55	55	☐☐☐☐☐
125	A42	25c	multicolored	55	55	☐☐☐☐☐
126	A42	25c	multicolored	55	55	☐☐☐☐☐
a.			Strip of 3, #124-126	1.65	1.65	☐☐☐☐☐
127	A43	45c	Gracillariidae	75	75	☐☐☐☐☐
128	A43	45c	Yponomeatidae	75	75	☐☐☐☐☐
129	A43	45c	shown	75	75	☐☐☐☐☐
130	A43	45c	Cosmopterigidae, diff. ...	75	75	☐☐☐☐☐
a.			Block of 4, #127-130	3.00	3.00	☐☐☐☐☐
131			Sheet of 9	3.50	3.50	☐☐☐☐☐
a.-i.	A44	25c	any single	40	40	☐☐☐☐☐
1991						
132			Sheet of 2	1.40	1.40	☐☐☐☐☐
a.	A45	25c	Executive Branch	50	50	☐☐☐☐☐
b.	A45	45c	Legislative, Judicial Branches	90	90	☐☐☐☐☐
133	A45	$1	New Capitol	2.00	2.00	☐☐☐☐☐
134	A47	29c	Hawksbill on beach	70	70	☐☐☐☐☐
135	A47	29c	Green	70	70	☐☐☐☐☐
a.			Pair, #134-135	1.40	1.40	☐☐☐☐☐
136	A47	50c	Hawksbill	1.15	1.15	☐☐☐☐☐
137	A47	50c	Leatherback	1.15	1.15	☐☐☐☐☐
a.			Pair, #136-137	2.30	2.30	☐☐☐☐☐
138	A47	29c	Battleship Missouri	60	60	☐☐☐☐☐
139	A47	29c	Multiple launch rocket system	60	60	☐☐☐☐☐
140	A47	29c	F-14 Tomcat	60	60	☐☐☐☐☐
141	A47	29c	E-3 Sentry (AWACS)	60	60	☐☐☐☐☐
a.			Block of 4, #138-141	2.40	2.40	☐☐☐☐☐
142	A47	$2.90	Frigatebird, flag	5.80	5.80	☐☐☐☐☐
a.			Souvenir sheet of 1	5.80	5.80	☐☐☐☐☐
143			Sheet of 3	1.75	1.75	☐☐☐☐☐
a.-c.	A48	29c	any single	58	58	☐☐☐☐☐
144			Sheet of 3	3.00	3.00	☐☐☐☐☐
a.-c.	A48	50c	any single	1.00	1.00	☐☐☐☐☐
145	A48	$1	multicolored	2.00	2.00	☐☐☐☐☐

Scott No.	Illus No.		Description	Unused Value	Used Value	//////
146	A49	29c	multicolored	58	58	☐☐☐☐☐
147	A49	40c	multicolored	80	80	☐☐☐☐☐
148	A49	50c	multicolored	1.00	1.00	☐☐☐☐☐
149			Sheet of 18	10.50	10.50	☐☐☐☐☐
a.-r.	A50	29c	any single	58	58	☐☐☐☐☐

1992

| 150 | A51 | 29c | Strip of 5, #a.-e. .... | 2.90 | 2.90 | ☐☐☐☐☐ |

Scott No.	Illus No.	Description	Unused Value	Used Value	——————

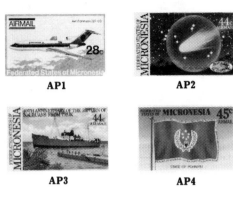

AP1

AP2

AP3

AP4

AP5

HOW TO USE THIS BOOK

The number in the first column is its Scott number or identifying number. The letter and number that come next (A41) indicate the design and refer to the illustration so designated. Following that is the denomination of the stamp and its color. Finally, the value, unused and used is shown.

MICRONESIA, AIR POST STAMPS

1984

Scott No.	Illus No.		Description	Unused Value	Used Value	
C1	AP1	28c	shown	55	55	☐☐☐☐☐
C2	AP1	35c	SA-16 Albatross, 1960	70	70	☐☐☐☐☐
C3	AP1	40c	PBY-5A Catalina, 1951 ...	80	80	☐☐☐☐☐
C4	A4	28c	multicolored	70	70	☐☐☐☐☐
C5	A4	35c	multicolored	90	90	☐☐☐☐☐
C6	A4	40c	multicolored	1.20	1.20	☐☐☐☐☐
C7	A5	28c	Illustrated Christmas text .	70	70	☐☐☐☐☐
C8	A5	35c	Decorated palm tree	90	90	☐☐☐☐☐
C9	A5	40c	Feast preparation	1.20	1.20	☐☐☐☐☐

1985

Scott No.	Illus No.		Description	Unused Value	Used Value	
C10	A6	33c	L'Astrolabe	70	70	☐☐☐☐☐
C11	A6	39c	La Coquille	1.00	1.00	☐☐☐☐☐
C12	A6	44c	Shenandoah	1.25	1.25	☐☐☐☐☐
C13	A7	33c	Dublon Protestant Church	70	70	☐☐☐☐☐
C14	A7	44c	Pohnpei Catholic Church	90	90	☐☐☐☐☐
C15	A8	44c	Sooty tern	1.20	1.20	☐☐☐☐☐
C16	A16	33c	Nan Tauas inner courtyard	70	70	☐☐☐☐☐
C17	A16	39c	Outer wall	80	80	☐☐☐☐☐
C18	A16	44c	Tomb	90	90	☐☐☐☐☐

1986

Scott No.	Illus No.		Description	Unused Value	Used Value	
C19	AP2	44c	dark blue, blue & black ...	1.25	1.25	☐☐☐☐☐
C20	AP3	44c	Ship in port	1.25	1.25	☐☐☐☐☐
C21	A18	33c	Forging Hawaiian stamp .	75	75	☐☐☐☐☐
C22	A18	39c	Sinking of the Leonora, Kosrae	90	90	☐☐☐☐☐
C23	A18	44c	Hayes escapes capture	1.00	1.00	☐☐☐☐☐
C24	A18	75c	Biography, by Louis Becke	1.90	1.90	☐☐☐☐☐
C25	A18	$1	Hayes ransoming chief	4.00	4.00	☐☐☐☐☐
C26	A20	33c	multicolored	1.00	1.00	☐☐☐☐☐
C27	A20	44c	multicolored	1.40	1.40	☐☐☐☐☐

1987

Scott No.	Illus No.		Description	Unused Value	Used Value	
C28	A21	33c	US currency, bicent.	80	80	☐☐☐☐☐
C29	A21	39c	1st American in orbit, 25th anniv.	1.25	1.25	☐☐☐☐☐
C30	A21	44c	US Constitution, bicent. ..	1.40	1.40	☐☐☐☐☐
C31	A22	33c	Holy Family	80	80	☐☐☐☐☐
C32	A22	39c	Shepherds	90	90	☐☐☐☐☐
C33	A22	44c	Three Wise Men	1.00	1.00	☐☐☐☐☐

Scott No.	Illus No.		Description	Unused Value	Used Value	/ / / / / /
1988						
C34	A9	33c	Great truk white-eye	55	55	☐☐☐☐☐
C35	A9	44c	Blue-faced parrotfinch	70	70	☐☐☐☐☐
C36	A9	$1	Yap monarch	1.75	1.75	☐☐☐☐☐
C37	A23	44c	Traditional skills (boat-building)	95	95	☐☐☐☐☐
C38	A23	44c	Modern Micronesia (tourism)	95	95	☐☐☐☐☐
a.			Pair, #C37-C38	1.90	1.90	☐☐☐☐☐
1989						
C39	AP4	45c	Pohnpei............................	90	90	☐☐☐☐☐
C40	AP4	45c	Truk	90	90	☐☐☐☐☐
C41	AP4	45c	Kosrae	90	90	☐☐☐☐☐
C42	AP4	45c	Yap	90	90	☐☐☐☐☐
a.			Block of 4, #C39-C42	3.60	3.60	☐☐☐☐☐
1990						
C43	AP5	22c	shown	45	45	☐☐☐☐☐
C44	AP5	36c	multi, diff.......................	72	72	☐☐☐☐☐
C45	AP5	39c	multi, diff.......................	80	80	☐☐☐☐☐
C46	AP5	45c	multi, diff.......................	90	90	☐☐☐☐☐
1992						
C47	AP5	40c	Propeller plane, outrigger canoe	75	75	☐☐☐☐☐
C48	AP5	50c	Passenger jet, sailboat	90	90	☐☐☐☐☐

Scott No.	Illus No.	Description	Unused Value	Used Value	/ / / / /
					☐☐☐☐☐
					☐☐☐☐☐
					☐☐☐☐☐
					☐☐☐☐☐
					☐☐☐☐☐
					☐☐☐☐☐
					☐☐☐☐☐
					☐☐☐☐☐
					☐☐☐☐☐
					☐☐☐☐☐
					☐☐☐☐☐
					☐☐☐☐☐
					☐☐☐☐☐
					☐☐☐☐☐
					☐☐☐☐☐
					☐☐☐☐☐
					☐☐☐☐☐
					☐☐☐☐☐
					☐☐☐☐☐
					☐☐☐☐☐
					☐☐☐☐☐
					☐☐☐☐☐
					☐☐☐☐☐
					☐☐☐☐☐
					☐☐☐☐☐
					☐☐☐☐☐
					☐☐☐☐☐
					☐☐☐☐☐
					☐☐☐☐☐
					☐☐☐☐☐
					☐☐☐☐☐
					☐☐☐☐☐
					☐☐☐☐☐
					☐☐☐☐☐
					☐☐☐☐☐
					☐☐☐☐☐
					☐☐☐☐☐
					☐☐☐☐☐
					☐☐☐☐☐
					☐☐☐☐☐
					☐☐☐☐☐
					☐☐☐☐☐
					☐☐☐☐☐
					☐☐☐☐☐
					☐☐☐☐☐
					☐☐☐☐☐
					☐☐☐☐☐

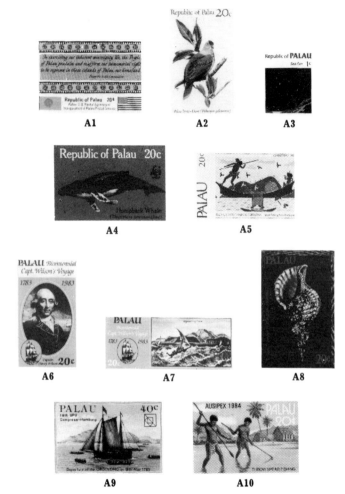

A1

A2

A3

A4

A5

A6

A7

A8

A9

A10

HOW TO USE THIS BOOK

The number in the first column is its Scott number or identifying number. The letter and number that come next (A41) indicate the design and refer to the illustration so designated. Following that is the denomination of the stamp and its color. Finally, the value, unused and used is shown.

Scott No.	Illus No.		Description	Unused Value	Used Value	//////
PALAU						
1983						
1	A1	20c	Constitution preamble	55	55	
2	A1	20c	Hunters	55	55	
3	A1	20c	Fish	55	55	
4	A1	20c	Preamble, diff.	55	55	
a.			Block of 4, #1-4	2.20	2.20	
5	A2	20c	shown	40	40	
6	A2	20c	Palau morningbird	40	40	
7	A2	20c	Giant white-eye	40	40	
8	A2	20c	Palau fantail....................	40	40	
a.			Block of 4, #5-8	1.65	1.65	
1983-84						
9	A3	1c	shown	15	15	
10	A3	3c	Map cowrie	15	15	
11	A3	5c	Jellyfish	15	15	
12	A3	10c	Hawksbill turtle	16	16	
13	A3	13c	Giant Clam	20	20	
a.			Booklet pane of 10	*9.00*	—	
b.			Bklt. pane, 5 #13, 5 #14 ..	*9.00*	—	
14	A3	20c	Parrotfish	35	35	
b.			Booklet pane of 10	*10.00*	—	
15	A3	28c	Chambered Nautilus	45	45	
16	A3	30c	Dappled sea cucumber	50	50	
17	A3	37c	Sea Urchin	55	55	
18	A3	50c	Starfish	85	85	
19	A3	$1	Squid	1.60	1.60	
20	A3	$2	Dugong	5.00	5.00	
21	A3	$5	Pink sponge	11.00	11.00	
1983						
24	A4	20c	shown	40	40	
25	A4	20c	Blue whale	40	40	
26	A4	20c	Fin whale	40	40	
27	A4	20c	Great sperm whale	40	40	
a.			Block of 4, #24-27	1.60	1.60	
28	A5	20c	First Child ceremony	50	50	
29	A5	20c	Spearfishing from Red Canoe	50	50	
30	A5	20c	Traditional feast at the Bai	50	50	
31	A5	20c	Taro gardening	50	50	
32	A5	20c	Spearfishing at New Moon	50	50	
a.			Strip of 5, #28-32	2.50	2.50	
33	A6	20c	Capt. Henry Wilson	50	50	

A12

A11

A13

A14

A15

A16

A17

A18

A19

A20

Scott No.	Illus No.		Description	Unused Value	Used Value	/ / / / / /
34	A7	20c	Approaching Pelew	50	50	☐☐☐☐☐
35	A7	20c	Englishmans Camp on Ulong	50	50	☐☐☐☐☐
36	A6	20c	Prince Lee Boo	50	50	☐☐☐☐☐
37	A6	20c	King Abba Thulle	50	50	☐☐☐☐☐
38	A7	20c	Mooring in Koror	50	50	☐☐☐☐☐
39	A7	20c	Village scene of Pelew Islands	50	50	☐☐☐☐☐
40	A6	20c	Ludee	50	50	☐☐☐☐☐
a.			Block or strip of 8, #33-40	4.00	4.00	☐☐☐☐☐

1984

41	A8	20c	Triton trumpet, d.	40	40	☐☐☐☐☐
42	A8	20c	Horned helmet, d.	40	40	☐☐☐☐☐
43	A8	20c	Giant clam, d.	40	40	☐☐☐☐☐
44	A8	20c	Laciniate conch, d.	40	40	☐☐☐☐☐
45	A8	20c	Royal cloak scallop, d.	40	40	☐☐☐☐☐
46	A8	20c	Triton trumpet, v.	40	40	☐☐☐☐☐
47	A8	20c	Horned helmet, v.	40	40	☐☐☐☐☐
48	A8	20c	Giant clam, v.	40	40	☐☐☐☐☐
49	A8	20c	Laciniate conch, v.	40	40	☐☐☐☐☐
50	A8	20c	Royal cloak scallop, v.	40	40	☐☐☐☐☐
a.			Block of 10, #41-50	4.00	4.00	☐☐☐☐☐
51	A9	40c	Oroolong, 1783	95	95	☐☐☐☐☐
52	A9	40c	Duff, 1797	95	95	☐☐☐☐☐
53	A9	40c	Peiho, 1908	95	95	☐☐☐☐☐
54	A9	40c	Albatross, 1885	95	95	☐☐☐☐☐
a.			Block of 4, #51-54	3.80	3.80	☐☐☐☐☐
55	A10	20c	Throw spear fishing	45	45	☐☐☐☐☐
56	A10	20c	Kite fishing	45	45	☐☐☐☐☐
57	A10	20c	Underwater spear fishing .	45	45	☐☐☐☐☐
58	A10	20c	Net fishing	45	45	☐☐☐☐☐
a.			Block of 4, #55-58	1.90	1.90	☐☐☐☐☐
59	A11	20c	Mountain Apple	45	45	☐☐☐☐☐
60	A11	20c	Beach Morning Glory	45	45	☐☐☐☐☐
61	A11	20c	Turmeric	45	45	☐☐☐☐☐
62	A11	20c	Plumeria	45	45	☐☐☐☐☐
a.			Block of 4, #59-62	1.90	1.90	☐☐☐☐☐

1985

63	A12	22c	Shearwater chick	60	60	☐☐☐☐☐
64	A12	22c	Shearwaters head	60	60	☐☐☐☐☐
65	A12	22c	Shearwater in flight	60	60	☐☐☐☐☐
66	A12	22c	Swimming	60	60	☐☐☐☐☐
a.			Block of 4, #63-66	2.40	2.40	☐☐☐☐☐
67	A13	22c	Cargo canoe	50	50	☐☐☐☐☐
68	A13	22c	War canoe	50	50	☐☐☐☐☐

A21

A22

A23

A24

A23a

A25

A26

A27

A28

342

Scott No.	Illus No.		Description	Unused Value	Used Value	//////
69	A13	22c	Bamboo raft	50	50	☐☐☐☐☐
70	A13	22c	Racing/sailing canoe	50	50	☐☐☐☐☐
a.			Block of 4, #67-70	2.00	2.00	☐☐☐☐☐
75	A3	14c	Trumpet triton	20	20	☐☐☐☐☐
a.			Booklet pane of 10	6.00	—	☐☐☐☐☐
76	A3	22c	Bumphead parrotfish	35	35	☐☐☐☐☐
a.			Booklet pane of 10	10.00	—	☐☐☐☐☐
b.			Bklt. pane, 5 14c, 5 22c ...	9.00	—	☐☐☐☐☐
77	A3	25c	Soft coral, damsel fish	40	40	☐☐☐☐☐
79	A3	33c	Sea anemone, clownfish ..	55	55	☐☐☐☐☐
80	A3	39c	Green sea turtle	65	65	☐☐☐☐☐
81	A3	44c	Pacific sailfish	70	70	☐☐☐☐☐
85	A3	$10	Spinner dolphins	15.00	15.00	☐☐☐☐☐
86	A14	44c	multicolored	75	75	☐☐☐☐☐
87	A14	44c	multicolored	75	75	☐☐☐☐☐
88	A14	44c	multicolored	75	75	☐☐☐☐☐
89	A14	44c	multicolored	75	75	☐☐☐☐☐
a.			Block of 4, #86-89	3.00	3.00	☐☐☐☐☐
90	A15	14c	multicolored	40	40	☐☐☐☐☐
91	A15	22c	multicolored	55	55	☐☐☐☐☐
92	A15	33c	multicolored	85	85	☐☐☐☐☐
93	A15	44c	multicolored	1.15	1.15	☐☐☐☐☐
94	A16	$1	multicolored	2.75	2.75	☐☐☐☐☐
95	A17	44c	Kaeb canoe, 1758	85	85	☐☐☐☐☐
96	A17	44c	U.S.S. Vincennes, 1835 ...	85	85	☐☐☐☐☐
97	A17	44c	S.M.S. Scharnhorst, 1910	85	85	☐☐☐☐☐
98	A17	44c	Yacht, 1986	85	85	☐☐☐☐☐
a.			Block of 4, #95-98	3.40	3.40	☐☐☐☐☐
1986						
99	A18	44c	Mangrove flycatcher	90	90	☐☐☐☐☐
100	A18	44c	Cardinal honeyeater.........	90	90	☐☐☐☐☐
101	A18	44c	Blue-faced parrotfinch	90	90	☐☐☐☐☐
102	A18	44c	Dusky and bridled white-eyes	90	90	☐☐☐☐☐
a.			Block of 4, #99-102	3.60	3.60	☐☐☐☐☐
103			Sheet of 40	40.00		☐☐☐☐☐
a.	A19	14c	any single	30	30	☐☐☐☐☐
104	A20	22c	Commercial trochus	55	55	☐☐☐☐☐
105	A20	22c	Marble cone	55	55	☐☐☐☐☐
106	A20	22c	Fluted giant clam	55	55	☐☐☐☐☐
107	A20	22c	Bullmouth helmet	55	55	☐☐☐☐☐
108	A20	22c	Golden cowrie	55	55	☐☐☐☐☐
a.			Strip of 5, #104-108	2.75	2.75	☐☐☐☐☐
109	A21	22c	Soldiers helmet	55	55	☐☐☐☐☐
110	A21	22c	Plane wreckage................	55	55	☐☐☐☐☐
111	A21	22c	Woman playing guitar	55	55	☐☐☐☐☐

A30

A32

A33

A34

A35

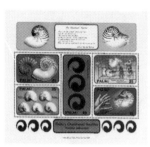

A36

A37

A38

Scott No.	Illus No.		Description	Unused Value	Used Value	/ / / / / /
112	A21	22c	Airai vista	55	55	
a.			Block of 4, #109-112	2.20	2.20	
113	A22	22c	Gecko	50	50	
114	A22	22c	Emerald tree skink	50	50	
115	A22	22c	Estuarine crocodile	50	50	
116	A22	22c	Leatherback turtle	50	50	
a.			Block of 4, #113-116	2.00	2.00	
117	A23	22c	multicolored	35	35	
118	A23	22c	multicolored	35	35	
119	A23	22c	multicolored	35	35	
120	A23	22c	multicolored	35	35	
121	A23	22c	multicolored	35	35	
a.			Strip of 5, #117-121	1.75	1.75	

1987

Scott No.	Illus No.		Description	Unused Value	Used Value	/ / / / / /
121B	A23a	44c	Tangadik, soursop	85	85	
121C	A23a	44c	Dira amartal, sweet orange	85	85	
121D	A23a	44c	Ilhuochel, swamp cabbage	85	85	
121E	A23a	44c	Bauosech, fig	85	85	
f.			Block of 4, #121B-121E ..	3.40	3.40	
122	A24	44c	In flight	90	90	
123	A24	44c	Hanging	90	90	
124	A24	44c	Eating	90	90	
125	A24	44c	Head	90	90	
a.			Block of 4, #122-125	3.60	3.60	

1987-88

Scott No.	Illus No.		Description	Unused Value	Used Value	/ / / / / /
126	A25	1c	Ixora casei	15	15	
127	A25	3c	Lumnitzera littorea	15	15	
128	A25	5c	Sonneratia alba	15	15	
129	A25	10c	Tristellateria australasiae .	16	16	
130	A25	14c	Bikkia palauensis	20	20	
a.			Booklet pane of 10	3.00	—	
131	A25	15c	Limnophila aromatica	22	22	
a.			Booklet pane of 10	2.25	—	
132	A25	22c	Bruguiera gymnorhiza	35	35	
a.			Booklet pane of 10	4.00	—	
b.			Booklet pane, 5 each 14c, 22c	4.00	—	
133	A25	25c	Fagraea ksid	40	40	
a.			Booklet pane of 10	4.00	—	
b.			Booklet pane, 5 each 15c, 25c	4.00	—	
137	A25	36c	Ophiorrhiza palauensis	55	55	
138	A25	39c	Cerbera manghas	60	60	
140	A25	44c	Sandera indica	70	70	

IN MEMORIAM

**Shōwa Emperor
Hirohito
1901–1989**

Thoughts
on an Exotic Bird

*He is a great lord,
with a mind that
flies as high
as that of the rukh,
so he will have
none of me,
who dares not climb
high.*

In Honor of
Emperor Akihito

平成
Heisei Era

*Kyōka verse and Print by
Andō, Hiroshige, 1797–1858*

PALAU

A39

A41

A42

A44

A45

A46

A49

A47

Scott No.	Illus No.		Description	Unused Value	Used Value	/ / / / / /
141	A25	45c	Maesa canfieldiae	72	72	☐☐☐☐☐
142	A25	50c	Dolichandrone spathacea .	85	85	☐☐☐☐☐
143	A25	$1	Barringtonia racemosa	1.60	1.60	☐☐☐☐☐
144	A25	$2	Nepenthes mirabilis	3.25	3.25	☐☐☐☐☐
145	A25	$5	Dendrobium palawense ...	8.00	8.00	☐☐☐☐☐
145A	A25	$10	Bouquet	15.00	15.00	☐☐☐☐☐
1987						
146	A26	22c	Babeldaob Is.	50	50	☐☐☐☐☐
147	A26	22c	Floating Garden Isls.	50	50	☐☐☐☐☐
148	A26	22c	Rock Is.	50	50	☐☐☐☐☐
149	A26	22c	Koror	50	50	☐☐☐☐☐
a.			Block of 4, #146-149	2.00	2.00	☐☐☐☐☐
150	A20	22c	Black-striped triton	55	55	☐☐☐☐☐
151	A20	22c	Tapestry turban	55	55	☐☐☐☐☐
152	A20	22c	Adusta murex	55	55	☐☐☐☐☐
153	A20	22c	Little fox miter	55	55	☐☐☐☐☐
154	A20	22c	Cardinal miter..................	55	55	☐☐☐☐☐
a.			Strip of 5, #150-154	2.75	2.75	☐☐☐☐☐
155	A27	14c	Art. VIII, Sec. 1, Palau	20	20	☐☐☐☐☐
156	A27	14c	Presidential seals	20	20	☐☐☐☐☐
157	A27	14c	Art. II, Sec. 1, US	20	20	☐☐☐☐☐
a.			Strip of 3, #155-157 + label	60	60	☐☐☐☐☐
158	A27	22c	Art. IX, Sec. 1, Palau	35	35	☐☐☐☐☐
159	A27	22c	Legislative seals	35	35	☐☐☐☐☐
160	A27	22c	Art. I, Sec. 1, US	35	35	☐☐☐☐☐
a.			Strip of 3, #158-160 + label	1.05	1.05	☐☐☐☐☐
161	A27	44c	Art X, Sec. 1, Palau	70	70	☐☐☐☐☐
162	A27	44c	Supreme Court seals	70	70	☐☐☐☐☐
163	A27	44c	Art. III, Sec. 1, US	70	70	☐☐☐☐☐
a.			Strip of 3, #161-163 + label	2.10	2.10	☐☐☐☐☐
164	A28	14c	multicolored	30	30	☐☐☐☐☐
165	A28	22c	multicolored	45	45	☐☐☐☐☐
166	A28	33c	multicolored	70	70	☐☐☐☐☐
167	A28	44c	multicolored	85	85	☐☐☐☐☐
168	A28	$1	multicolored	2.30	2.30	☐☐☐☐☐
173	A30	22c	I saw...	55	55	☐☐☐☐☐
174	A30	22c	And what was...	55	55	☐☐☐☐☐
175	A30	22c	Twas Joseph...	55	55	☐☐☐☐☐
176	A30	22c	Saint Michael...	55	55	☐☐☐☐☐
177	A30	22c	And all the bells...............	55	55	☐☐☐☐☐
a.			Strip of 5, #173-177	2.75	2.75	☐☐☐☐☐
178	A31	22c	multicolored	55	55	☐☐☐☐☐
179	A31	22c	multicolored	55	55	☐☐☐☐☐
180	A31	22c	multicolored	55	55	☐☐☐☐☐
181	A31	22c	multicolored	55	55	☐☐☐☐☐
182	A31	22c	multicolored	55	55	☐☐☐☐☐
a.			Strip of 5, #178-182	2.75	2.75	☐☐☐☐☐

347

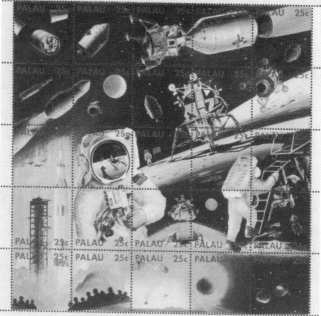

THE SEA OF TRANQUILLITY
'Houston. Tranquillity Base here. The Eagle has landed.'
20th July 1969 - 20:17:43. Greenwich Mean Time

20th Anniversary APOLLO 11 - First Manned Lunar Landing
Astronauts : Neil A. Armstrong, commander; Edwin Aldrin, lunar module pilot;
Michael Collins, command module pilot.

A40

A48

A50

Scott No.	Illus No.		Description	Unused Value	Used Value	/ / / / / /
1988						
183	A23a	44c	multicolored	85	85	
184	A23a	44c	multicolored	85	85	
185	A23a	44c	multicolored	85	85	
186	A23a	44c	multicolored	85	85	
a.			Block of 4, #183-186	3.40	3.40	
187	A32	44c	Whimbrel	85	85	
188	A32	44c	Yellow bittern	85	85	
189	A32	44c	Rufous night-heron	85	85	
190	A32	44c	Banded rail	85	85	
a.			Block of 4, #187-190	3.40	3.40	
191	A20	25c	Striped engina	55	55	
192	A20	25c	Ivory cone	55	55	
193	A20	25c	Plaited miter	55	55	
194	A20	25c	Episcopal miter	55	55	
195	A20	25c	Isabelle cowrie	55	55	
a.			Strip of 5, #191-195	2.75	2.75	
196			Sheet of 6	3.00	3.00	
a.-f.	A33	25c	multicolored	50	50	
197	A34		Sheet of 6	4.80	4.80	
a.-f.		45c	any single	80	80	
198	A35	25c	multicolored	50	50	
199	A35	25c	multicolored	50	50	
200	A35	25c	multicolored	50	50	
201	A35	25c	multicolored	50	50	
202	A35	25c	multicolored	50	50	
a.			Strip of 5, #199-202	2.50	2.50	
203	A36		Sheet of 5	2.75	2.75	
a.-e.		25c	multicolored	55	55	
1989						
204	A37	45c	Nicobar pigeon	85	85	
205	A37	45c	Ground dove	85	85	
206	A37	45c	Micronesian megapode	85	85	
207	A37	45c	Owl	85	85	
a.			Block of 4, #204-207	3.40	3.40	
208	A38	45c	Gilled auricularia	85	85	
209	A38	45c	Rock mushroom	85	85	
210	A38	45c	Polyporous	85	85	
211	A38	45c	Veiled stinkhorn	85	85	
a.			Block of 4, #208-211	3.40	3.40	
212	A20	25c	Robin redbreast triton	55	55	
213	A20	25c	Hebrew cone	55	55	
214	A20	25c	Tadpole triton	55	55	
215	A20	25c	Lettered cone	55	55	
216	A20	25c	Rugose miter	55	55	
a.			Strip of 5, #212-216	2.75	2.75	
217	A39	$1	multicolored	2.25	2.25	

PALAU'S STILT MANGROVE:
An Environmental Portrait

A43

PALAU

MAIL DELIVERY 1890

45c

A52

25 PALAU

A53

U. S. FORCES in PALAU · WORLD WAR II

PALAU 45c

B-24 S OVER PELELIU, 1944

A54

Scott No.	Illus No.		Description	Unused Value	Used Value	/ / / / / /
218	A40		Sheet of 25	11.00	11.00	
a.-y.		25c	any single	44	44	
219	A41	$2.40	multicolored	4.00	4.00	
220			Block of 10	4.25	4.25	
a.-j.	A42	25c	any single	42	42	
221	A43		Block of 20	8.50	8.50	
a.-t.		25c	any single	42	42	
222	A44	25c	multicolored	50	50	
223	A44	25c	multicolored	50	50	
224	A44	25c	multicolored	50	50	
225	A44	25c	multicolored	50	50	
226	A44	25c	multicolored	50	50	
a.			Strip of 5, #222-226	2.50	2.50	
1990						
227	A45	25c	Pink coral	50	50	
228	A45	25c	Pink & violet coral	50	50	
229	A45	25c	Yellow coral	50	50	
230	A45	25c	Red coral	50	50	
a.			Block of 4, #227-230	2.00	2.00	
231	A46	45c	Siberian rubythroat	80	80	
232	A46	45c	Palau bush-warbler	80	80	
233	A46	45c	Micronesian starling	80	80	
234	A46	45c	Cicadabird	80	80	
a.			Block of 4, #231-234	3.20	3.20	
235			Sheet of 9	3.75	3.75	
a.-i.	A47	25c	any single	40	40	
236	A48	$1	Great Britain #1	2.00	2.00	
237	A49	45c	Corymborkis veratrifolia	70	70	
238	A49	45c	Malaxis setipes	70	70	
239	A49	45c	Dipodium freycinetianum	70	70	
240	A49	45c	Bulbophyllum micronesiacum	70	70	
241	A49	45c	Vanda teres and hookeriana	70	70	
a.			Strip of 5, #237-241	3.50	3.50	
242	A50	45c	Wedelia strigulosa	70	70	
243	A50	45c	Erthrina variegata	70	70	
244	A50	45c	Clerodendrum inerme	70	70	
245	A50	45c	Vigna marina	70	70	
a.			Block of 4, #242-245	2.80	2.80	
246	A51	25c	Sheet of 25, #a.-y.	10.50	10.50	
247	A52	45c	Mailship, 1890	1.00	1.00	
248	A52	45c	US #803 on cover, forklift, plane	1.00	1.00	
a.			Pair, #247-248	2.00	2.00	
249	A53	25c	multicolored	50	50	
250	A53	25c	multicolored	50	50	

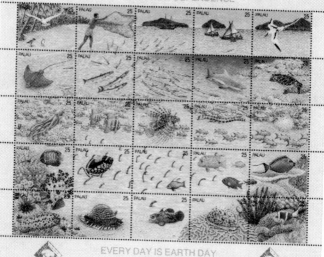

A51

A56

Scott No.	Illus No.		Description	Unused Value	Used Value	//////
251	A53	25c	multicolored	50	50	☐☐☐☐☐
252	A53	25c	multicolored	50	50	☐☐☐☐☐
253	A53	25c	multicolored	50	50	☐☐☐☐☐
a.			Strip of 5, #249-253	2.50	2.50	☐☐☐☐☐
254	A54	45c	multicolored	90	90	☐☐☐☐☐
255	A54	45c	multicolored	90	90	☐☐☐☐☐
256	A54	45c	multicolored	90	90	☐☐☐☐☐
257	A54	45c	multicolored	90	90	☐☐☐☐☐
a.			Block of 4, #254-257	3.60	3.60	☐☐☐☐☐
258	A54	$1	multicolored	2.00	2.00	☐☐☐☐☐

1991

Scott No.	Illus No.		Description	Unused Value	Used Value	//////
259	A55	30c	Staghorn	60	60	☐☐☐☐☐
260	A55	30c	Velvet Leather	60	60	☐☐☐☐☐
261	A55	30c	Van Goghs Cypress	60	60	☐☐☐☐☐
262	A55	30c	Violet Lace	60	60	☐☐☐☐☐
a.			Block of 4, #259-262	2.40	2.40	☐☐☐☐☐
263	A56	30c	Sheet of 16, #a.-p.	7.50	7.50	☐☐☐☐☐

1991-92

Scott No.	Illus No.		Description	Unused Value	Used Value	//////
264	A57	1c	Palau bush-warbler	15	15	☐☐☐☐☐
266	A57	4c	Common moorhen	15	15	☐☐☐☐☐
267	A57	6c	Banded rail	15	15	☐☐☐☐☐
270	A57	19c	Palau fantail	38	38	☐☐☐☐☐
270A	A57	20c	Mangrove flycatcher	40	40	☐☐☐☐☐
271	A57	23c	Purple swamphen	46	46	☐☐☐☐☐
272	A57	29c	Palau fruit dove	58	58	☐☐☐☐☐
274	A57	35c	Great crested tern	70	70	☐☐☐☐☐
275	A57	40c	Pacific reef heron	80	80	☐☐☐☐☐
276	A57	45c	Micronesian pigeon	90	90	☐☐☐☐☐
277	A57	50c	Great frigatebird	1.00	1.00	☐☐☐☐☐
278	A57	52c	Little pied cormorant	1.05	1.05	☐☐☐☐☐
280	A57	75c	Jungle night jar	1.50	1.50	☐☐☐☐☐
281	A57	95c	Cattle egret	1.90	1.90	☐☐☐☐☐
283	A57	$1.34	Great sulphur-crested cockatoo	2.68	2.68	☐☐☐☐☐
285	A57	$2	Blue-faced parrotfinch	4.00	4.00	☐☐☐☐☐
286	A57	$5	Eclectus parrot	10.00	10.00	☐☐☐☐☐
287	A57	$10	Palau bush warbler	20.00	20.00	☐☐☐☐☐

1991

Scott No.	Illus No.		Description	Unused Value	Used Value	//////
288	A58	29c	Sheet of 6, #a.-f.	3.00	3.00	☐☐☐☐☐
289	A59	29c	Sheet of 20, #a.-t.	11.60	11.60	☐☐☐☐☐
290	A60	20c	Sheet of 9, #a.-i.	4.00	4.00	☐☐☐☐☐
291	A60	$2.90	Fairy tern, yellow ribbon .	4.25	4.25	☐☐☐☐☐
292	A60	$2.90	like #291	4.25	4.25	☐☐☐☐☐
293	A61	29c	Sheet of 8, #a.-h.	4.60	4.60	☐☐☐☐☐
294	A62	50c	Sheet of 5, #a.-e.	5.00	5.00	☐☐☐☐☐

A55

A57

A58

A60

A61

A62

A59

A63

A64

A65

A66

A67

A68

PALAU SALUTES THE OLYMPIAN INNOVATORS

A71

A70

A72

A73

A69

Scott No.	Illus No.		Description	Unused Value	Used Value	/ / / / / /
1991						
295	A63	29c	Sheet of 6, #a.-f.	3.50	3.50	☐☐☐☐☐☐
296	A63	$1	multicolored	2.00	2.00	☐☐☐☐☐☐
297	A64	29c	Sheet of 6, #a.-f.	3.50	3.50	☐☐☐☐☐☐
298	A65	29c	Strip of 5, #a.-e.	2.90	2.90	☐☐☐☐☐☐
299	A66	29c	Sheet of 10, #a.-j.	5.80	5.80	☐☐☐☐☐☐
1992						
300	A67	50c	Block of 4, #a.-d.	3.75	3.75	☐☐☐☐☐☐
301	A68	29c	Strip of 5, #a.-e.	2.65	2.65	☐☐☐☐☐☐
302	A69	29c	Sheet of 20, #a.-t.	11.60	11.60	☐☐☐☐☐☐
303	A70	29c	Sheet of 24, #a.-x.	14.00	14.00	☐☐☐☐☐☐
304	A71	50c	Dawn Fraser	1.00	1.00	☐☐☐☐☐☐
305	A71	50c	Olga Korbut	1.00	1.00	☐☐☐☐☐☐
306	A71	50c	Bob Beamon	1.00	1.00	☐☐☐☐☐☐
307	A71	50c	Carl Lewis	1.00	1.00	☐☐☐☐☐☐
308	A71	50c	Dick Fosbury	1.00	1.00	☐☐☐☐☐☐
309	A71	50c	Greg Louganis	1.00	1.00	☐☐☐☐☐☐
310	A72	29c	Sheet of 9, #a.-i.	5.25	5.25	☐☐☐☐☐☐
311	A66	50c	Sheet of 10, #a.-j.	10.00	10.00	☐☐☐☐☐☐
312	A73	29c	Strip of 5, #a.-e.	2.65	2.65	☐☐☐☐☐☐

SP1

Scott No.	Illus No.		Description	Unused Value	Used Value	/ / / / / /
PALAU, SEMI-POSTAL STAMPS						
1988						
B1	SP1	25c	5c Baseball glove, player .	50	50	☐☐☐☐☐
B2	SP1	25c	5c Running shoe, athlete .	50	50	☐☐☐☐☐
a.			Pair, #B1-B2	1.00	1.00	☐☐☐☐☐
B3	SP1	45c	5c Goggles, swimmer	1.00	1.00	☐☐☐☐☐
B4	SP1	45c	5c Gold medal, diver	1.00	1.00	☐☐☐☐☐
a.			Pair, #B3-B4	2.00	2.00	☐☐☐☐☐

AP1

AP2

AP3

AP4

AP5

HOW TO USE THIS BOOK

The number in the first column is its Scott number or identifying number. The letter and number that come next (A41) indicate the design and refer to the illustration so designated. Following that is the denomination of the stamp and its color. Finally, the value, unused and used is shown.

360

Scott No.	Illus No.	Description	Unused Value	Used Value	//////
PALAU, AIR POST STAMPS					
1984					
C1	AP1	40c shown	75	75	☐☐☐☐☐
C2	AP1	40c Fairy tern	75	75	☐☐☐☐☐
C3	AP1	40c Black noddy	75	75	☐☐☐☐☐
C4	AP1	40c Black-naped tern	75	75	☐☐☐☐☐
a.		Block of 4, #C1-C4	3.00	3.00	☐☐☐☐☐
1985					
C5	A12	44c Audubons Shearwater	70	70	☐☐☐☐☐
C6	AP2	44c multicolored	90	90	☐☐☐☐☐
C7	AP2	44c multicolored	90	90	☐☐☐☐☐
C8	AP2	44c multicolored	90	90	☐☐☐☐☐
C9	AP2	44c multicolored	90	90	☐☐☐☐☐
a.		Block of 4, #C6-C9	3.60	3.60	☐☐☐☐☐
C10	A16	44c multicolored	80	80	☐☐☐☐☐
C11	A16	44c multicolored	80	80	☐☐☐☐☐
C12	A16	44c multicolored	80	80	☐☐☐☐☐
C13	A16	44c multicolored	80	80	☐☐☐☐☐
a.		Block of 4, #C10-C13	3.20	3.20	☐☐☐☐☐
1986					
C14	AP3	44c multicolored	1.20	1.20	☐☐☐☐☐
C15	AP3	44c multicolored	1.20	1.20	☐☐☐☐☐
C16	AP3	44c multicolored	1.20	1.20	☐☐☐☐☐
a.		Strip of 3, #C14-C16	3.60	3.60	☐☐☐☐☐
C17	AP4	44c multicolored	90	90	☐☐☐☐☐
1989					
C18	AP5	36c Cessna 207 Skywagon	70	70	☐☐☐☐☐
a.		Booklet pane of 10	7.00	—	☐☐☐☐☐
C19	AP5	39c Embraer EMB-110 Bandeirante	80-	80	☐☐☐☐☐
a.		Booklet pane of 10	8.00	—	☐☐☐☐☐
C20	AP5	45c Boeing 727	90	90	☐☐☐☐☐
a.		Booklet pane of 10	9.00	—	☐☐☐☐☐
b.		Booklet pane, 5 each 36c, 45c	8.00	—	☐☐☐☐☐
1991					
C21	A61	50c like #293a	1.10	1.10	☐☐☐☐☐
					☐☐☐☐☐
					☐☐☐☐☐
					☐☐☐☐☐
					☐☐☐☐☐
					☐☐☐☐☐
					☐☐☐☐☐

Scott No.	Illus No.	Description	Unused Value	Used Value	/ / / / / /

Scott No.	Illus No.	Description	Unused Value	Used Value	/ / / / / /

INDEX TO ADVERTISERS

★ ★ ★ ★ ★ ★ ★ ★ ★ ★ ★ ★

Scott Advertising Opportunities